MY Lovey-Dovey Wife IS A STONE COLD KILLER

story & art by
Donten Kosaka

2

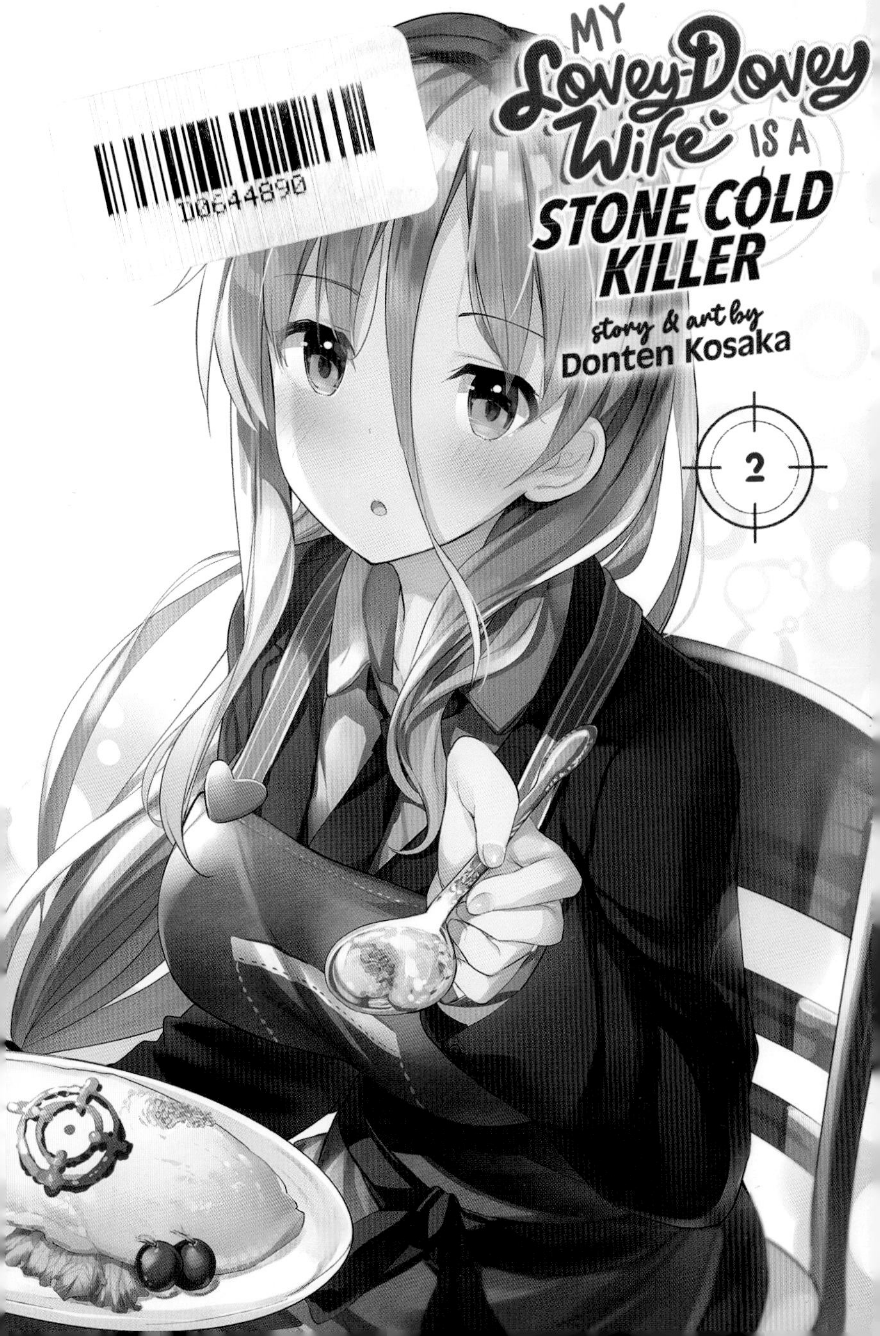

Contents

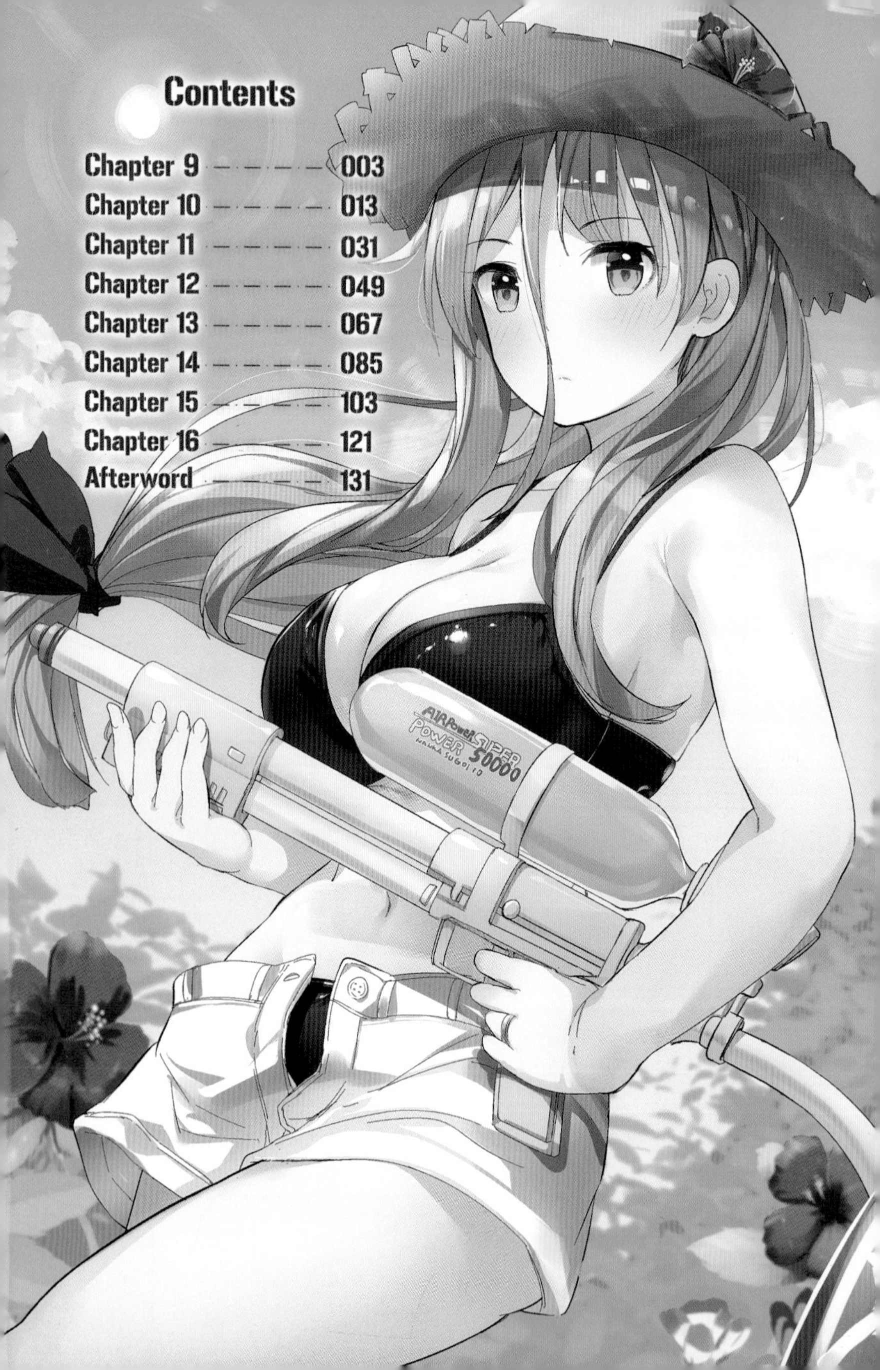

AIR Power SUPER
POWER 50000

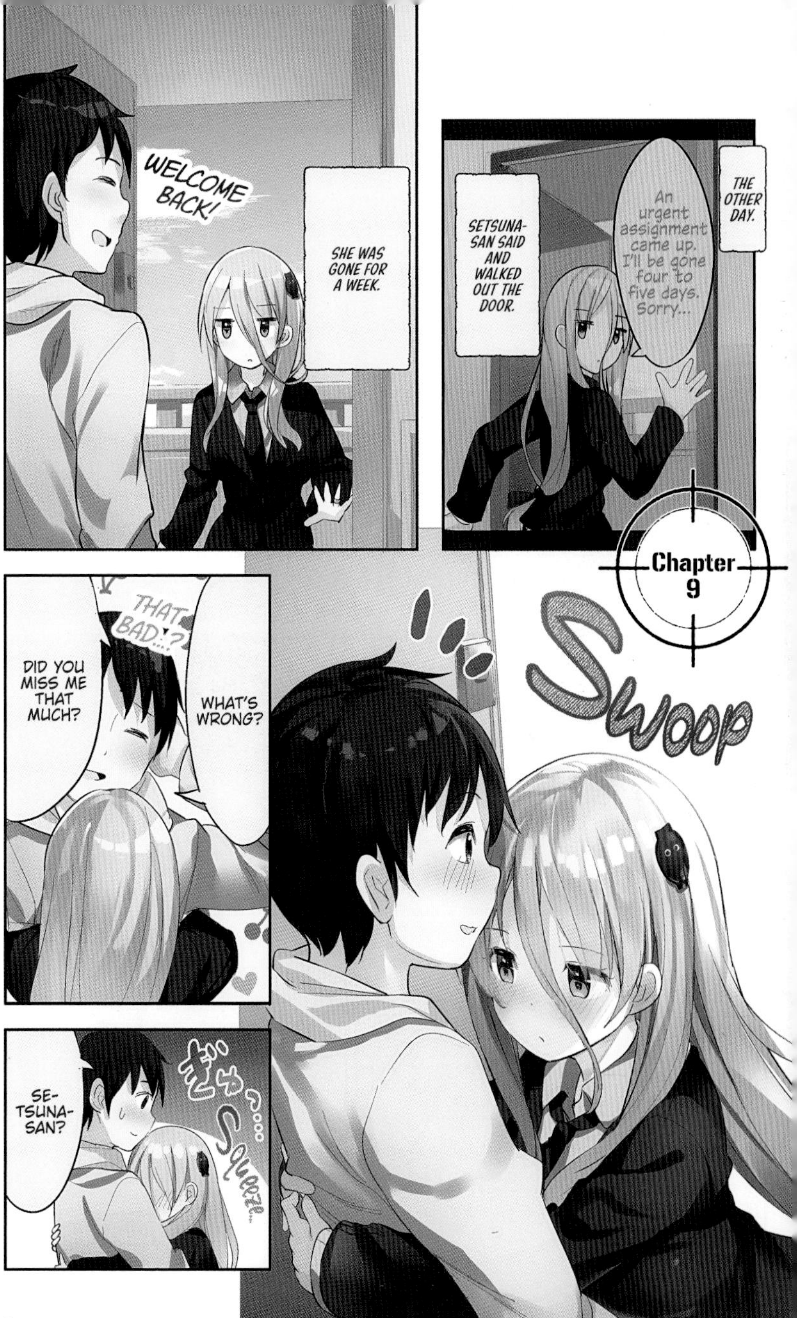
THE OTHER DAY.
An urgent assignment came up. I'll be gone four to five days. Sorry...
SETSUNA-SAN SAID AND WALKED OUT THE DOOR.
SHE WAS GONE FOR A WEEK.
WELCOME BACK!
Chapter 9
SWOOP
WHAT'S WRONG?
THAT BAD...?
DID YOU MISS ME THAT MUCH?
SQUEEZE...
SE-TSUNA-SAN?

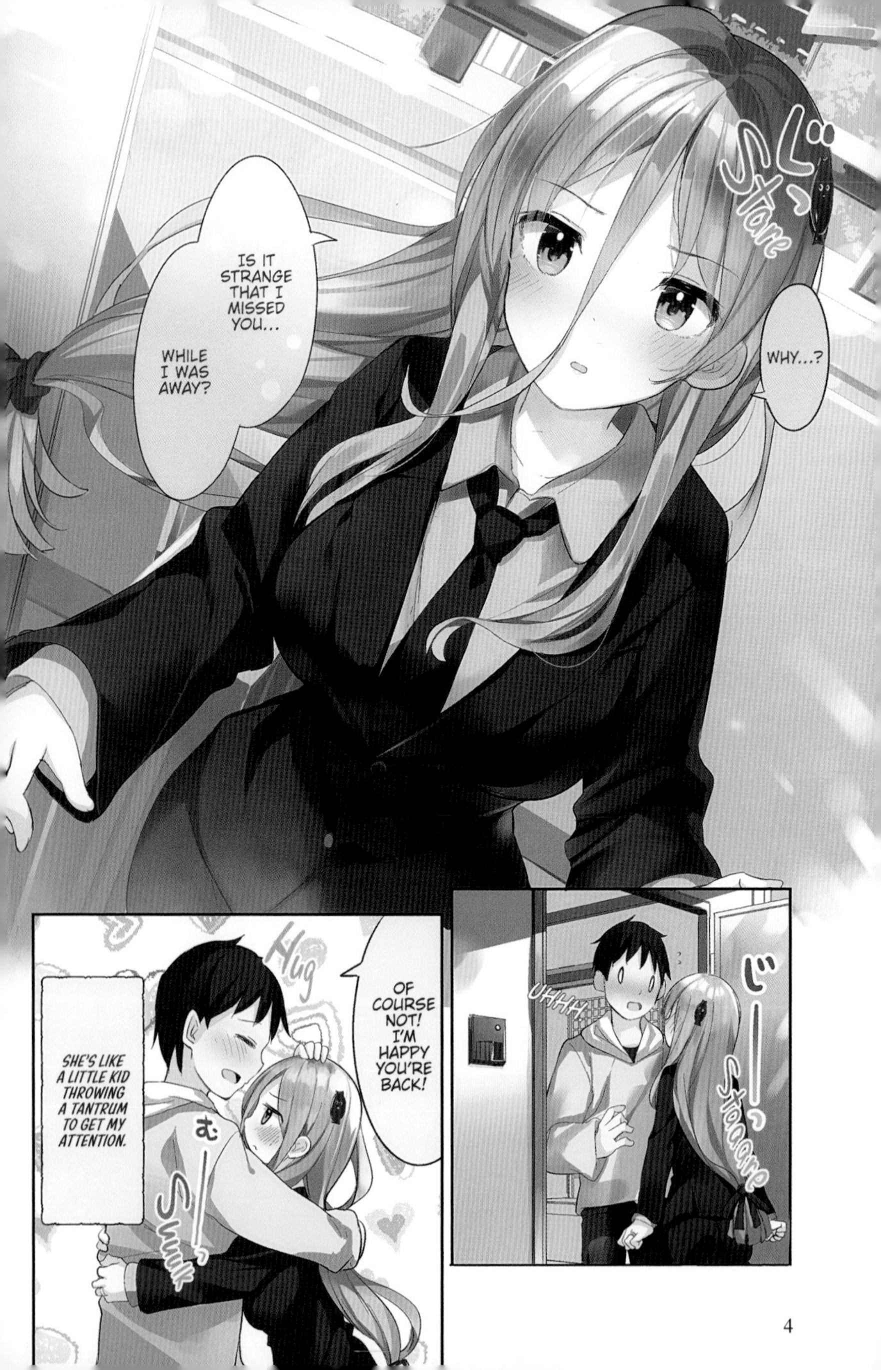
じ
Stare
WHY...?
IS IT STRANGE THAT I MISSED YOU... WHILE I WAS AWAY?
UHHH
じーっ
Staaare
Hug
OF COURSE NOT! I'M HAPPY YOU'RE BACK!
SHE'S LIKE A LITTLE KID THROWING A TANTRUM TO GET MY ATTENTION.
むーっ
Suulk

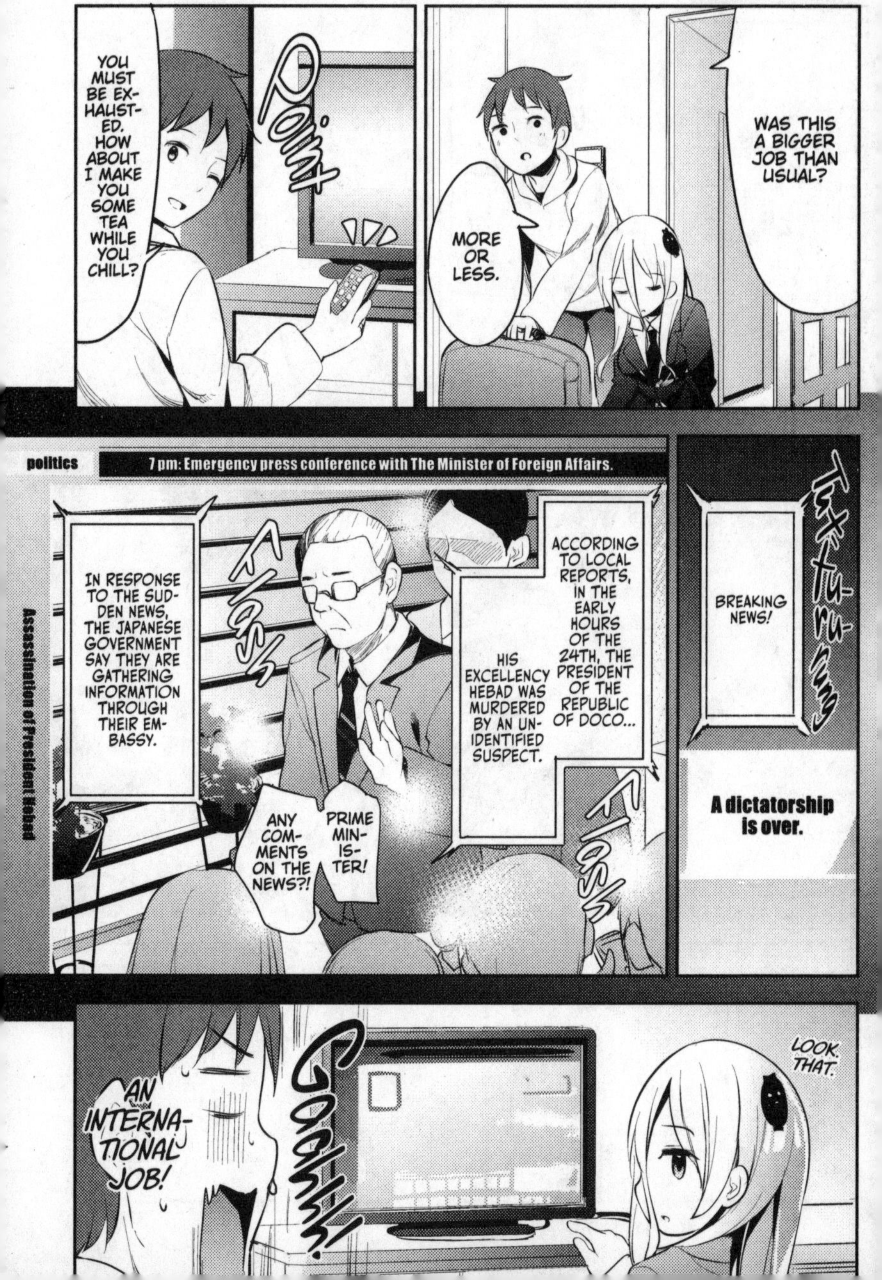
WAS THIS A BIGGER JOB THAN USUAL?
MORE OR LESS.
Point
YOU MUST BE EX-HAUST-ED. HOW ABOUT I MAKE YOU SOME TEA WHILE YOU CHILL?
Tu-tu-tu-ru-rung
BREAKING NEWS!
A dictatorship is over.
politics
7 pm: Emergency press conference with The Minister of Foreign Affairs.
Assassination of President Hebad
Flash
ACCORDING TO LOCAL REPORTS, IN THE EARLY HOURS OF THE 24TH, THE PRESIDENT OF THE REPUBLIC OF DOCO...
HIS EXCELLENCY HEBAD WAS MURDERED BY AN UN-IDENTIFIED SUSPECT.
IN RESPONSE TO THE SUD-DEN NEWS, THE JAPANESE GOVERNMENT SAY THEY ARE GATHERING INFORMATION THROUGH THEIR EM-BASSY.
Flash
PRIME MIN-IS-TER!
ANY COM-MENTS ON THE NEWS?!
LOOK. THAT.
Gaahhh!
AN INTERNA-TIONAL JOB!

SETSUNA-SAN'S BONUS PAY.

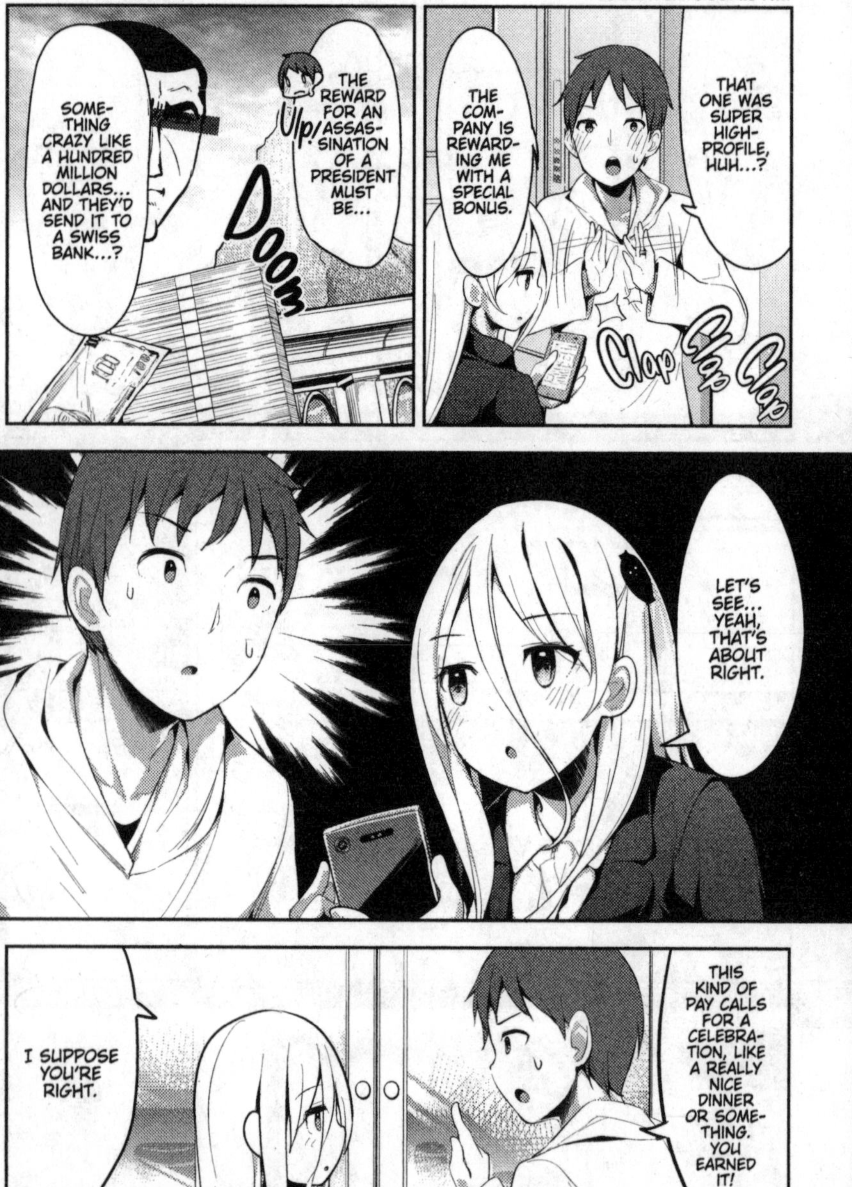

THAT ONE WAS SUPER HIGH-PROFILE, HUH...?
THE COMPANY IS REWARDING ME WITH A SPECIAL BONUS.
Clap Clap Clap
THE REWARD FOR AN ASSASSINATION OF A PRESIDENT MUST BE...
Ulp!
SOMETHING CRAZY LIKE A HUNDRED MILLION DOLLARS... AND THEY'D SEND IT TO A SWISS BANK...?
Doom
LET'S SEE... YEAH, THAT'S ABOUT RIGHT.
THIS KIND OF PAY CALLS FOR A CELEBRATION, LIKE A REALLY NICE DINNER OR SOMETHING. YOU EARNED IT!
I SUPPOSE YOU'RE RIGHT.

TIRED SETSUNA-SAN.

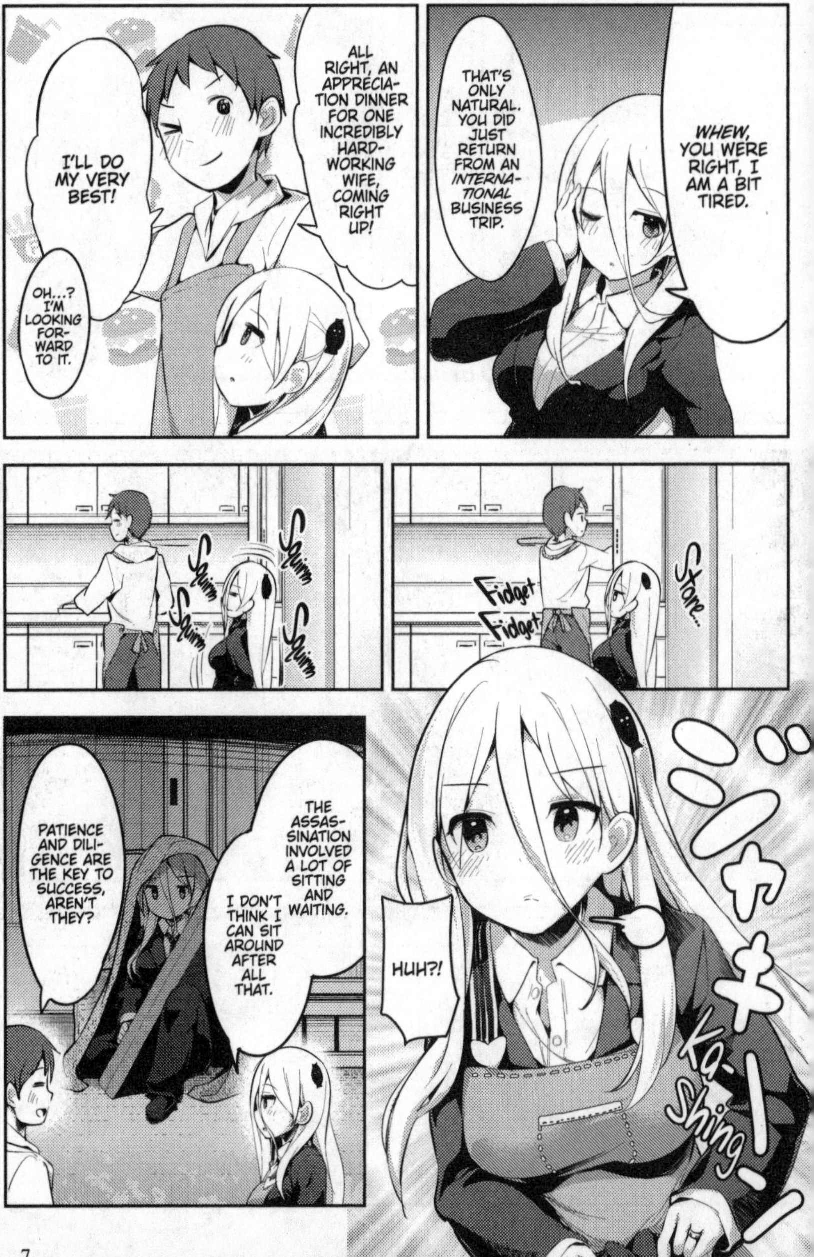
WHEW, YOU WERE RIGHT, I AM A BIT TIRED.
THAT'S ONLY NATURAL. YOU DID JUST RETURN FROM AN *INTERNATIONAL* BUSINESS TRIP.
ALL RIGHT, AN APPRECIATION DINNER FOR ONE INCREDIBLY HARD-WORKING WIFE, COMING RIGHT UP!
I'LL DO MY VERY BEST!
OH...? I'M LOOKING FORWARD TO IT.
Stare...
Fidget Fidget
Squirm Squirm
Squirm Squirm
ジャキ
Ka-Shing-!
HUH?!
THE ASSASSINATION INVOLVED A LOT OF SITTING AND WAITING.
I DON'T THINK I CAN SIT AROUND AFTER ALL THAT.
PATIENCE AND DILIGENCE ARE THE KEY TO SUCCESS, AREN'T THEY?

COOKING WITH SETSUNA-SAN.

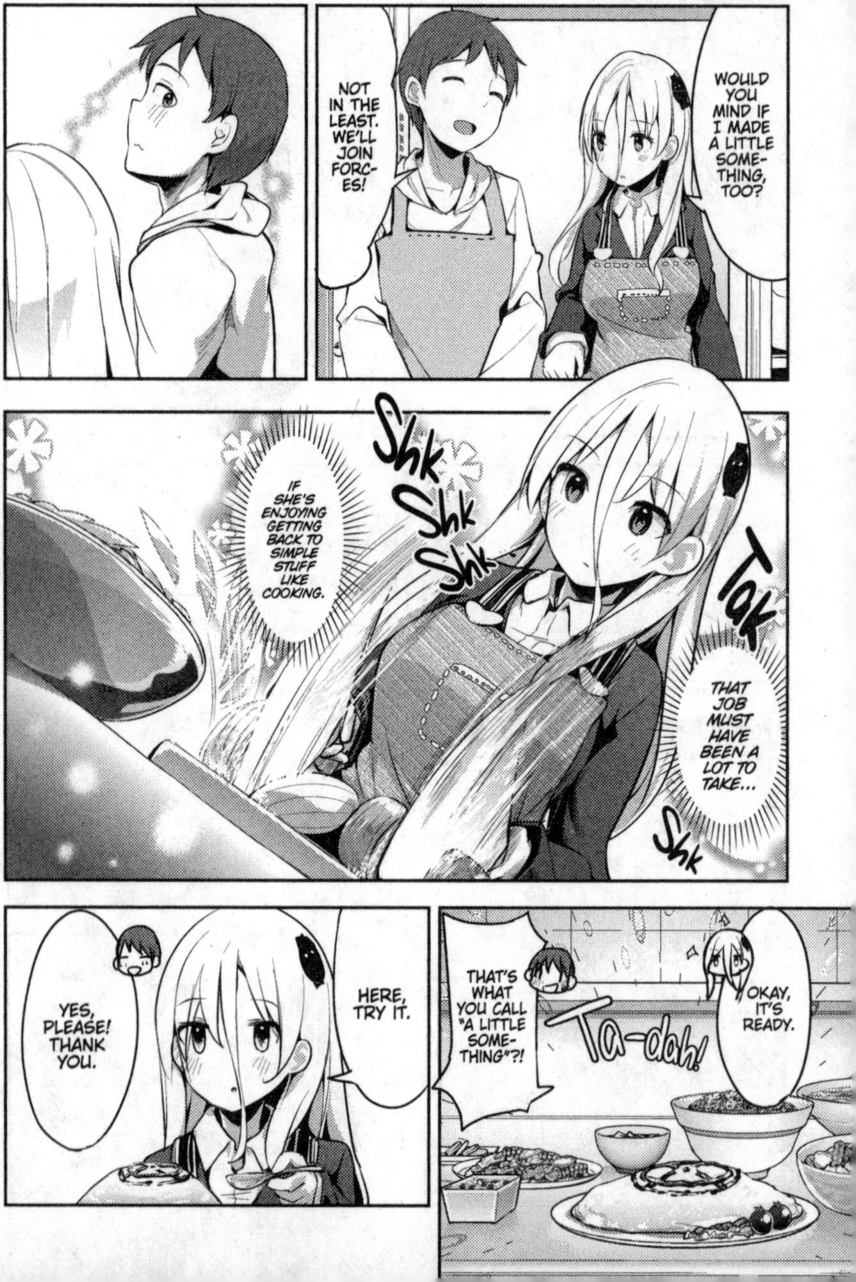
WOULD YOU MIND IF I MADE A LITTLE SOME-THING, TOO?
NOT IN THE LEAST. WE'LL JOIN FORC-ES!
Shk Shk Shk
Tak
THAT JOB MUST HAVE BEEN A LOT TO TAKE...
IF SHE'S ENJOYING GETTING BACK TO SIMPLE STUFF LIKE COOKING.
Shk
OKAY, IT'S READY.
Ta-dah!
THAT'S WHAT YOU CALL "A LITTLE SOME-THING"?!
HERE, TRY IT.
YES, PLEASE! THANK YOU.

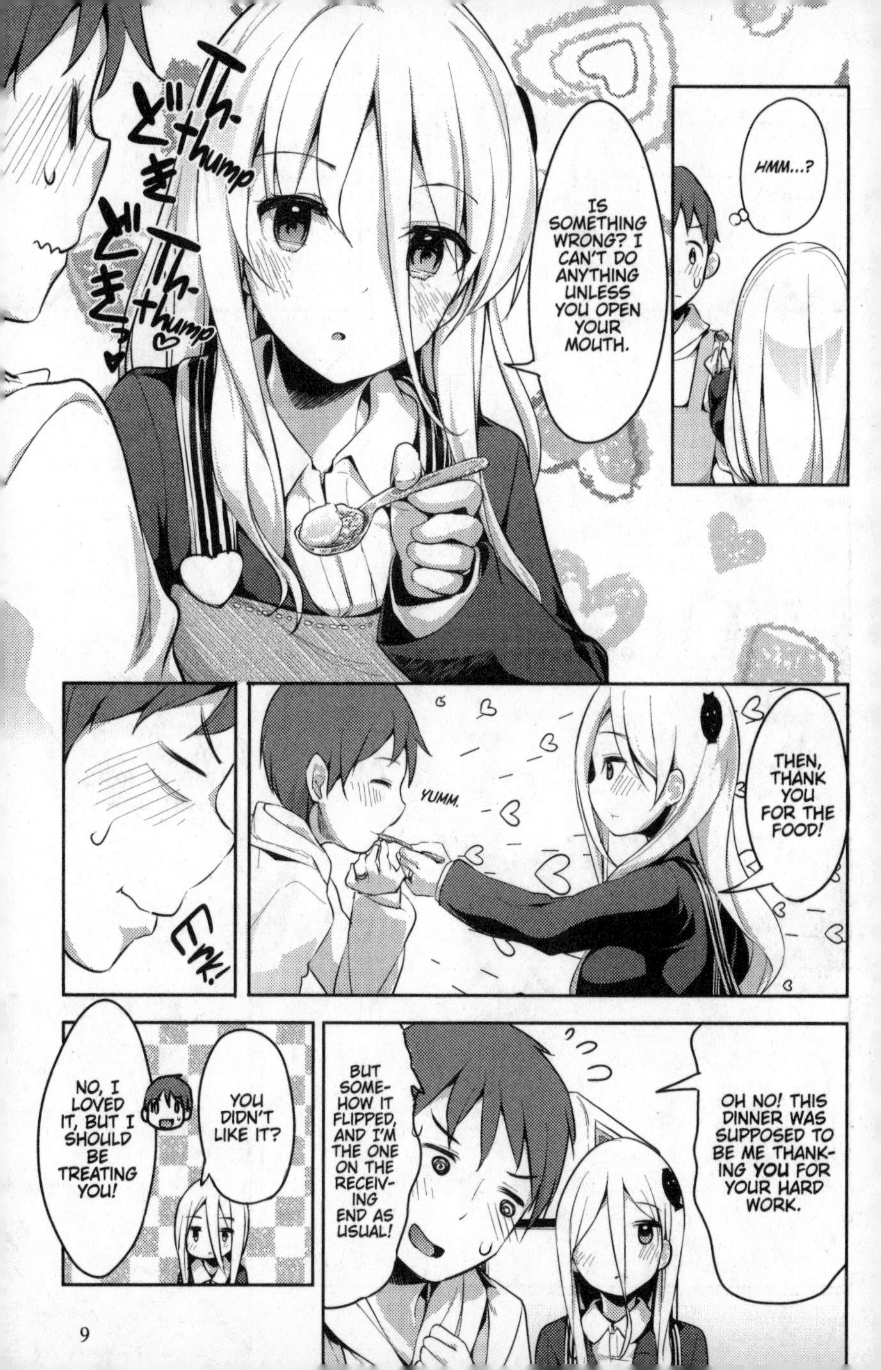
HMM...?
IS SOMETHING WRONG? I CAN'T DO ANYTHING UNLESS YOU OPEN YOUR MOUTH.
Th-thump
どきどきっ
Th-thump
THEN, THANK YOU FOR THE FOOD!
YUMM.
Erk!
OH NO! THIS DINNER WAS SUPPOSED TO BE ME THANKING YOU FOR YOUR HARD WORK.
BUT SOMEHOW IT FLIPPED, AND I'M THE ONE ON THE RECEIVING END AS USUAL!
YOU DIDN'T LIKE IT?
NO, I LOVED IT, BUT I SHOULD BE TREATING YOU!

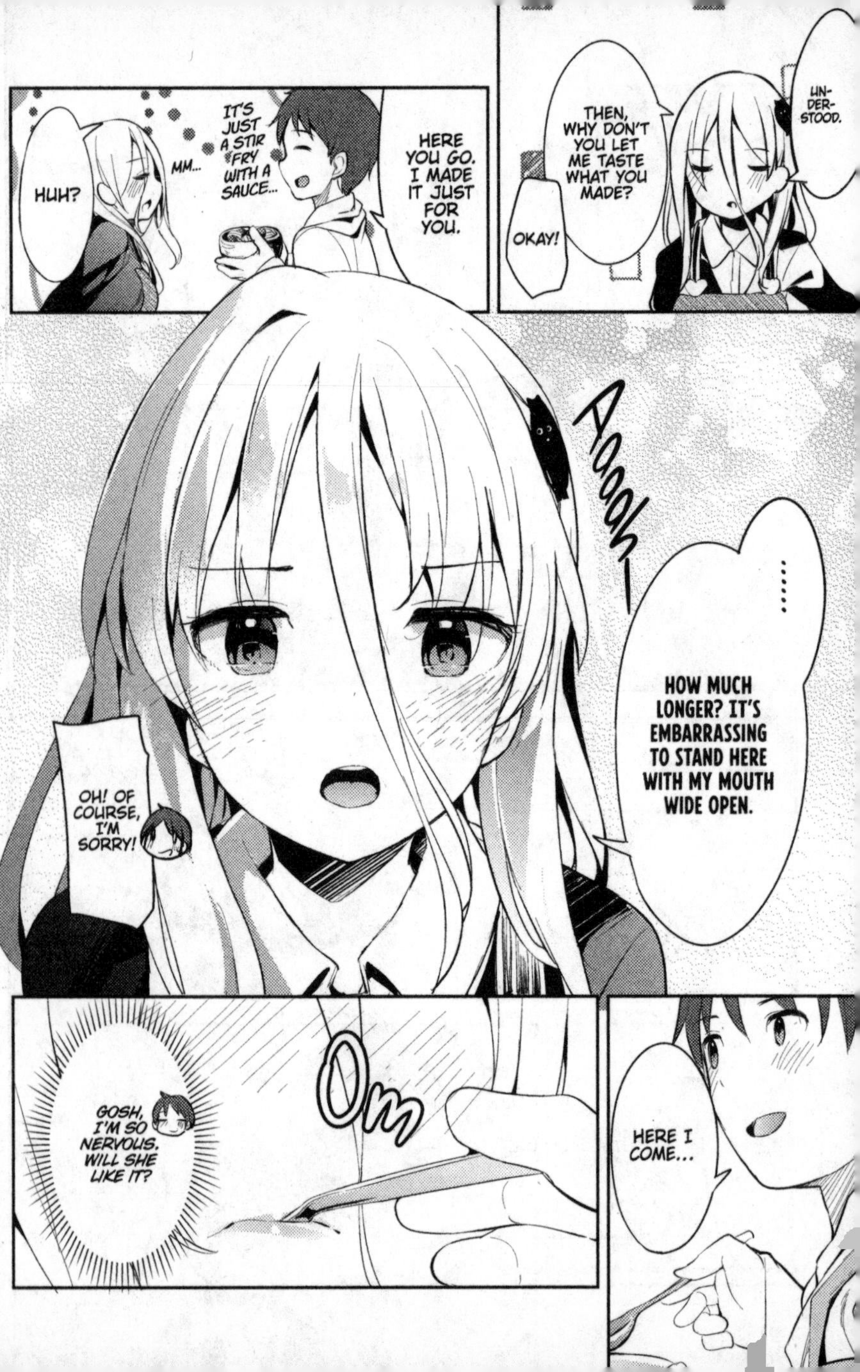
UN-DER-STOOD.
THEN, WHY DON'T YOU LET ME TASTE WHAT YOU MADE?
OKAY!
HERE YOU GO. I MADE IT JUST FOR YOU.
IT'S JUST A STIR FRY WITH A SAUCE...
MM...
HUH?
Aaaah–
......
HOW MUCH LONGER? IT'S EMBARRASSING TO STAND HERE WITH MY MOUTH WIDE OPEN.
OH! OF COURSE, I'M SORRY!
HERE I COME...
Om
GOSH, I'M SO NERVOUS. WILL SHE LIKE IT?

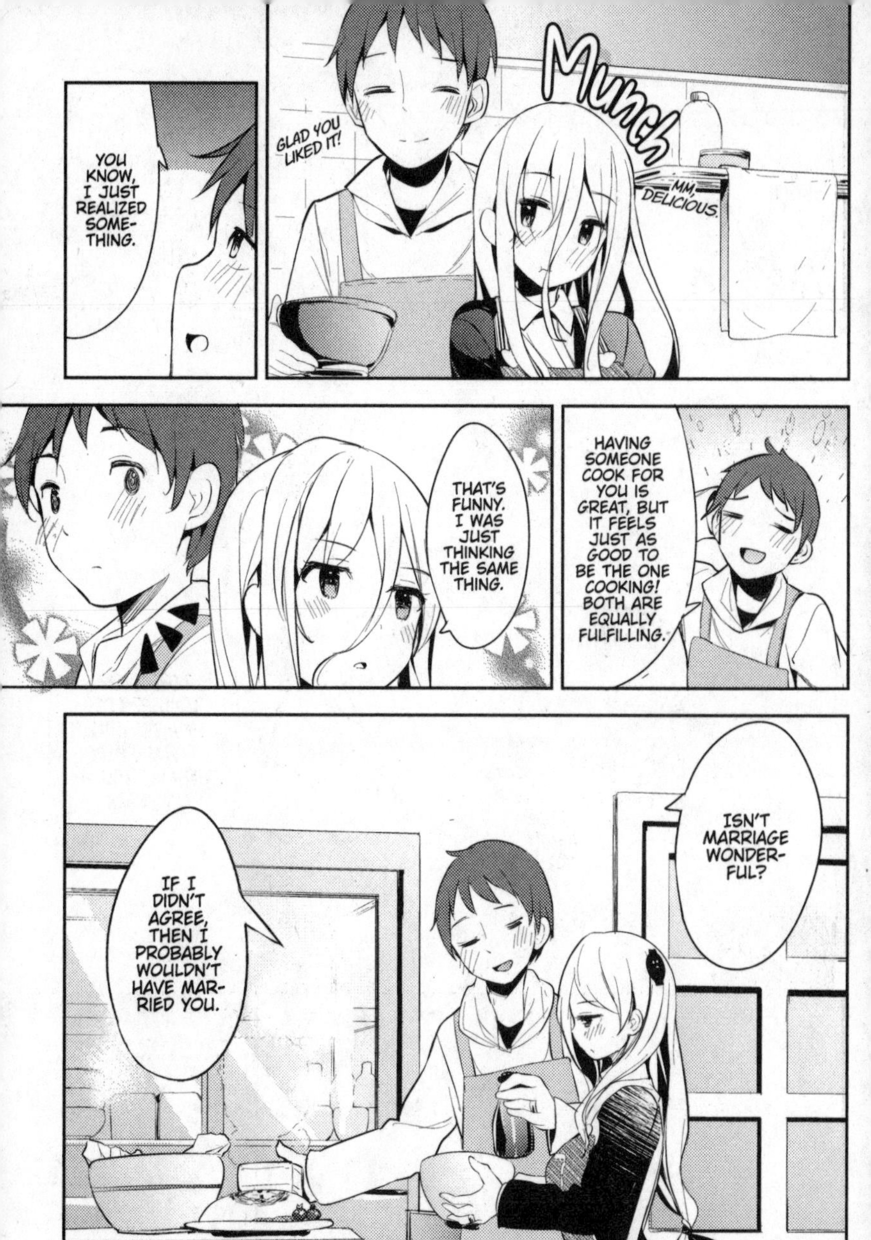
Munch
MM, DELICIOUS.
GLAD YOU LIKED IT!
YOU KNOW, I JUST REALIZED SOME-THING.
HAVING SOMEONE COOK FOR YOU IS GREAT, BUT IT FEELS JUST AS GOOD TO BE THE ONE COOKING! BOTH ARE EQUALLY FULFILLING.
THAT'S FUNNY. I WAS JUST THINKING THE SAME THING.
ISN'T MARRIAGE WONDER-FUL?
IF I DIDN'T AGREE, THEN I PROBABLY WOULDN'T HAVE MAR-RIED YOU.

MY Lovey-Dovey Wife IS A STONE COLD KILLER

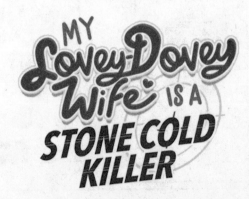

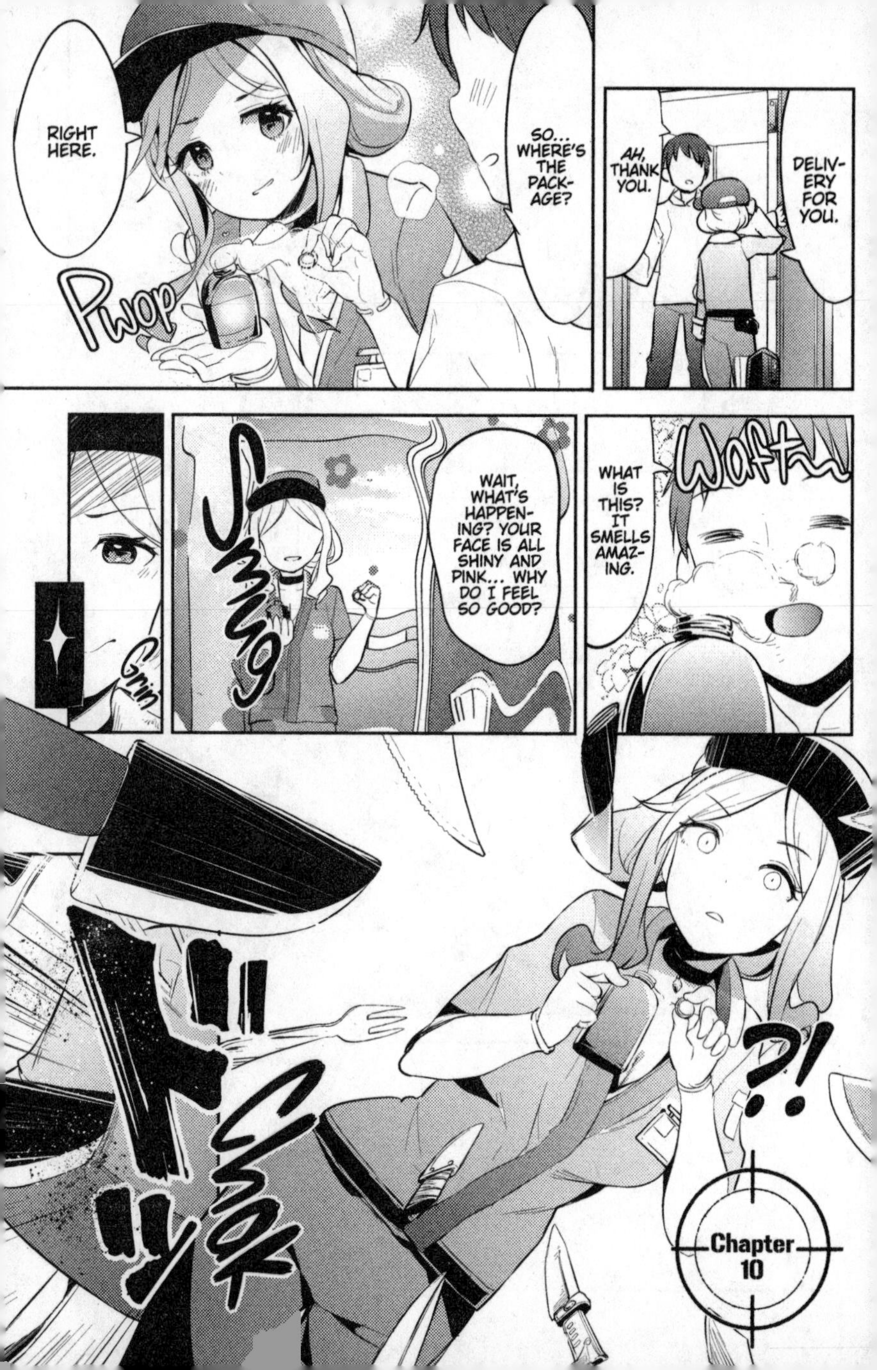
DELIVERY FOR YOU.
AH, THANK YOU.
SO... WHERE'S THE PACKAGE?
RIGHT HERE.
Pwop
Wofth
WHAT IS THIS? IT SMELLS AMAZING.
WAIT, WHAT'S HAPPENING? YOUR FACE IS ALL SHINY AND PINK... WHY DO I FEEL SO GOOD?
Smug
Grin
?!
Chapter 10

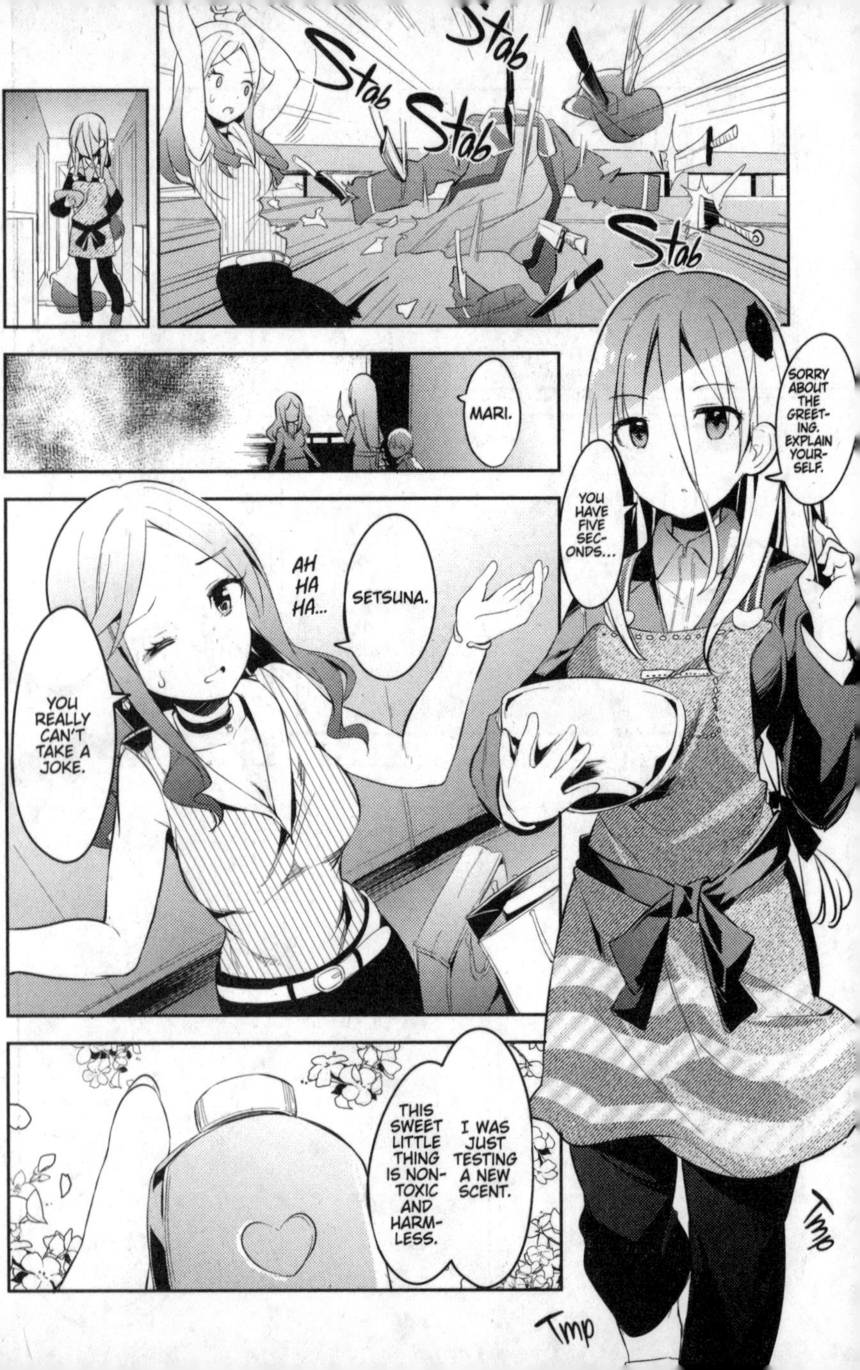
Stab
Stab
Stab
Stab
SORRY ABOUT THE GREETING. EXPLAIN YOURSELF.
YOU HAVE FIVE SECONDS...
Tmp
Tmp
MARI.
SETSUNA.
AH HA HA...
YOU REALLY CAN'T TAKE A JOKE.
I WAS JUST TESTING A NEW SCENT.
THIS SWEET LITTLE THING IS NON-TOXIC AND HARMLESS.

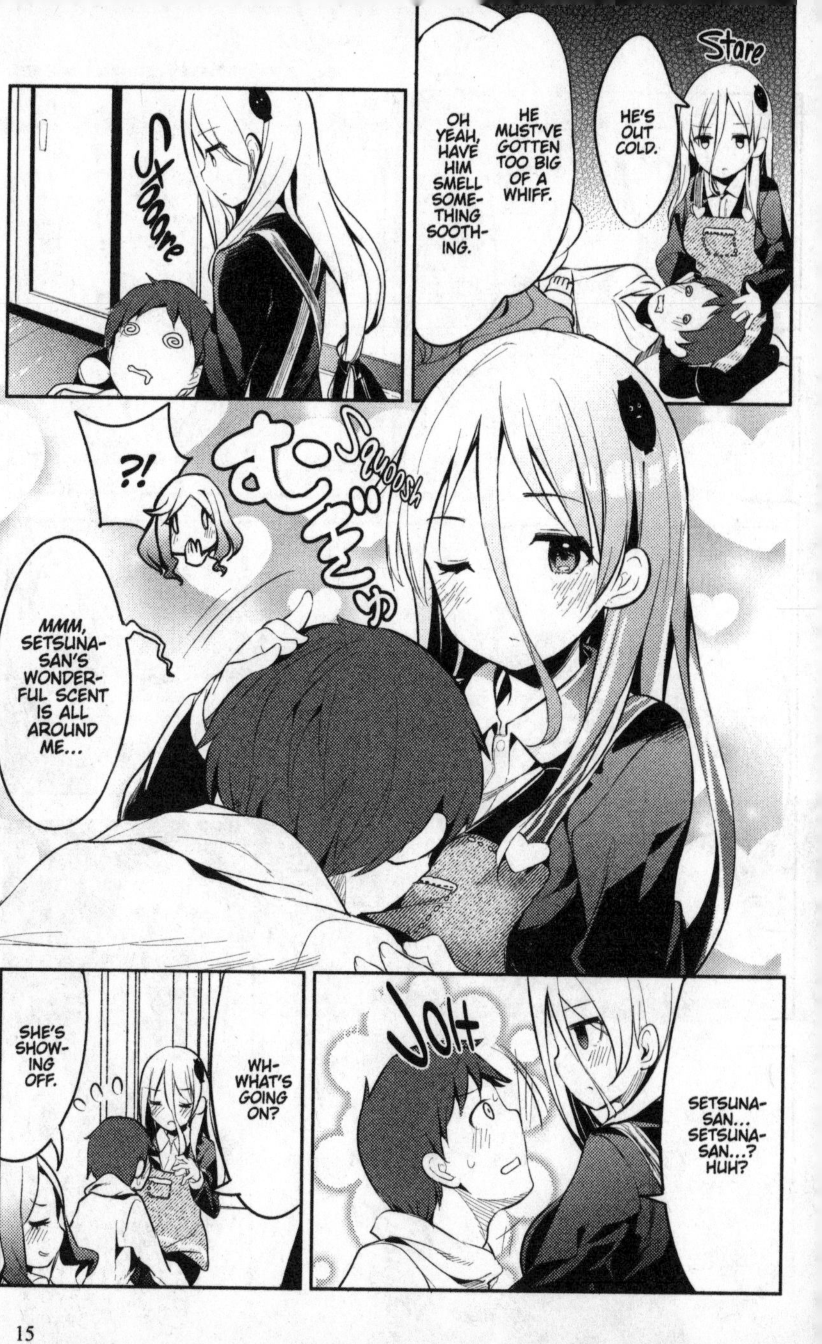
Stare
HE'S OUT COLD.
HE MUST'VE GOTTEN TOO BIG OF A WHIFF.
OH YEAH, HAVE HIM SMELL SOMETHING SOOTHING.
Stooare
むぎゅ
Squoosh
?!
MMM, SETSUNA-SAN'S WONDERFUL SCENT IS ALL AROUND ME...
Jolt
SETSUNA-SAN... SETSUNA-SAN...? HUH?
WH-WHAT'S GOING ON?
SHE'S SHOWING OFF.

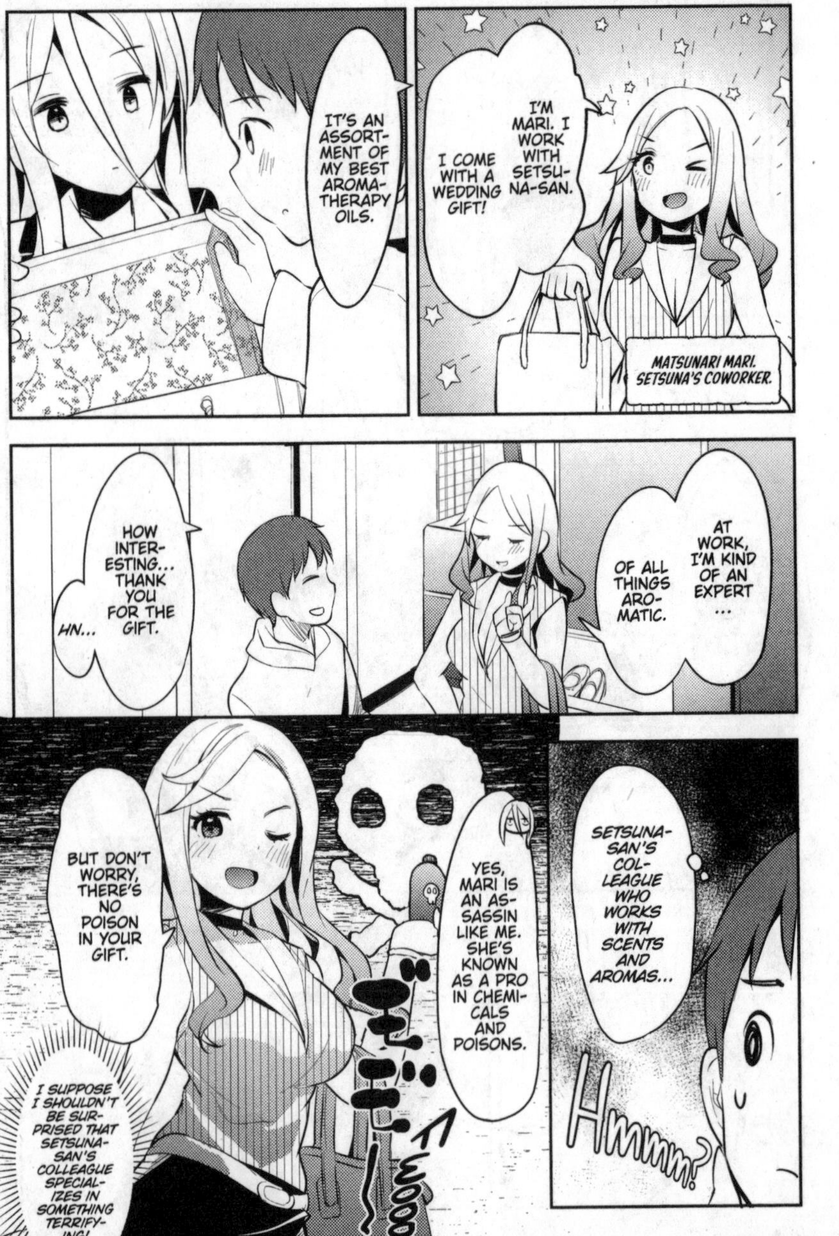
I'M MARI. I WORK WITH SETSUNA-SAN.
I COME WITH A WEDDING GIFT!
MATSUNARI MARI. SETSUNA'S COWORKER.
IT'S AN ASSORTMENT OF MY BEST AROMATHERAPY OILS.
AT WORK, I'M KIND OF AN EXPERT ...
OF ALL THINGS AROMATIC.
HOW INTERESTING... THANK YOU FOR THE GIFT.
HN...
SETSUNA-SAN'S COLLEAGUE WHO WORKS WITH SCENTS AND AROMAS...
Hmmmm?
YES, MARI IS AN ASSASSIN LIKE ME. SHE'S KNOWN AS A PRO IN CHEMICALS AND POISONS.
BUT DON'T WORRY, THERE'S NO POISON IN YOUR GIFT.
FWOOOM
I SUPPOSE I SHOULDN'T BE SURPRISED THAT SETSUNA-SAN'S COLLEAGUE SPECIALIZES IN SOMETHING TERRIFYING!

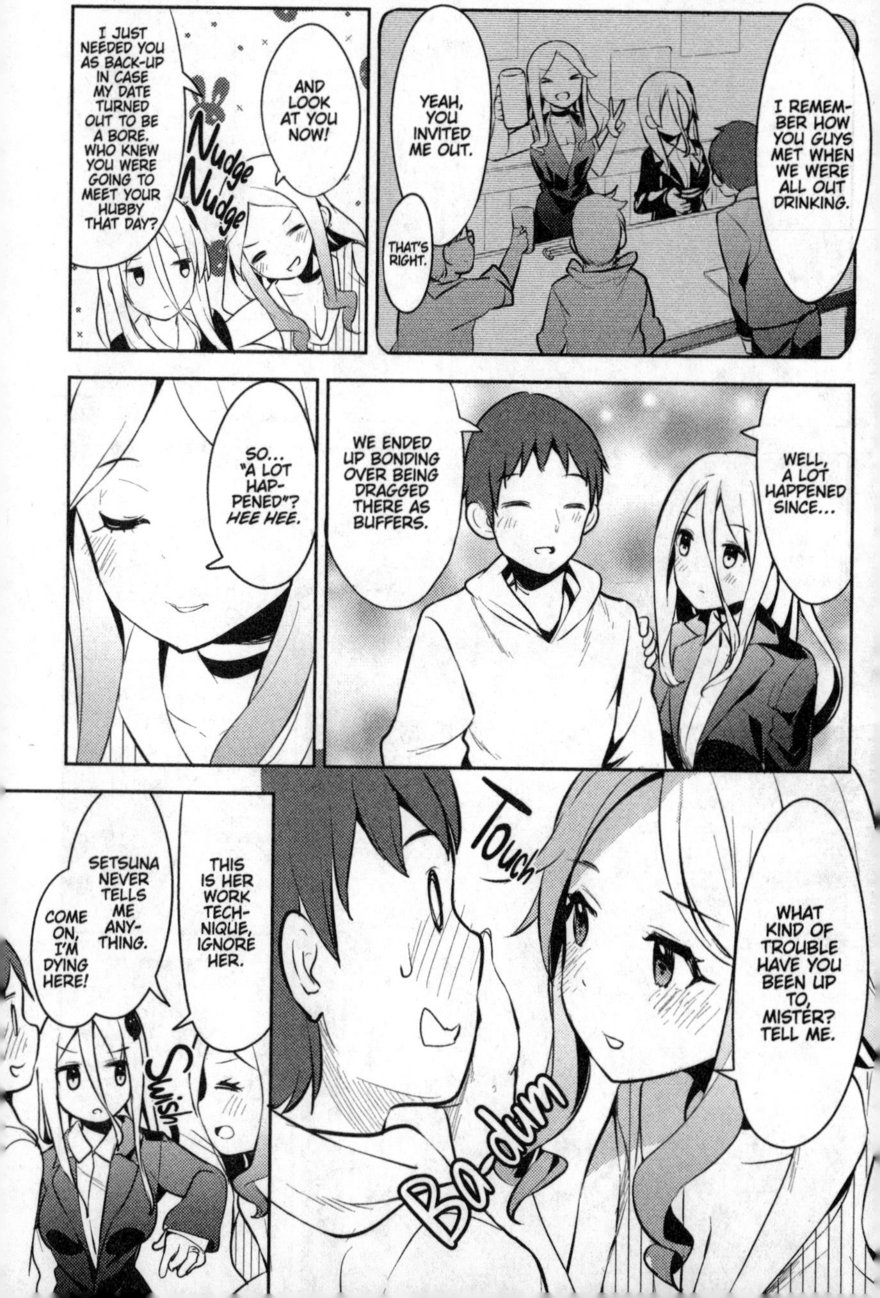
I REMEMBER HOW YOU GUYS MET WHEN WE WERE ALL OUT DRINKING.
YEAH, YOU INVITED ME OUT.
THAT'S RIGHT.
AND LOOK AT YOU NOW!
I JUST NEEDED YOU AS BACK-UP IN CASE MY DATE TURNED OUT TO BE A BORE. WHO KNEW YOU WERE GOING TO MEET YOUR HUBBY THAT DAY?
Nudge Nudge
WELL, A LOT HAPPENED SINCE...
WE ENDED UP BONDING OVER BEING DRAGGED THERE AS BUFFERS.
SO... "A LOT HAPPENED"? HEE HEE.
WHAT KIND OF TROUBLE HAVE YOU BEEN UP TO, MISTER? TELL ME.
Touch
Ba-dum
THIS IS HER WORK TECHNIQUE, IGNORE HER.
SETSUNA NEVER TELLS ME ANYTHING.
COME ON, I'M DYING HERE!
Swish

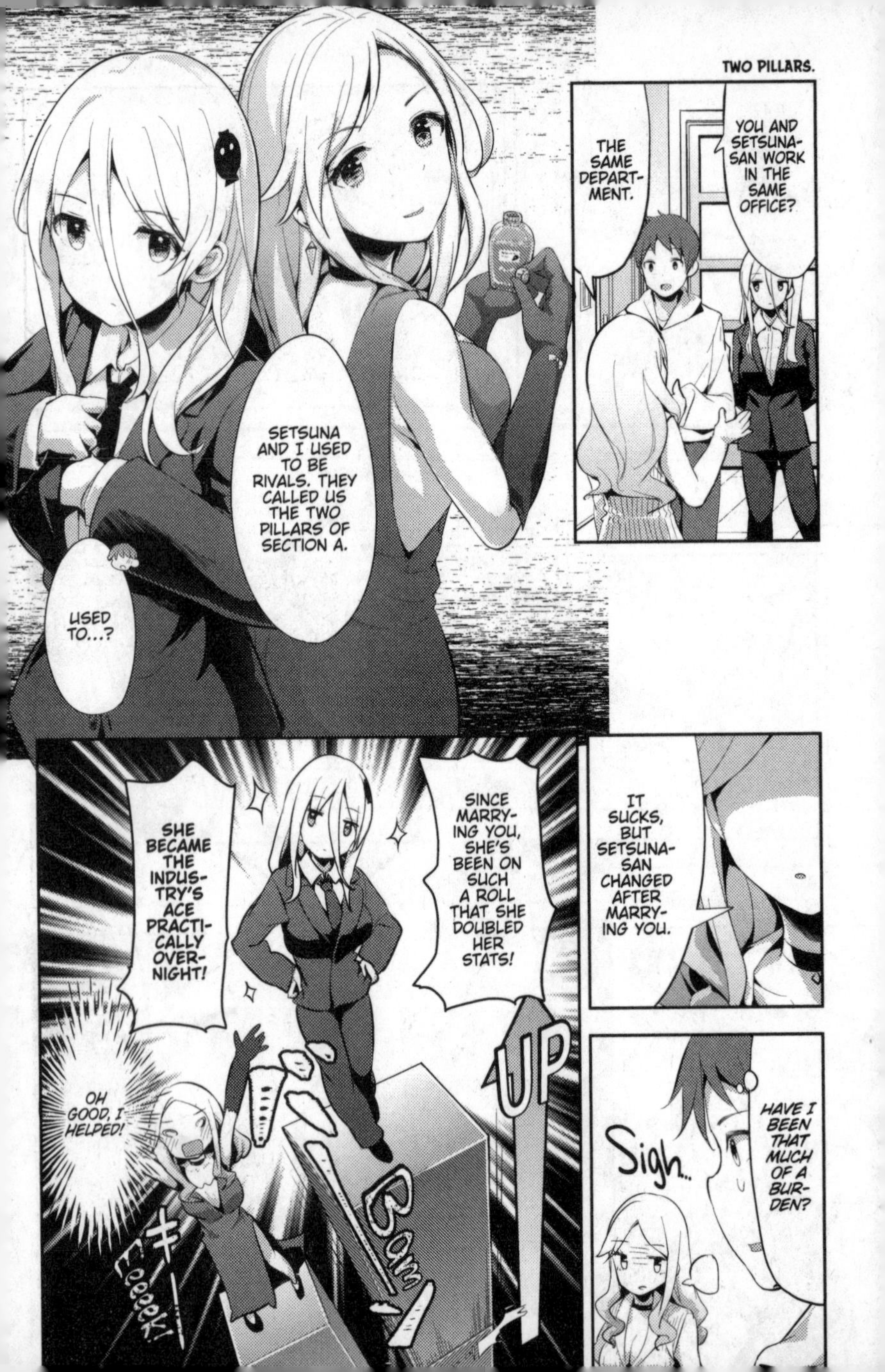
TWO PILLARS.
YOU AND SETSUNA-SAN WORK IN THE SAME OFFICE?
THE SAME DEPARTMENT.
SETSUNA AND I USED TO BE RIVALS. THEY CALLED US THE TWO PILLARS OF SECTION A.
USED TO...?
IT SUCKS, BUT SETSUNA-SAN CHANGED AFTER MARRYING YOU.
HAVE I BEEN THAT MUCH OF A BURDEN?
Sigh..
SINCE MARRYING YOU, SHE'S BEEN ON SUCH A ROLL THAT SHE DOUBLED HER STATS!
SHE BECAME THE INDUSTRY'S ACE PRACTICALLY OVERNIGHT!
UP
OH GOOD, I HELPED!
Bam
Eeeeek!

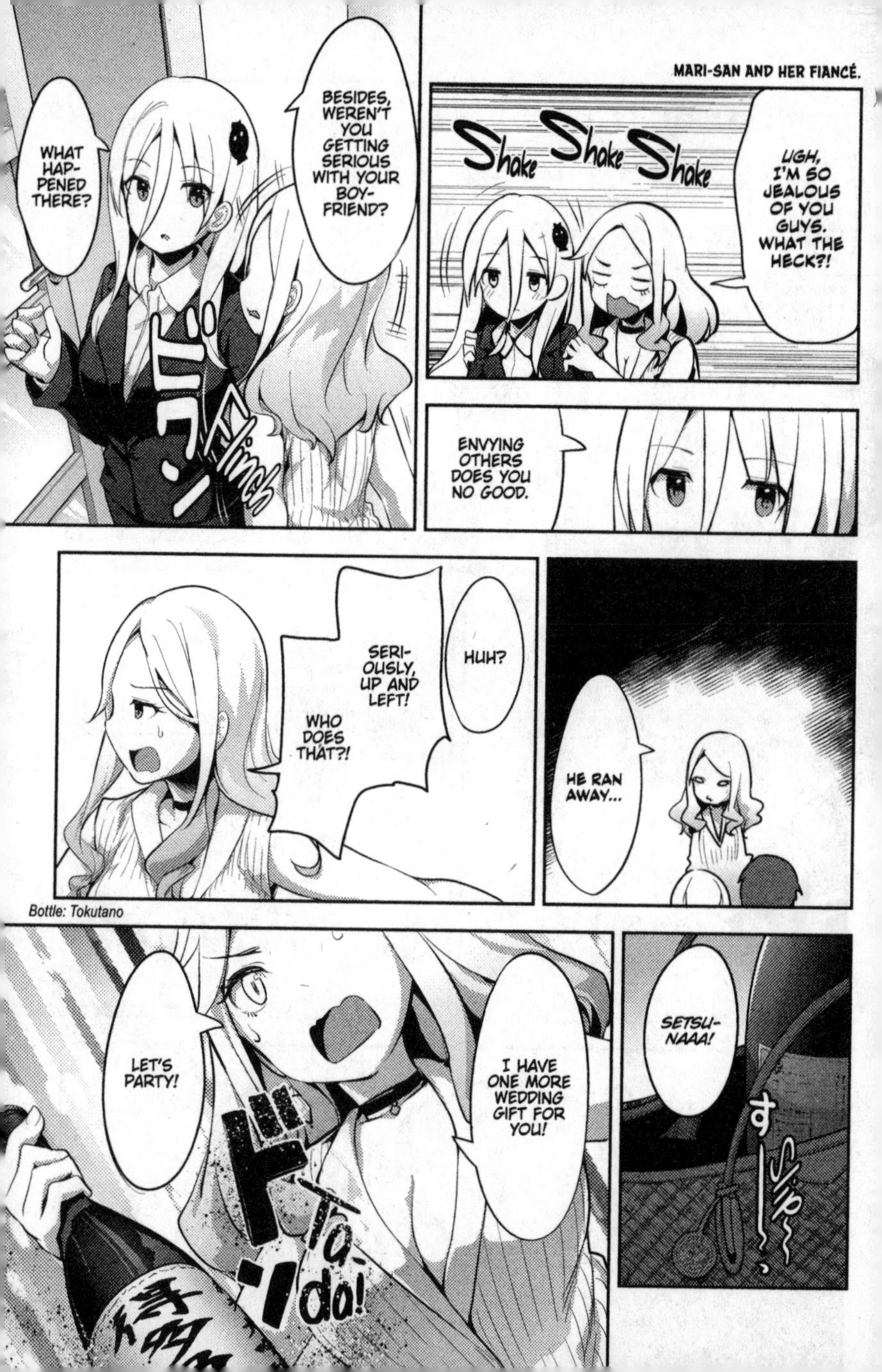
Shake Shake Shake
UGH, I'M SO JEALOUS OF YOU GUYS. WHAT THE HECK?!
ENVYING OTHERS DOES YOU NO GOOD.
BESIDES, WEREN'T YOU GETTING SERIOUS WITH YOUR BOY-FRIEND?
WHAT HAP-PENED THERE?
Flinch
HE RAN AWAY...
HUH?
SERI-OUSLY, UP AND LEFT!
WHO DOES THAT?!
SETSU-NAAA!
Slip~
I HAVE ONE MORE WEDDING GIFT FOR YOU!
LET'S PARTY!
Ta-da!
Bottle: Tokutano

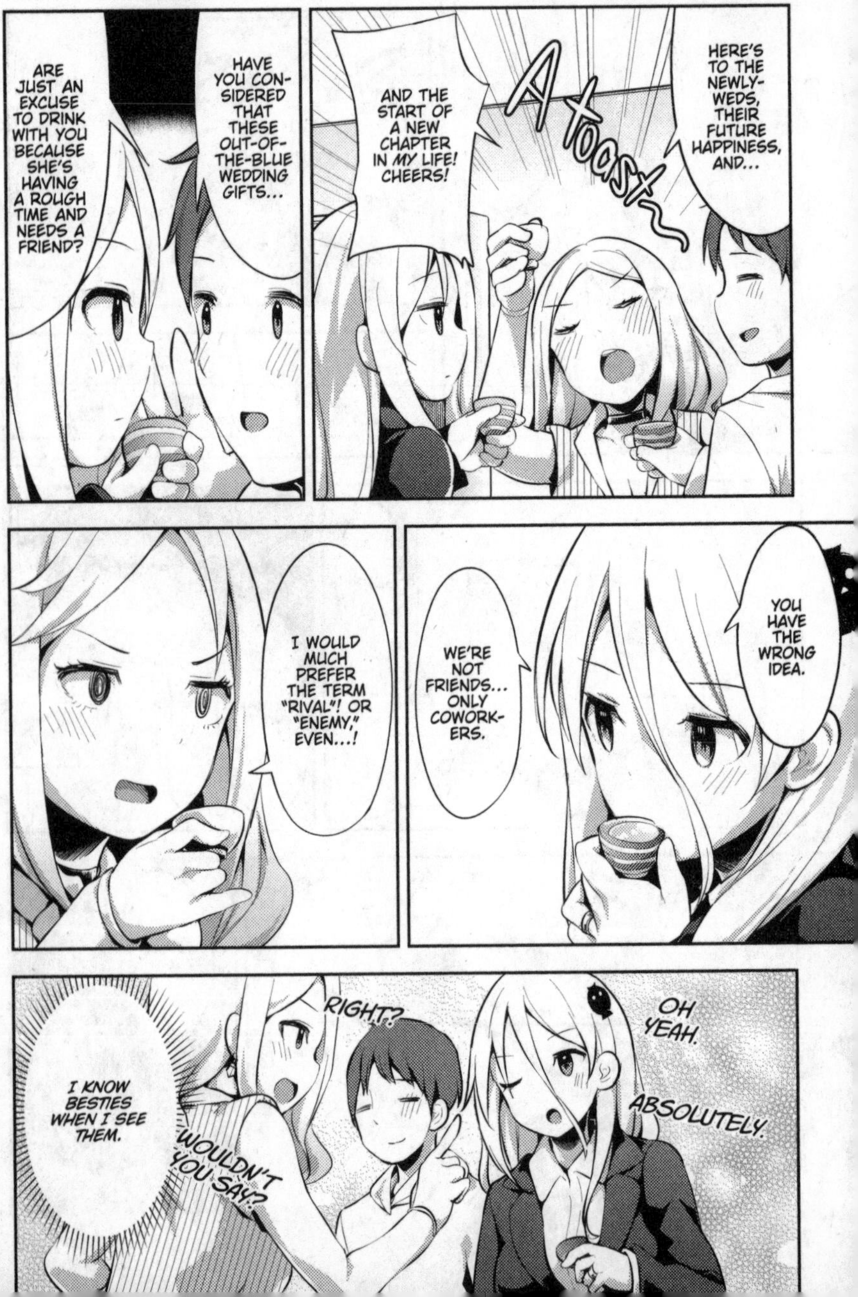
HERE'S TO THE NEWLYWEDS, THEIR FUTURE HAPPINESS, AND...
A toast~
AND THE START OF A NEW CHAPTER IN *MY* LIFE! CHEERS!
HAVE YOU CONSIDERED THAT THESE OUT-OF-THE-BLUE WEDDING GIFTS...
ARE JUST AN EXCUSE TO DRINK WITH YOU BECAUSE SHE'S HAVING A ROUGH TIME AND NEEDS A FRIEND?
YOU HAVE THE WRONG IDEA.
WE'RE NOT FRIENDS... ONLY COWORKERS.
I WOULD MUCH PREFER THE TERM "RIVAL"! OR "ENEMY," EVEN...!
OH YEAH.
RIGHT?
ABSOLUTELY.
WOULDN'T YOU SAY?
I KNOW BESTIES WHEN I SEE THEM.

S-RANK POISON IMMUNITY.

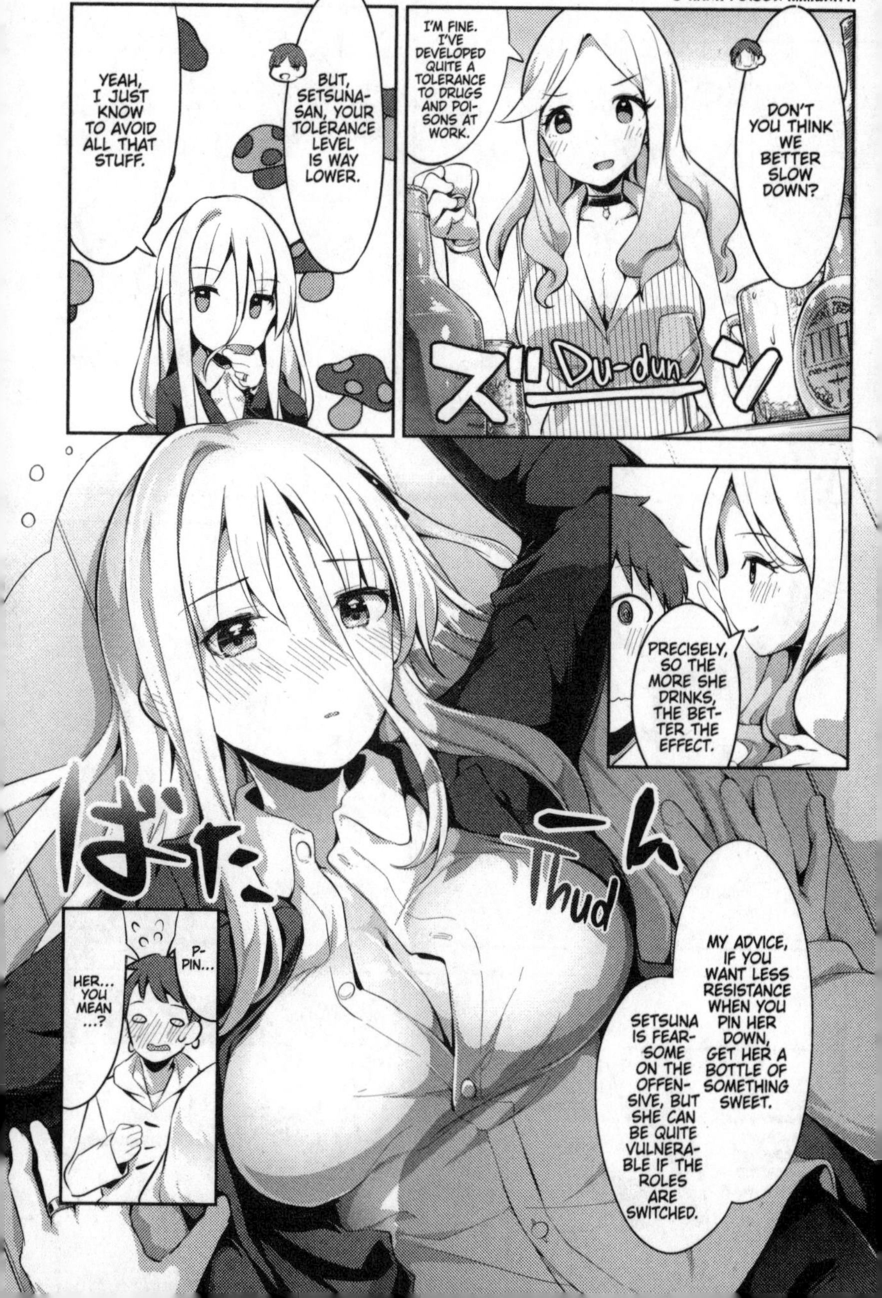
DON'T YOU THINK WE BETTER SLOW DOWN?
I'M FINE. I'VE DEVELOPED QUITE A TOLERANCE TO DRUGS AND POI-SONS AT WORK.
Du-dun
BUT, SETSUNA-SAN, YOUR TOLERANCE LEVEL IS WAY LOWER.
YEAH, I JUST KNOW TO AVOID ALL THAT STUFF.
PRECISELY, SO THE MORE SHE DRINKS, THE BET-TER THE EFFECT.
Thud
MY ADVICE, IF YOU WANT LESS RESISTANCE WHEN YOU PIN HER DOWN, GET HER A BOTTLE OF SOMETHING SWEET.
SETSUNA IS FEAR-SOME ON THE OFFEN-SIVE, BUT SHE CAN BE QUITE VULNERA-BLE IF THE ROLES ARE SWITCHED.
P-PIN...
HER... YOU MEAN ...?

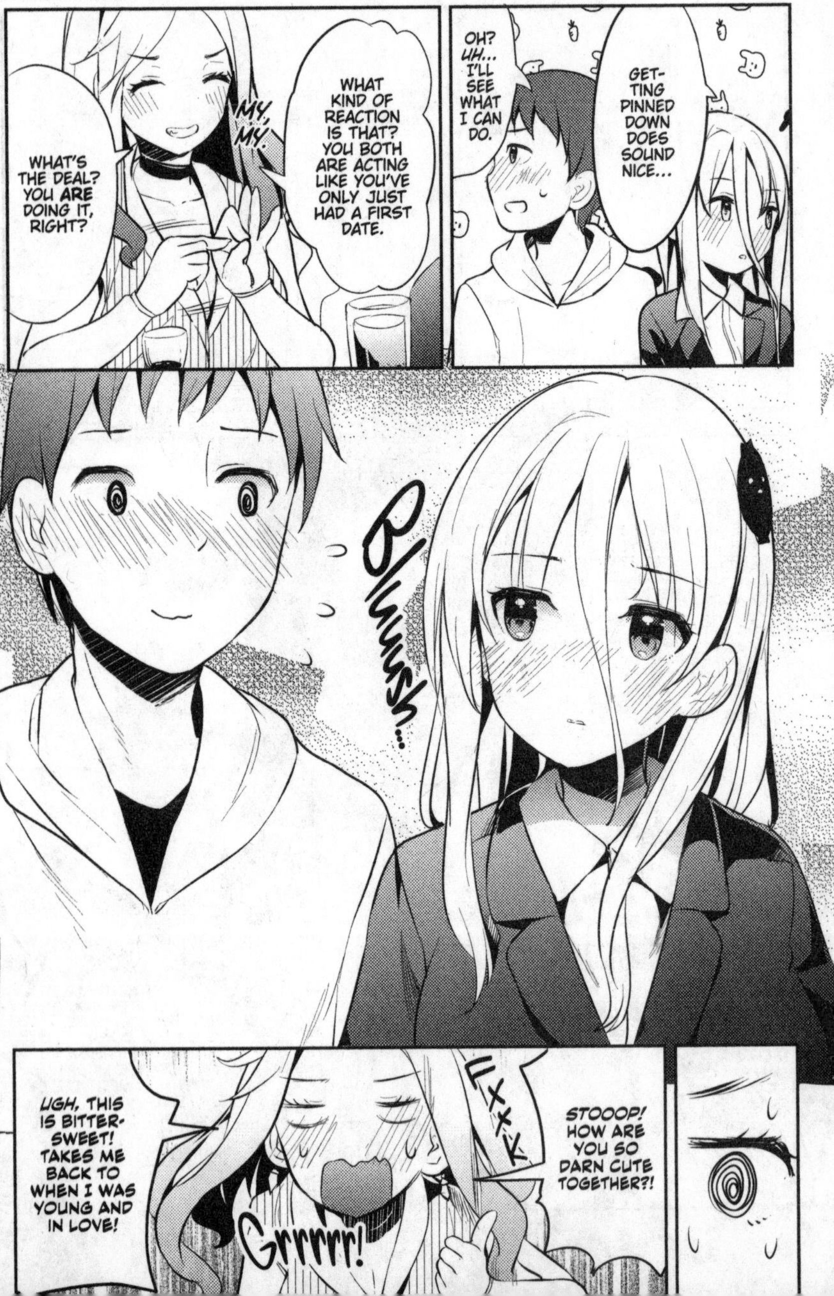
GET-TING PINNED DOWN DOES SOUND NICE...
OH? UH... I'LL SEE WHAT I CAN DO.
WHAT KIND OF REACTION IS THAT? YOU BOTH ARE ACTING LIKE YOU'VE ONLY JUST HAD A FIRST DATE.
MY, MY.
WHAT'S THE DEAL? YOU ARE DOING IT, RIGHT?
Bluuush...
STOOOP! HOW ARE YOU SO DARN CUTE TOGETHER?!
F-X-X-K
UGH, THIS IS BITTER-SWEET! TAKES ME BACK TO WHEN I WAS YOUNG AND IN LOVE!
Grrrrr!

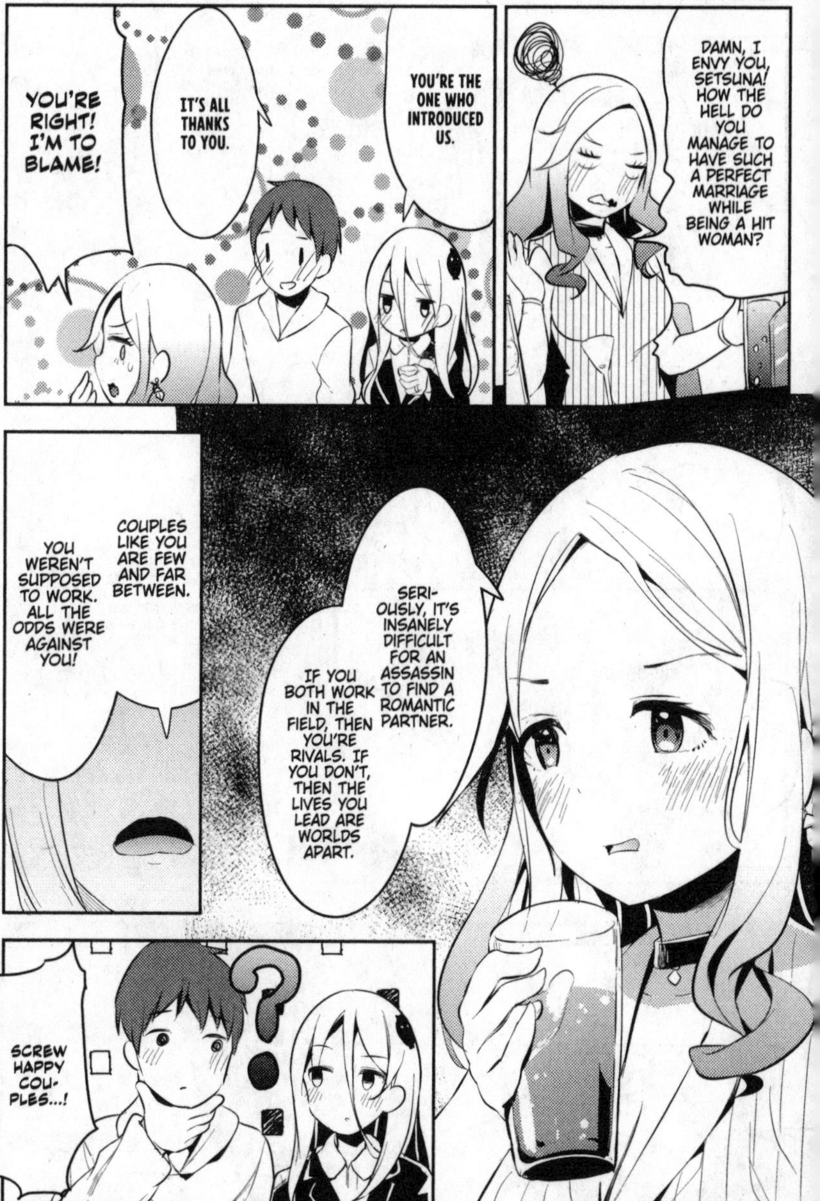
DAMN, I ENVY YOU, SETSUNA! HOW THE HELL DO YOU MANAGE TO HAVE SUCH A PERFECT MARRIAGE WHILE BEING A HIT WOMAN?
YOU'RE THE ONE WHO INTRODUCED US.
IT'S ALL THANKS TO YOU.
YOU'RE RIGHT! I'M TO BLAME!
SERI-OUSLY, IT'S INSANELY DIFFICULT FOR AN ASSASSIN TO FIND A ROMANTIC PARTNER.
IF YOU BOTH WORK IN THE FIELD, THEN YOU'RE RIVALS. IF YOU DON'T, THEN THE LIVES YOU LEAD ARE WORLDS APART.
COUPLES LIKE YOU ARE FEW AND FAR BETWEEN.
YOU WEREN'T SUPPOSED TO WORK. ALL THE ODDS WERE AGAINST YOU!
SCREW HAPPY COU-PLES...!

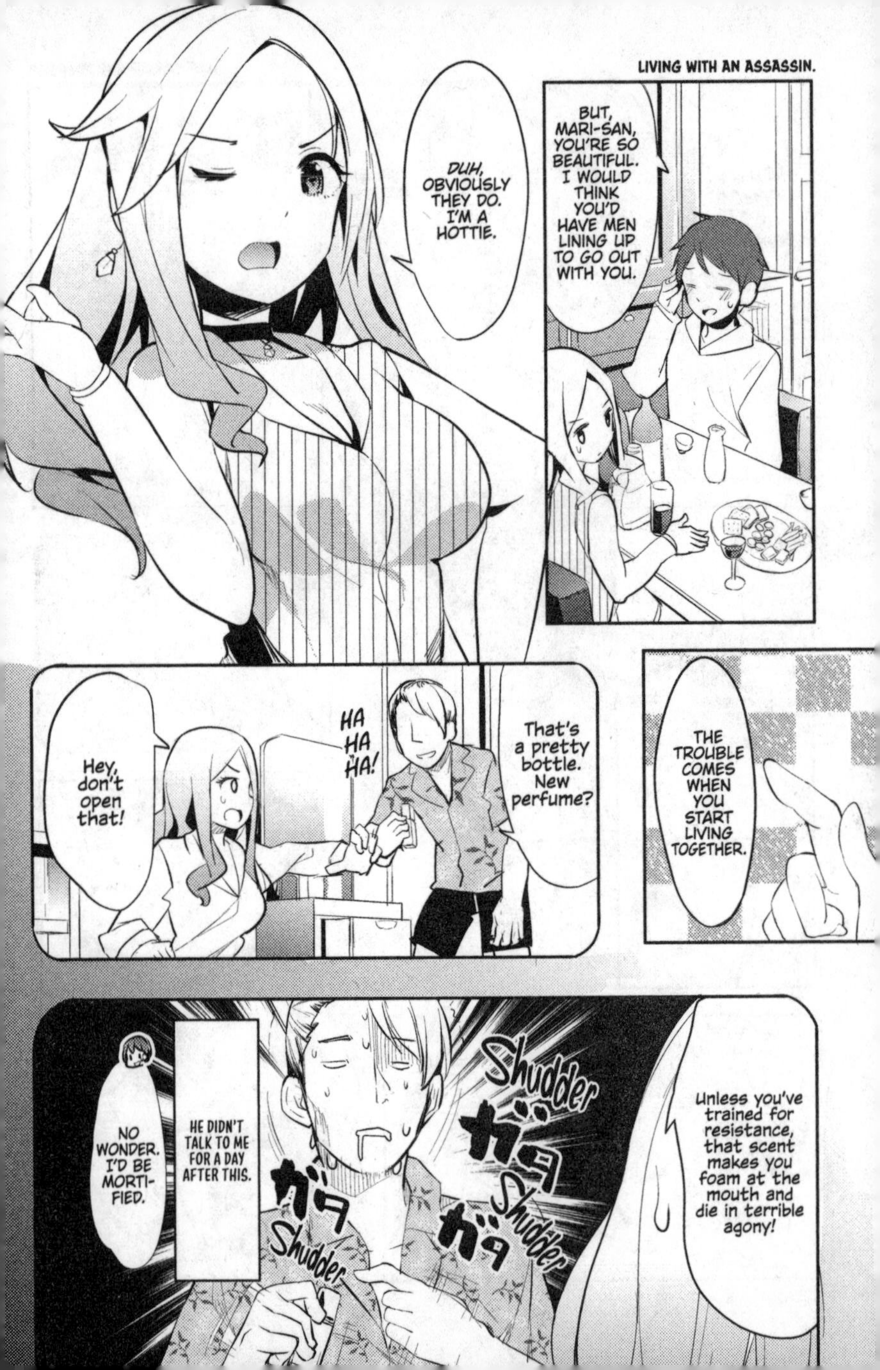
BUT, MARI-SAN, YOU'RE SO BEAUTIFUL. I WOULD THINK YOU'D HAVE MEN LINING UP TO GO OUT WITH YOU.
DUH, OBVIOUSLY THEY DO. I'M A HOTTIE.
THE TROUBLE COMES WHEN YOU START LIVING TOGETHER.
That's a pretty bottle. New perfume?
HA HA HA!
Hey, don't open that!
Unless you've trained for resistance, that scent makes you foam at the mouth and die in terrible agony!
Shudder ガタ
Shudder ガタ
ガタ Shudder
HE DIDN'T TALK TO ME FOR A DAY AFTER THIS.
NO WONDER. I'D BE MORTIFIED.

EVEN ASSASSINS NEED PRAISE.

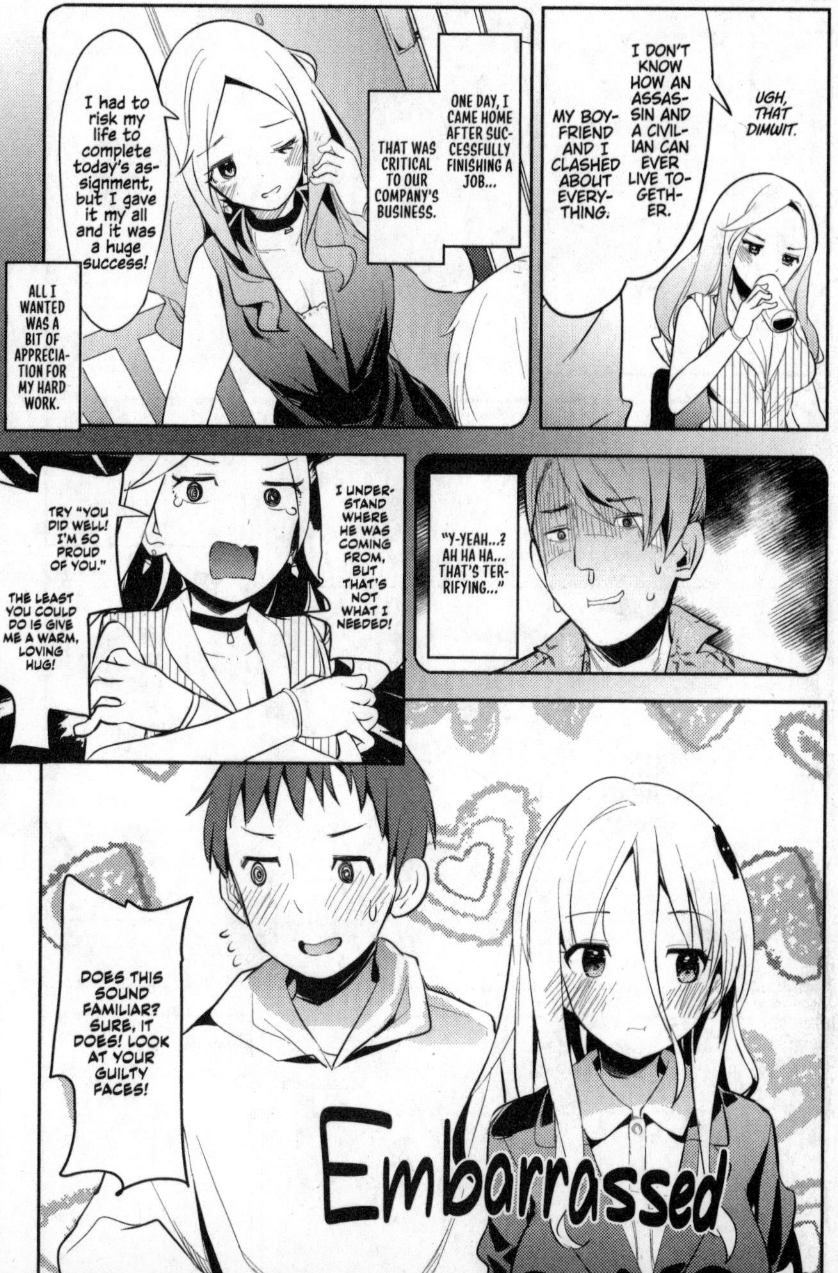

UGH, THAT DIMWIT.
I DON'T KNOW HOW AN ASSASSIN AND A CIVILIAN CAN EVER LIVE TOGETHER.
MY BOYFRIEND AND I CLASHED ABOUT EVERYTHING.
ONE DAY, I CAME HOME AFTER SUCCESSFULLY FINISHING A JOB...
THAT WAS CRITICAL TO OUR COMPANY'S BUSINESS.
I had to risk my life to complete today's assignment, but I gave it my all and it was a huge success!
ALL I WANTED WAS A BIT OF APPRECIATION FOR MY HARD WORK.
"Y-YEAH...? AH HA HA... THAT'S TERRIFYING..."
I UNDERSTAND WHERE HE WAS COMING FROM, BUT THAT'S NOT WHAT I NEEDED!
TRY "YOU DID WELL! I'M SO PROUD OF YOU."
THE LEAST YOU COULD DO IS GIVE ME A WARM, LOVING HUG!
DOES THIS SOUND FAMILIAR? SURE, IT DOES! LOOK AT YOUR GUILTY FACES!
Embarrassed

THE WHOLE STORY.

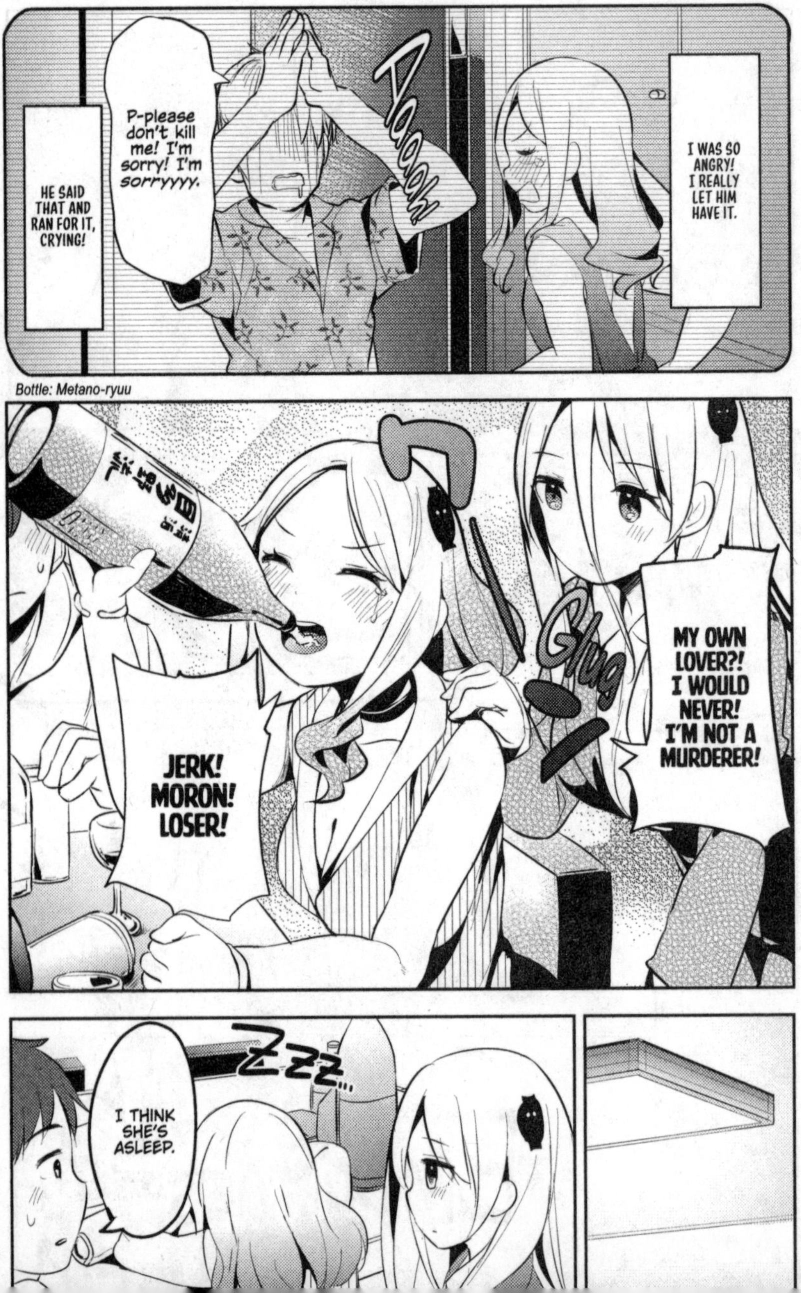
I WAS SO ANGRY! I REALLY LET HIM HAVE IT.
Aaaah!
P-please don't kill me! I'm sorry! I'm sorryyyy.
HE SAID THAT AND RAN FOR IT, CRYING!
MY OWN LOVER?! I WOULD NEVER! I'M NOT A MURDERER!
Glug
JERK! MORON! LOSER!
Zzz...
I THINK SHE'S ASLEEP.

Bottle: Metano-ryuu

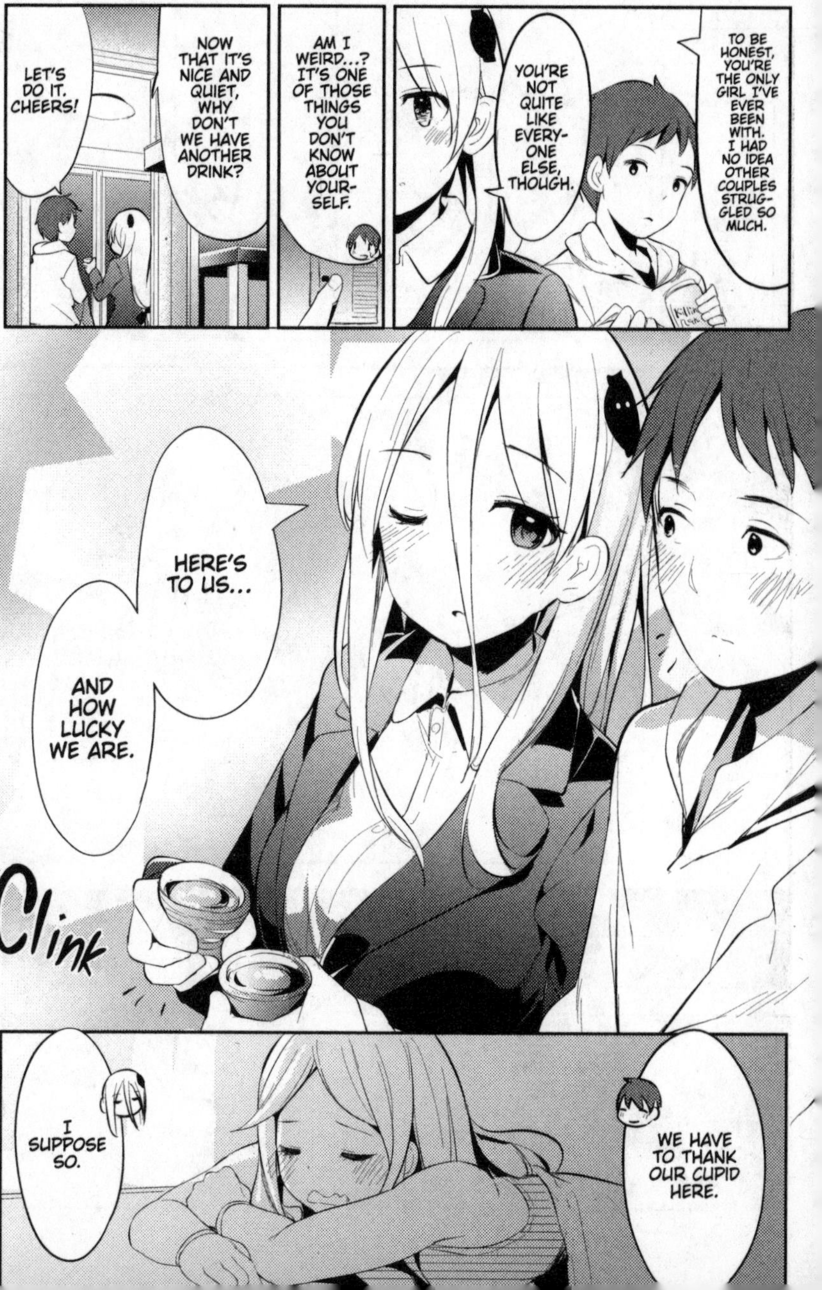
TO BE HONEST, YOU'RE THE ONLY GIRL I'VE EVER BEEN WITH. I HAD NO IDEA OTHER COUPLES STRUGGLED SO MUCH.
YOU'RE NOT QUITE LIKE EVERYONE ELSE, THOUGH.
AM I WEIRD...? IT'S ONE OF THOSE THINGS YOU DON'T KNOW ABOUT YOURSELF.
NOW THAT IT'S NICE AND QUIET, WHY DON'T WE HAVE ANOTHER DRINK?
LET'S DO IT. CHEERS!
HERE'S TO US...
AND HOW LUCKY WE ARE.
Clink
WE HAVE TO THANK OUR CUPID HERE.
I SUPPOSE SO.

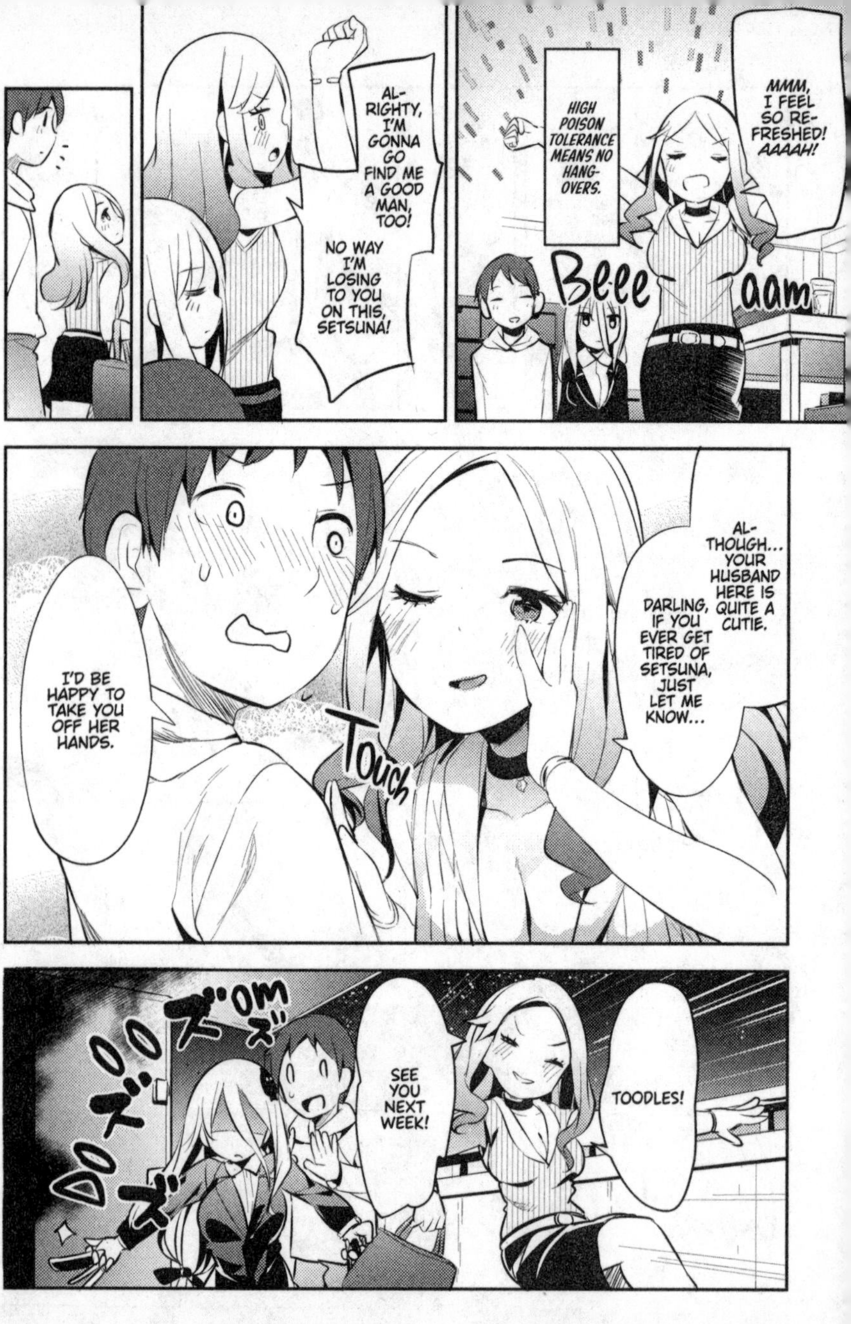
MMM, I FEEL SO RE-FRESHED! AAAAH!
HIGH POISON TOLERANCE MEANS NO HANG-OVERS.
Be-ee aam
AL-RIGHTY, I'M GONNA GO FIND ME A GOOD MAN, TOO!
NO WAY I'M LOSING TO YOU ON THIS, SETSUNA!
AL-THOUGH... YOUR HUSBAND HERE IS QUITE A CUTIE.
DARLING, IF YOU EVER GET TIRED OF SETSUNA, JUST LET ME KNOW...
Touch
I'D BE HAPPY TO TAKE YOU OFF HER HANDS.
TOODLES!
SEE YOU NEXT WEEK!
ズom ズ
DOO ズ

MARI-SAN'S GLAMOUROUS LIFE AS A SINGLE LADY-ASSASSIN.

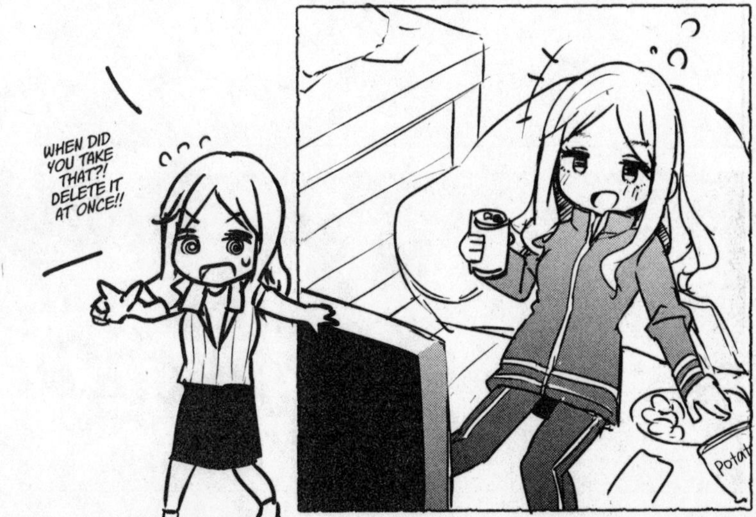
WHEN DID YOU TAKE THAT?! DELETE IT AT ONCE!!
Potat

MY Lovey-Dovey Wife IS A STONE COLD KILLER

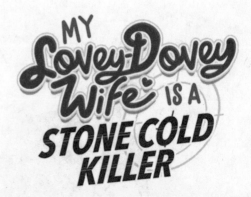

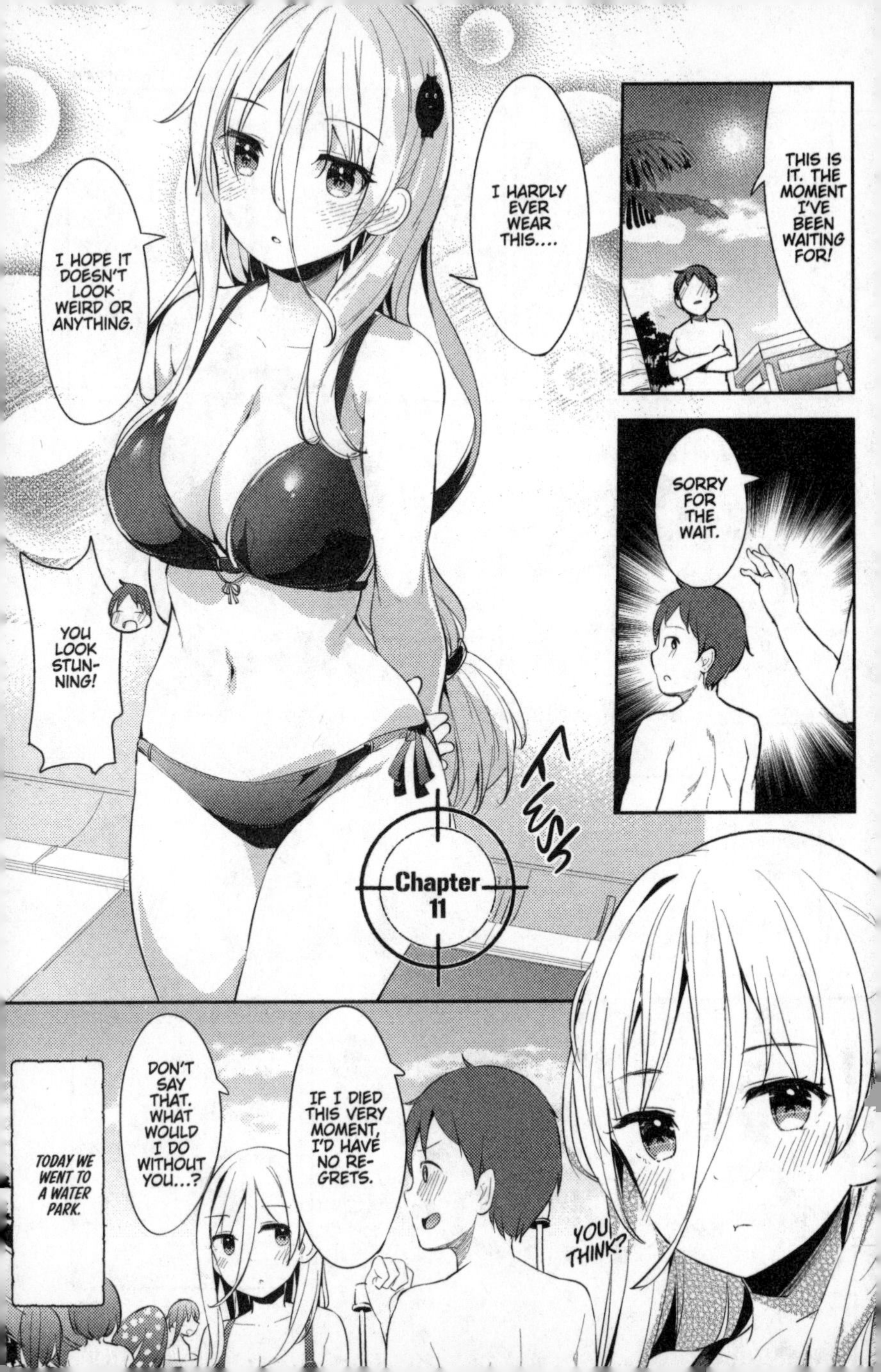
THIS IS IT. THE MOMENT I'VE BEEN WAITING FOR!
SORRY FOR THE WAIT.
I HARDLY EVER WEAR THIS....
I HOPE IT DOESN'T LOOK WEIRD OR ANYTHING.
YOU LOOK STUN-NING!
Flush
Chapter 11
YOU THINK?
IF I DIED THIS VERY MOMENT, I'D HAVE NO RE-GRETS.
DON'T SAY THAT. WHAT WOULD I DO WITHOUT YOU...?
TODAY WE WENT TO A WATER PARK.

FAMILY TIME AT A WATER PARK.

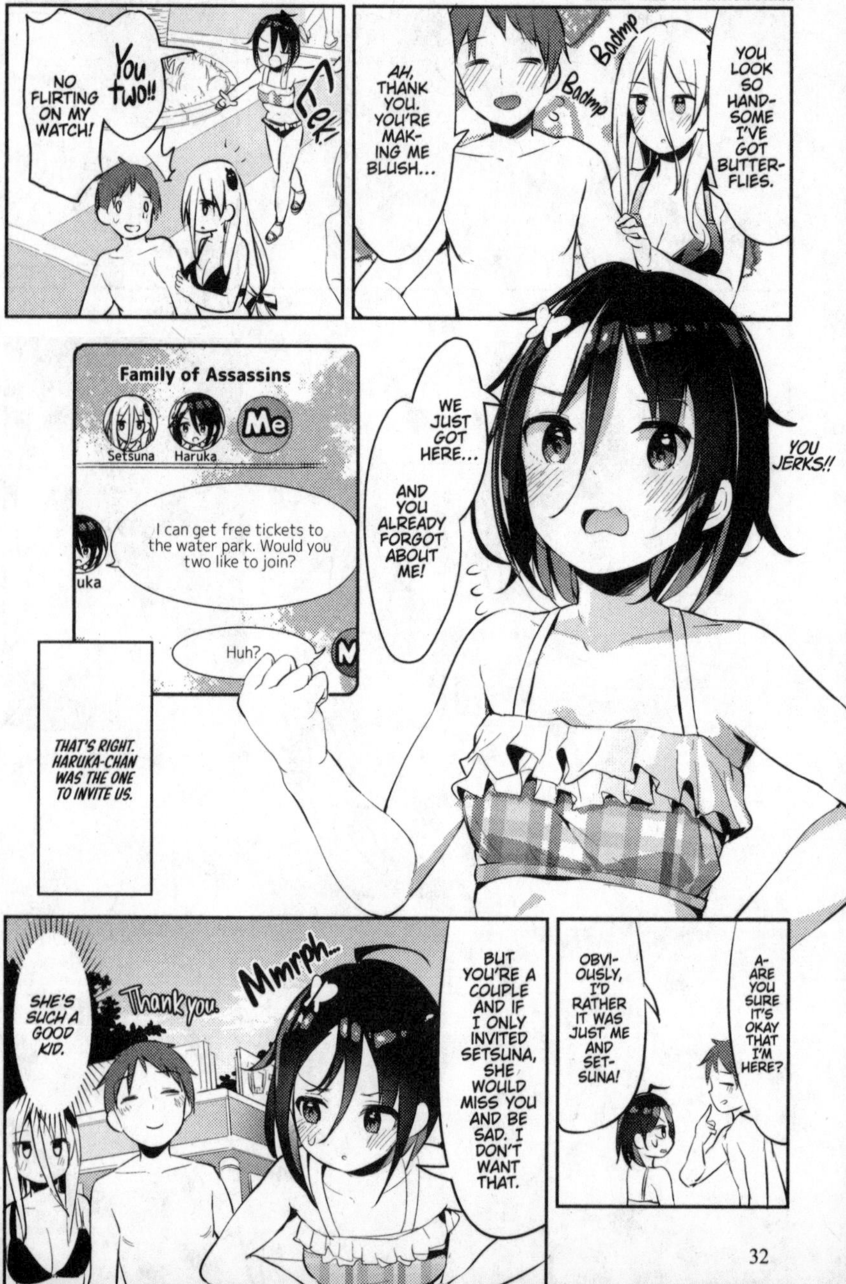
Badmp
Badmp
YOU LOOK SO HANDSOME I'VE GOT BUTTERFLIES.
AH, THANK YOU. YOU'RE MAKING ME BLUSH...
Eek!
You two!!
NO FLIRTING ON MY WATCH!
WE JUST GOT HERE...
AND YOU ALREADY FORGOT ABOUT ME!
YOU JERKS!!
Family of Assassins
Setsuna
Haruka
Me
I can get free tickets to the water park. Would you two like to join?
Huh?
THAT'S RIGHT. HARUKA-CHAN WAS THE ONE TO INVITE US.
A-ARE YOU SURE IT'S OKAY THAT I'M HERE?
OBVIOUSLY, I'D RATHER IT WAS JUST ME AND SETSUNA!
BUT YOU'RE A COUPLE AND IF I ONLY INVITED SETSUNA, SHE WOULD MISS YOU AND BE SAD. I DON'T WANT THAT.
Mmrph...
Thank you.
SHE'S SUCH A GOOD KID.

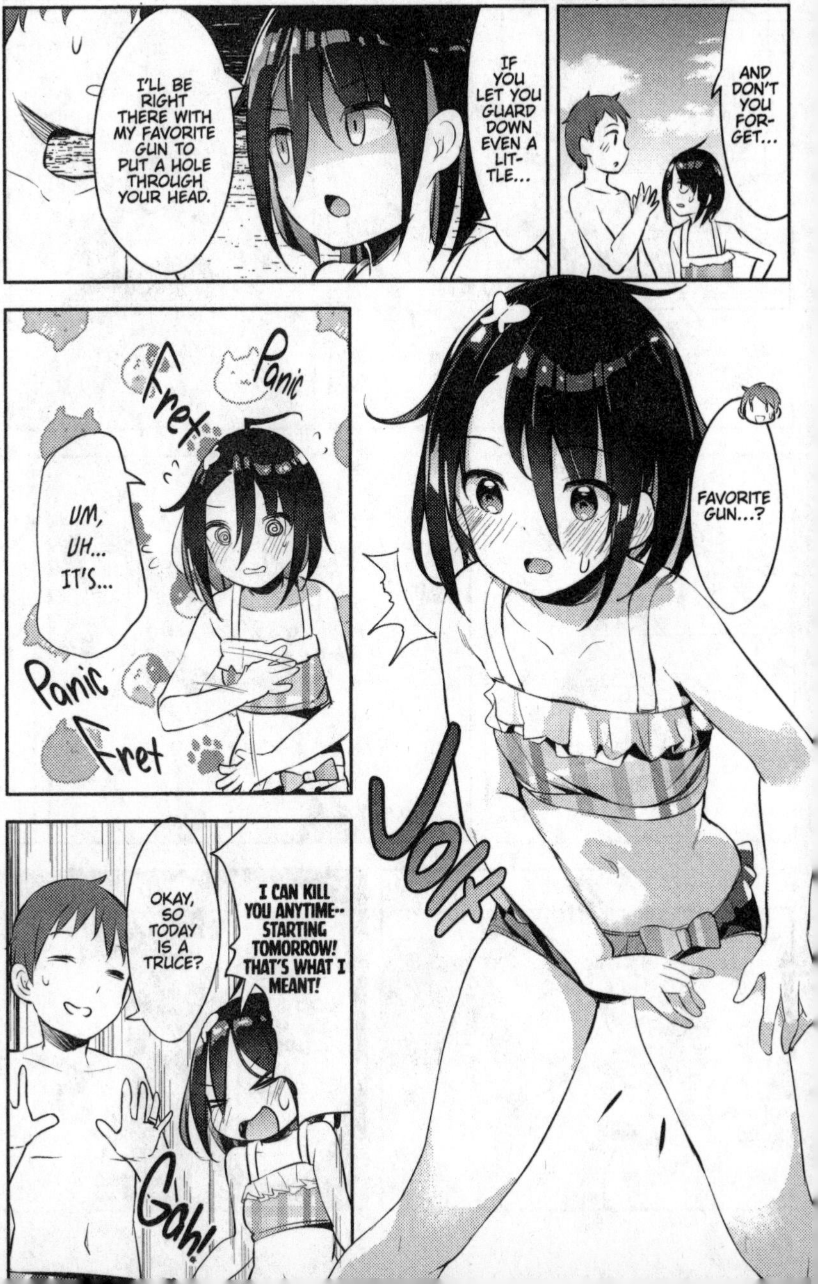
AND DON'T YOU FOR-GET...
IF YOU LET YOU GUARD DOWN EVEN A LIT-TLE...
I'LL BE RIGHT THERE WITH MY FAVORITE GUN TO PUT A HOLE THROUGH YOUR HEAD.
FAVORITE GUN...?
Jolt
Panic
Fret
UM, UH... IT'S...
Panic
Fret
I CAN KILL YOU ANYTIME-- STARTING TOMORROW! THAT'S WHAT I MEANT!
OKAY, SO TODAY IS A TRUCE?
Gah!

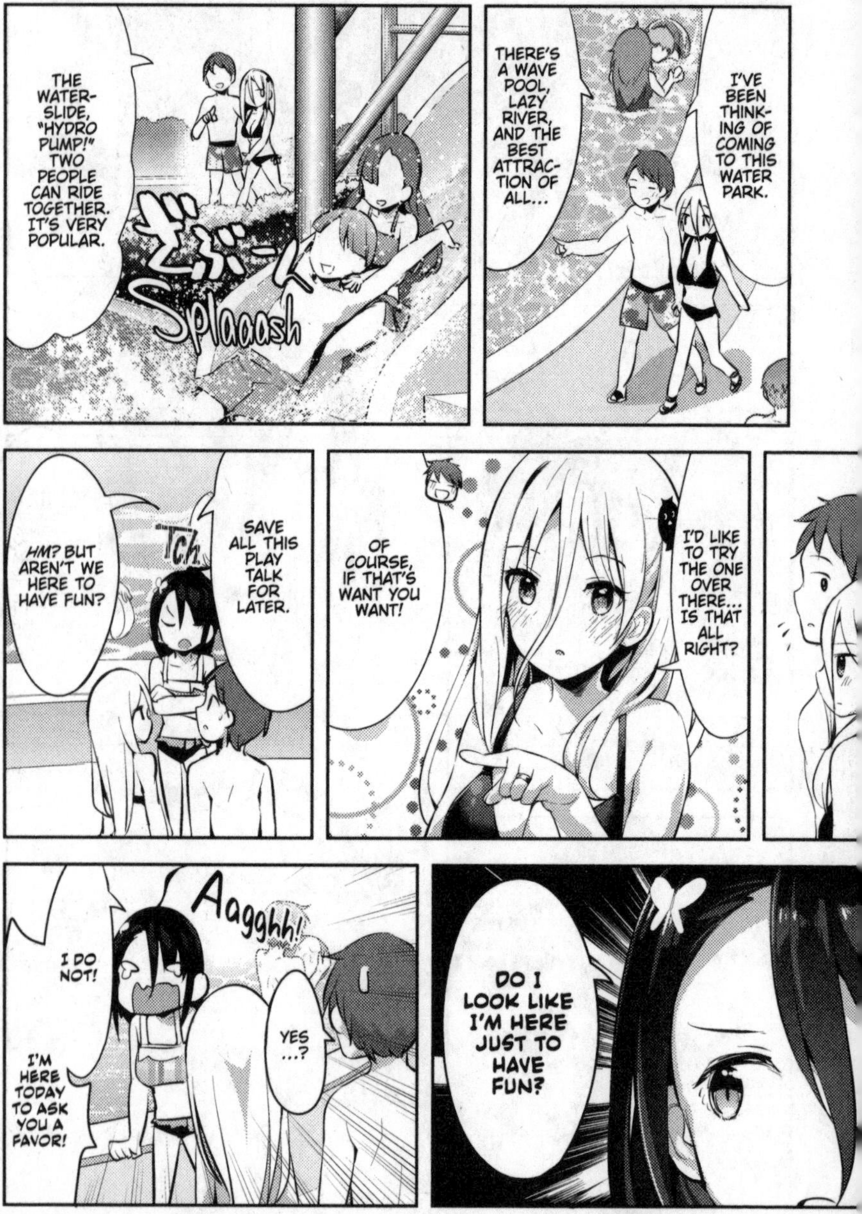
I'VE BEEN THINKING OF COMING TO THIS WATER PARK.
THERE'S A WAVE POOL, LAZY RIVER, AND THE BEST ATTRACTION OF ALL...
THE WATER-SLIDE, "HYDRO PUMP!" TWO PEOPLE CAN RIDE TOGETHER. IT'S VERY POPULAR.
Splaaash
I'D LIKE TO TRY THE ONE OVER THERE... IS THAT ALL RIGHT?
OF COURSE, IF THAT'S WANT YOU WANT!
SAVE ALL THIS PLAY TALK FOR LATER.
Tch
HM? BUT AREN'T WE HERE TO HAVE FUN?
DO I LOOK LIKE I'M HERE JUST TO HAVE FUN?
YES ...?
Aagghh!
I DO NOT!
I'M HERE TODAY TO ASK YOU A FAVOR!

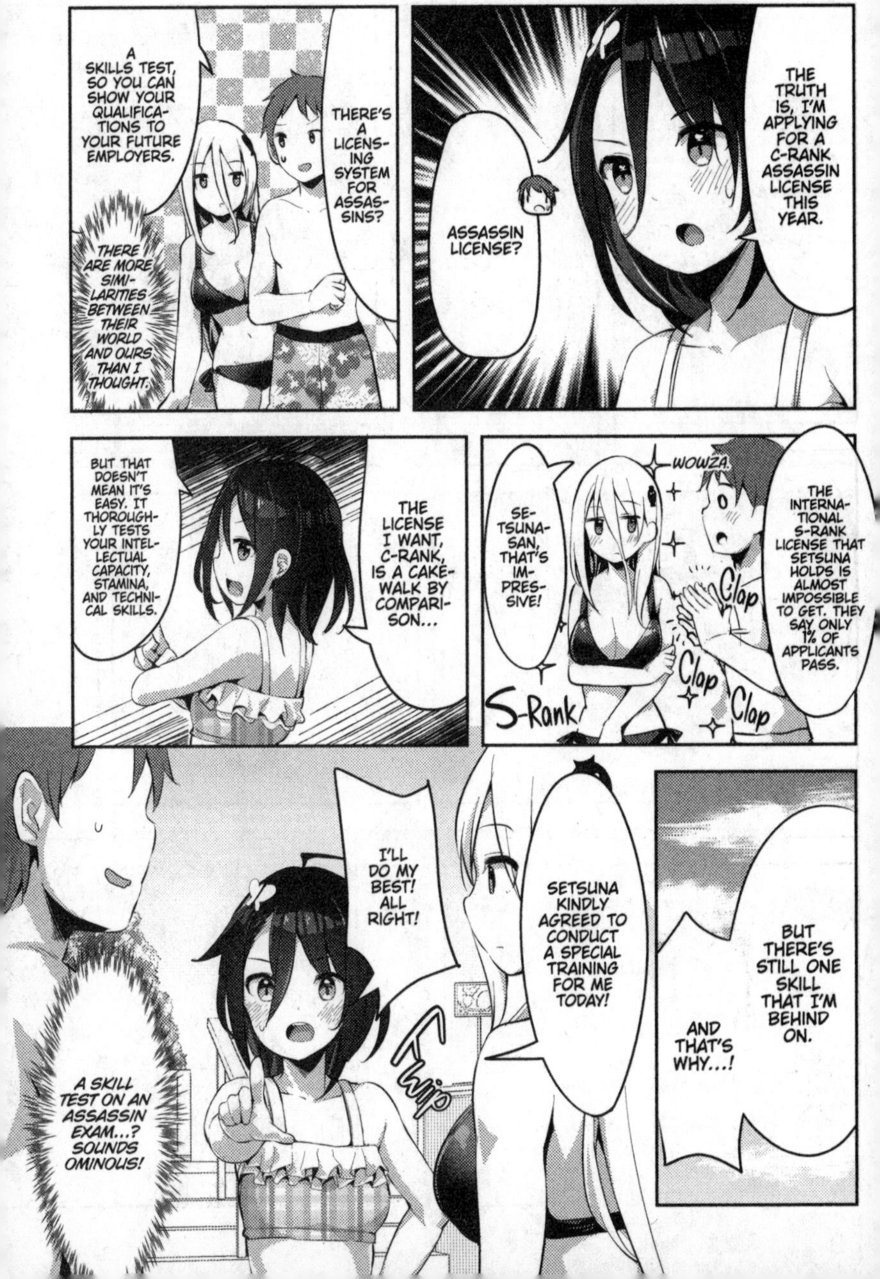
THE TRUTH IS, I'M APPLYING FOR A C-RANK ASSASSIN LICENSE THIS YEAR.
ASSASSIN LICENSE?
THERE'S A LICENSING SYSTEM FOR ASSASSINS?
A SKILLS TEST, SO YOU CAN SHOW YOUR QUALIFICATIONS TO YOUR FUTURE EMPLOYERS.
THERE ARE MORE SIMILARITIES BETWEEN THEIR WORLD AND OURS THAN I THOUGHT.
THE INTERNATIONAL S-RANK LICENSE THAT SETSUNA HOLDS IS ALMOST IMPOSSIBLE TO GET. THEY SAY ONLY 1% OF APPLICANTS PASS.
WOWZA.
SETSUNA-SAN, THAT'S IMPRESSIVE!
Clap
Clap
Clap
S-Rank
THE LICENSE I WANT, C-RANK, IS A CAKEWALK BY COMPARISON...
BUT THAT DOESN'T MEAN IT'S EASY. IT THOROUGHLY TESTS YOUR INTELLECTUAL CAPACITY, STAMINA, AND TECHNICAL SKILLS.
BUT THERE'S STILL ONE SKILL THAT I'M BEHIND ON.
AND THAT'S WHY...!
SETSUNA KINDLY AGREED TO CONDUCT A SPECIAL TRAINING FOR ME TODAY!
I'LL DO MY BEST! ALL RIGHT!
Flip
A SKILL TEST ON AN ASSASSIN EXAM...? SOUNDS OMINOUS!

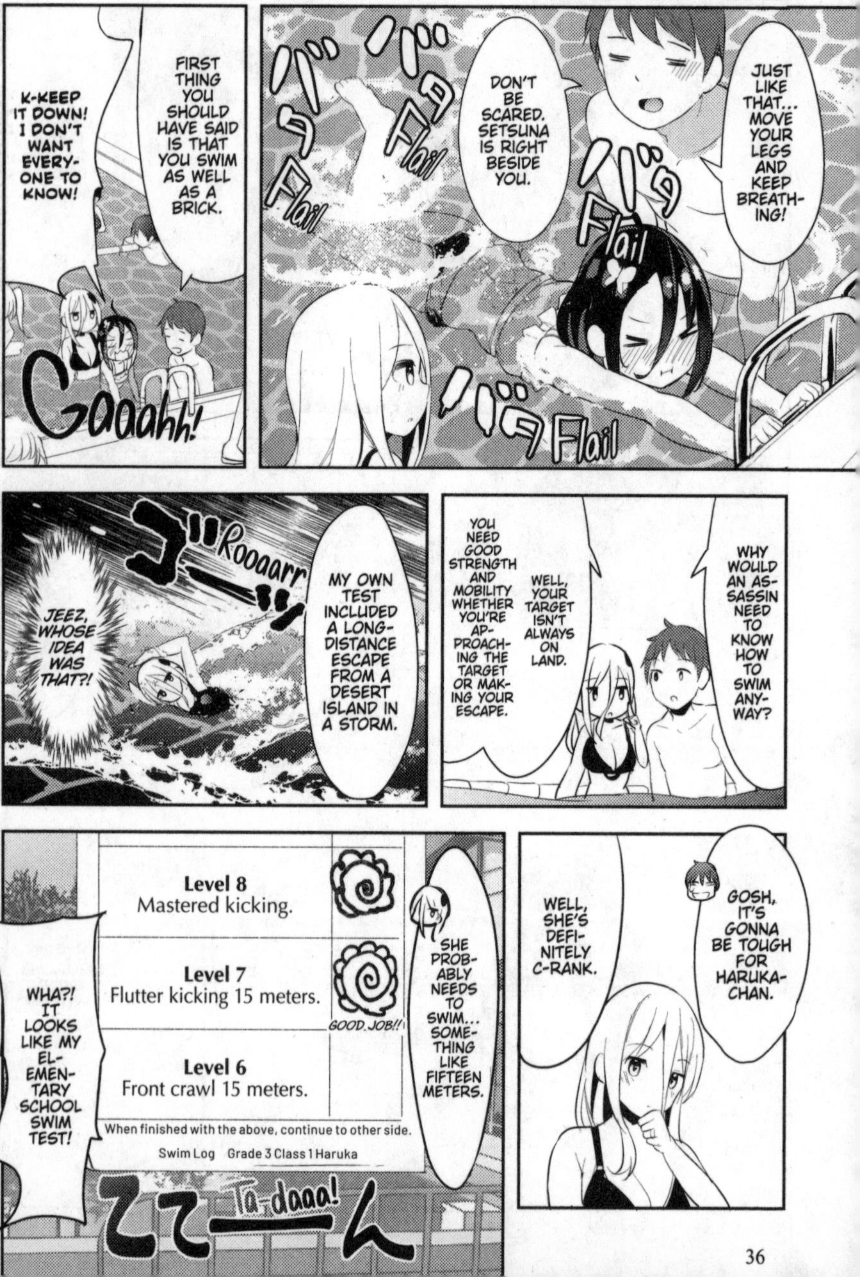
JUST LIKE THAT... MOVE YOUR LEGS AND KEEP BREATHING!
バタ Flail
DON'T BE SCARED. SETSUNA IS RIGHT BESIDE YOU.
バタ Flail
バタ Flail
バタ Flail
FIRST THING YOU SHOULD HAVE SAID IS THAT YOU SWIM AS WELL AS A BRICK.
K-KEEP IT DOWN! I DON'T WANT EVERYONE TO KNOW!
Gaaahh!
WHY WOULD AN ASSASSIN NEED TO KNOW HOW TO SWIM ANYWAY?
WELL, YOUR TARGET ISN'T ALWAYS ON LAND.
YOU NEED GOOD STRENGTH AND MOBILITY WHETHER YOU'RE APPROACHING THE TARGET OR MAKING YOUR ESCAPE.
MY OWN TEST INCLUDED A LONG-DISTANCE ESCAPE FROM A DESERT ISLAND IN A STORM.
ゴー Rooaarr
JEEZ, WHOSE IDEA WAS THAT?!
GOSH, IT'S GONNA BE TOUGH FOR HARUKA-CHAN.
WELL, SHE'S DEFINITELY C-RANK.
SHE PROBABLY NEEDS TO SWIM... SOMETHING LIKE FIFTEEN METERS.
Level 8
Mastered kicking.
Level 7
Flutter kicking 15 meters.
GOOD. JOB!!
Level 6
Front crawl 15 meters.
When finished with the above, continue to other side.
Swim Log Grade 3 Class 1 Haruka
WHA?! IT LOOKS LIKE MY ELEMENTARY SCHOOL SWIM TEST!
ててーん Ta-daaa!

MRS. S-RANK'S SWIMMING TECHNIQUE.

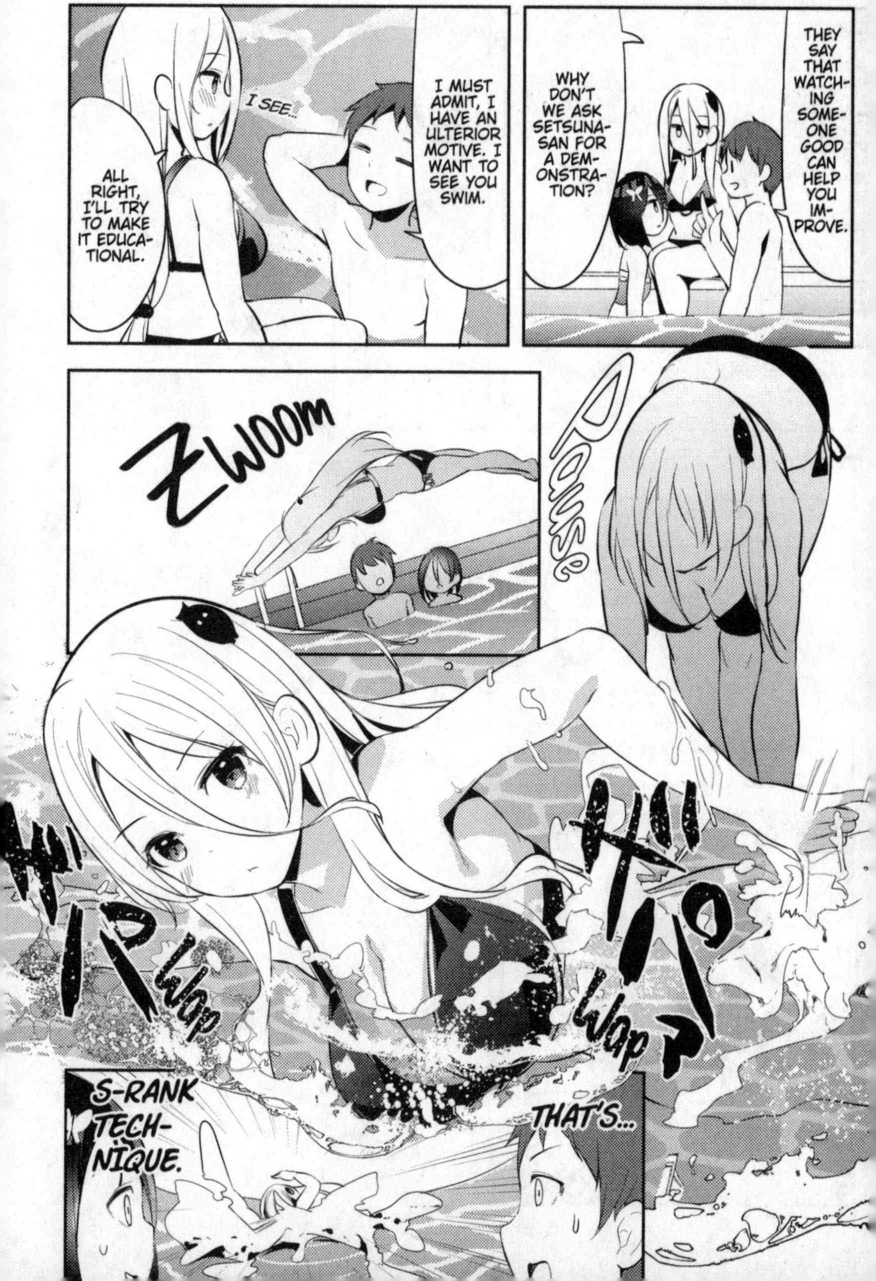
THEY SAY THAT WATCHING SOMEONE GOOD CAN HELP YOU IMPROVE.
WHY DON'T WE ASK SETSUNA-SAN FOR A DEMONSTRATION?
I MUST ADMIT, I HAVE AN ULTERIOR MOTIVE. I WANT TO SEE YOU SWIM.
I SEE...
ALL RIGHT, I'LL TRY TO MAKE IT EDUCATIONAL.
Pause
ZWOOM
Wap
Wap
THAT'S...
S-RANK TECHNIQUE.

SETSUNA-SAN DRAWS A CROWD.

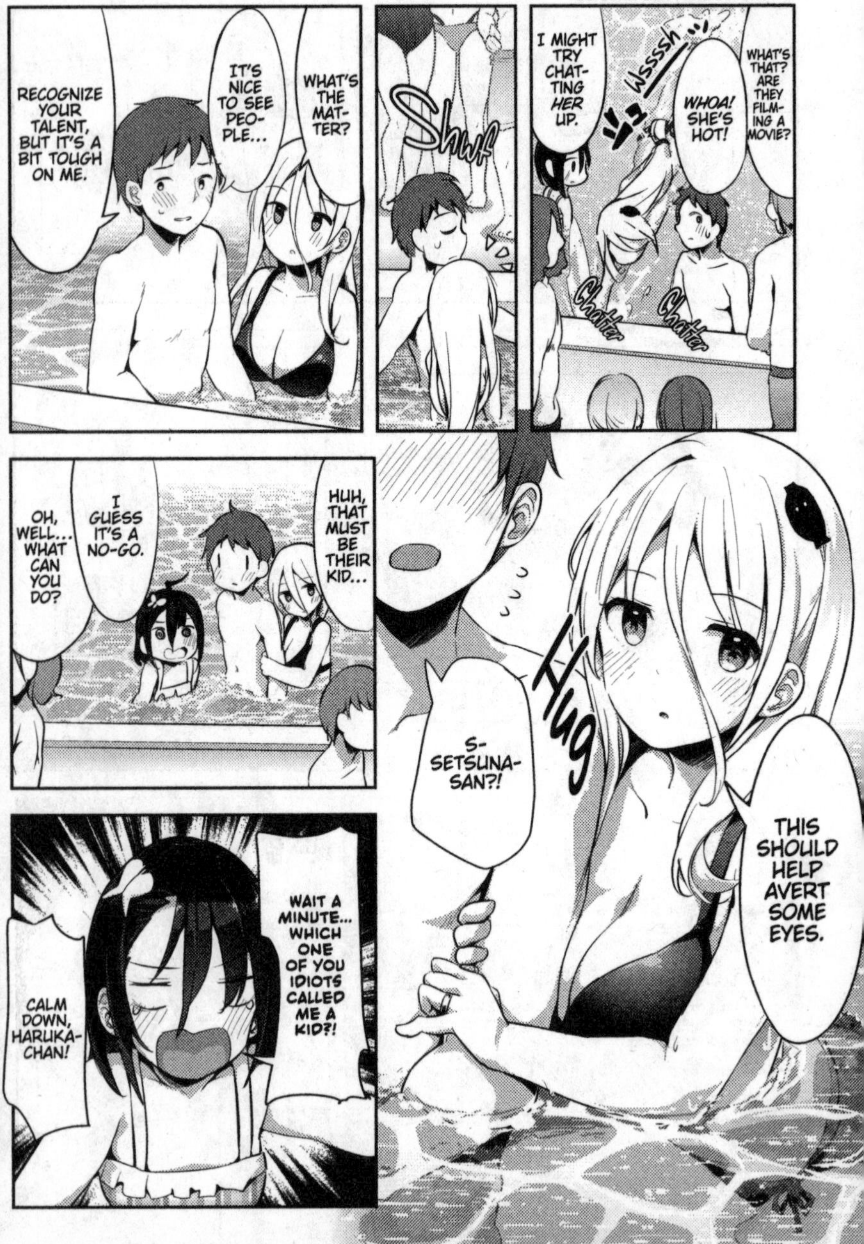
WHAT'S THAT? ARE THEY FILMING A MOVIE?
WHOA! SHE'S HOT!
Wssssh
I MIGHT TRY CHATTING HER UP.
Chatter
Chatter
Shwf
WHAT'S THE MATTER?
IT'S NICE TO SEE PEOPLE...
RECOGNIZE YOUR TALENT, BUT IT'S A BIT TOUGH ON ME.
Hug
THIS SHOULD HELP AVERT SOME EYES.
S-SETSUNA-SAN?!
HUH, THAT MUST BE THEIR KID...
I GUESS IT'S A NO-GO.
OH, WELL... WHAT CAN YOU DO?
WAIT A MINUTE... WHICH ONE OF YOU IDIOTS CALLED ME A KID?!
CALM DOWN, HARUKA-CHAN!

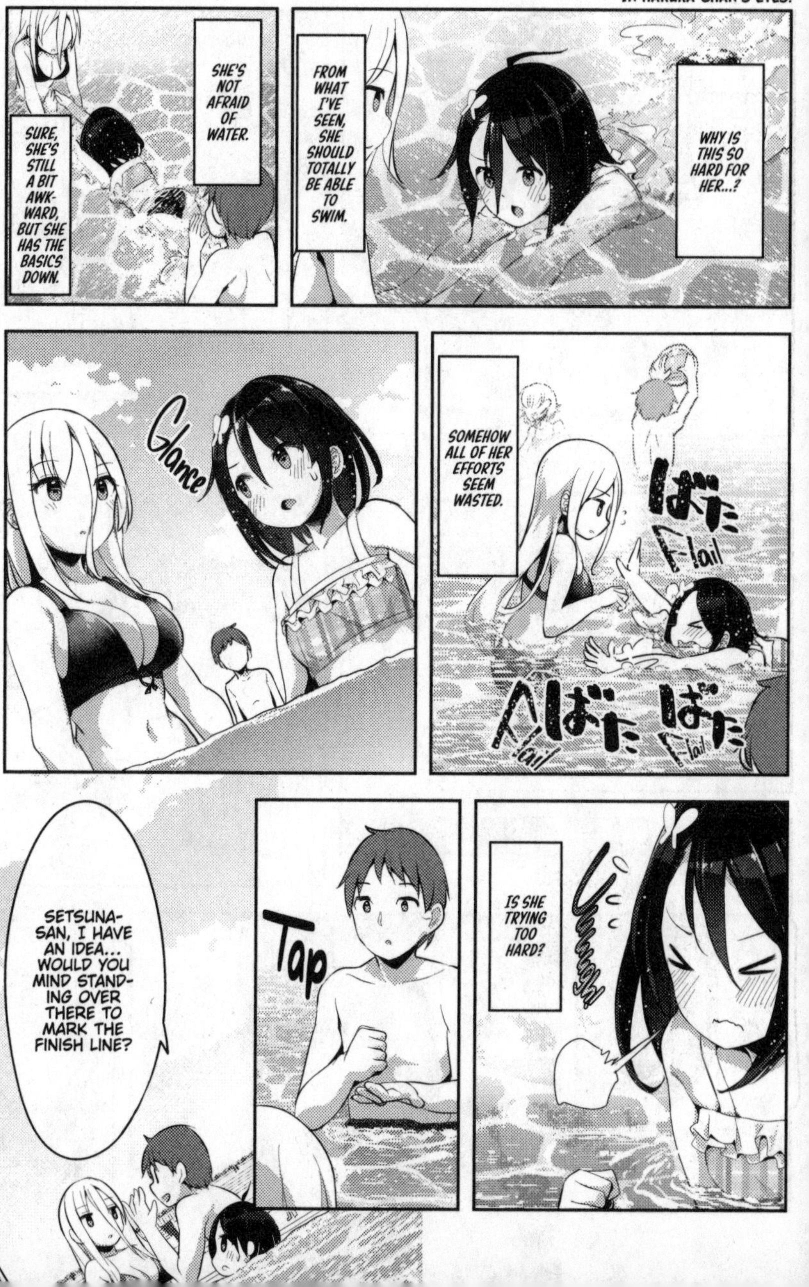
WHY IS THIS SO HARD FOR HER...?
FROM WHAT I'VE SEEN, SHE SHOULD TOTALLY BE ABLE TO SWIM.
SHE'S NOT AFRAID OF WATER.
SURE, SHE'S STILL A BIT AWK-WARD, BUT SHE HAS THE BASICS DOWN.
SOMEHOW ALL OF HER EFFORTS SEEM WASTED.
Flail
Flail
Flail
Glance
IS SHE TRYING TOO HARD?
Tap
SETSUNA-SAN, I HAVE AN IDEA... WOULD YOU MIND STANDING OVER THERE TO MARK THE FINISH LINE?

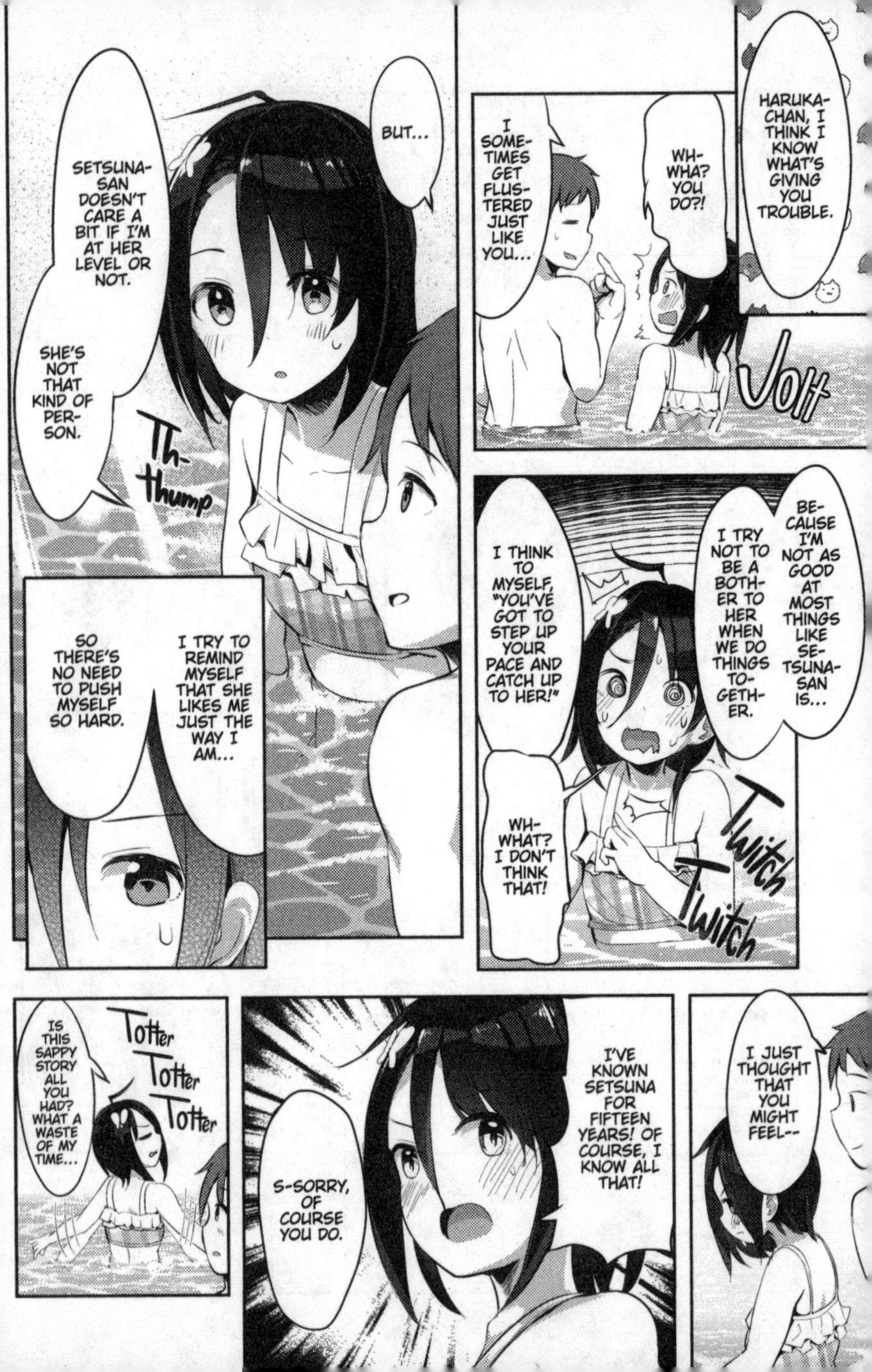
HARUKA-CHAN, I THINK I KNOW WHAT'S GIVING YOU TROUBLE.
Jolt
WH-WHAT? YOU DO?!
I SOMETIMES GET FLUSTERED JUST LIKE YOU...
BECAUSE I'M NOT AS GOOD AT MOST THINGS LIKE SETSUNA-SAN IS...
I TRY NOT TO BE A BOTHER TO HER WHEN WE DO THINGS TOGETHER.
I THINK TO MYSELF, "YOU'VE GOT TO STEP UP YOUR PACE AND CATCH UP TO HER!"
WH-WHAT? I DON'T THINK THAT!
Twitch Twitch
BUT...
SETSUNA-SAN DOESN'T CARE A BIT IF I'M AT HER LEVEL OR NOT.
SHE'S NOT THAT KIND OF PERSON.
Th-thump
I TRY TO REMIND MYSELF THAT SHE LIKES ME JUST THE WAY I AM...
SO THERE'S NO NEED TO PUSH MYSELF SO HARD.
I JUST THOUGHT THAT YOU MIGHT FEEL--
I'VE KNOWN SETSUNA FOR FIFTEEN YEARS! OF COURSE, I KNOW ALL THAT!
S-SORRY, OF COURSE YOU DO.
Totter Totter Totter
IS THIS SAPPY STORY ALL YOU HAD? WHAT A WASTE OF MY TIME...

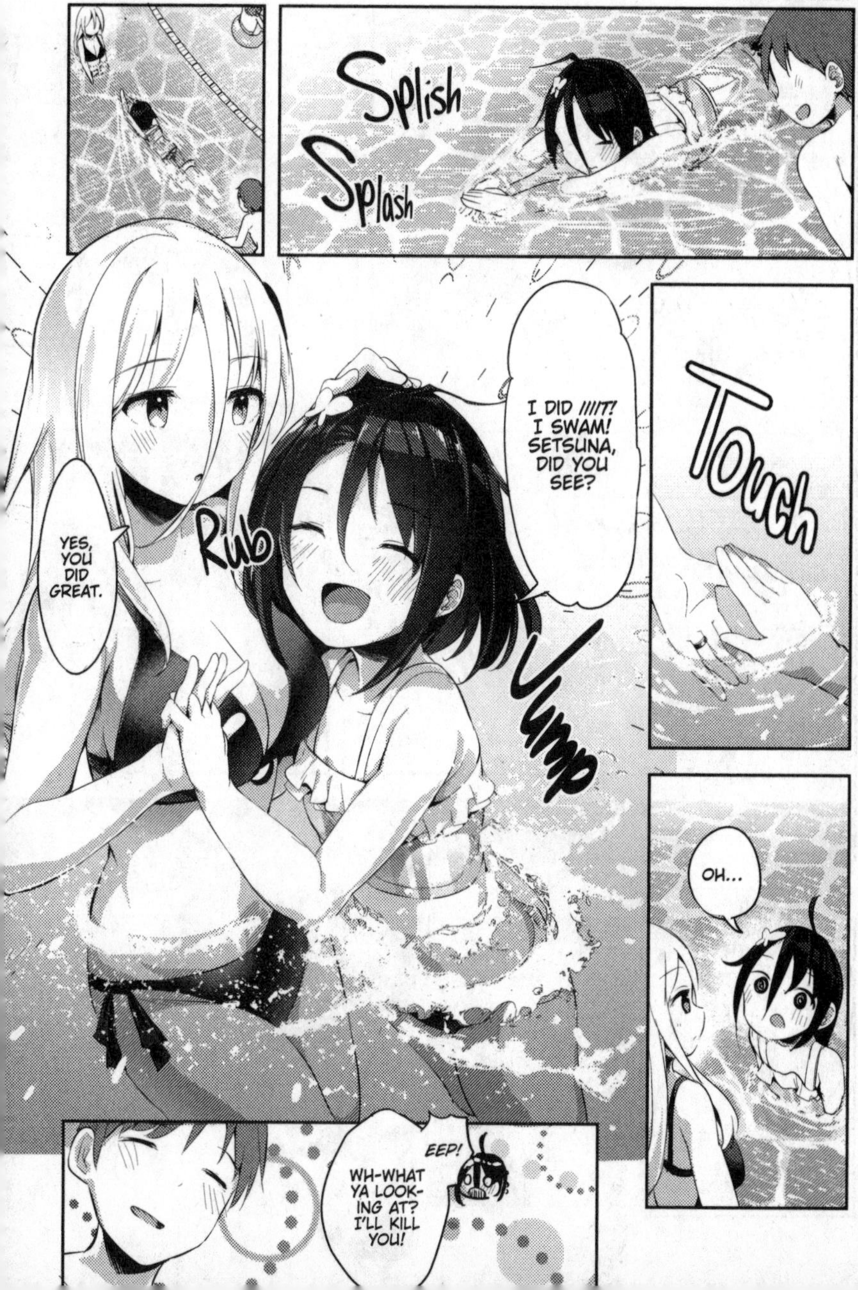
Splish
Splash
Touch
OH...
I DID IIIIT! I SWAM! SETSUNA, DID YOU SEE?
Jump
Rub
YES, YOU DID GREAT.
EEP!
WH-WHAT YA LOOKING-ING AT? I'LL KILL YOU!

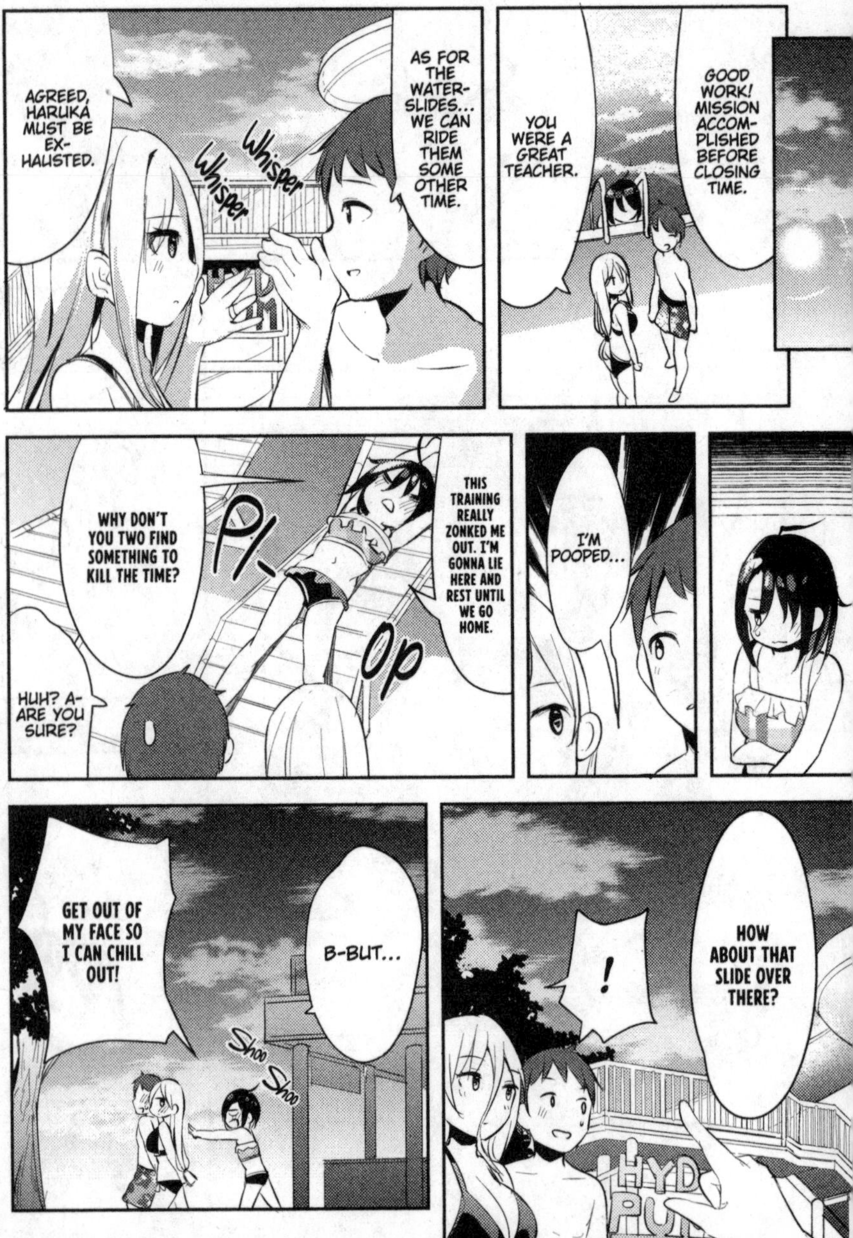
GOOD WORK! MISSION ACCOMPLISHED BEFORE CLOSING TIME.
YOU WERE A GREAT TEACHER.
AS FOR THE WATER-SLIDES... WE CAN RIDE THEM SOME OTHER TIME.
Whisper
Whisper
AGREED, HARUKA MUST BE EX-HAUSTED.
I'M POOPED...
THIS TRAINING REALLY ZONKED ME OUT. I'M GONNA LIE HERE AND REST UNTIL WE GO HOME.
Pl_op
WHY DON'T YOU TWO FIND SOMETHING TO KILL THE TIME?
HUH? A-ARE YOU SURE?
HOW ABOUT THAT SLIDE OVER THERE?
!
B-BUT...
GET OUT OF MY FACE SO I CAN CHILL OUT!
Shoo
Shoo

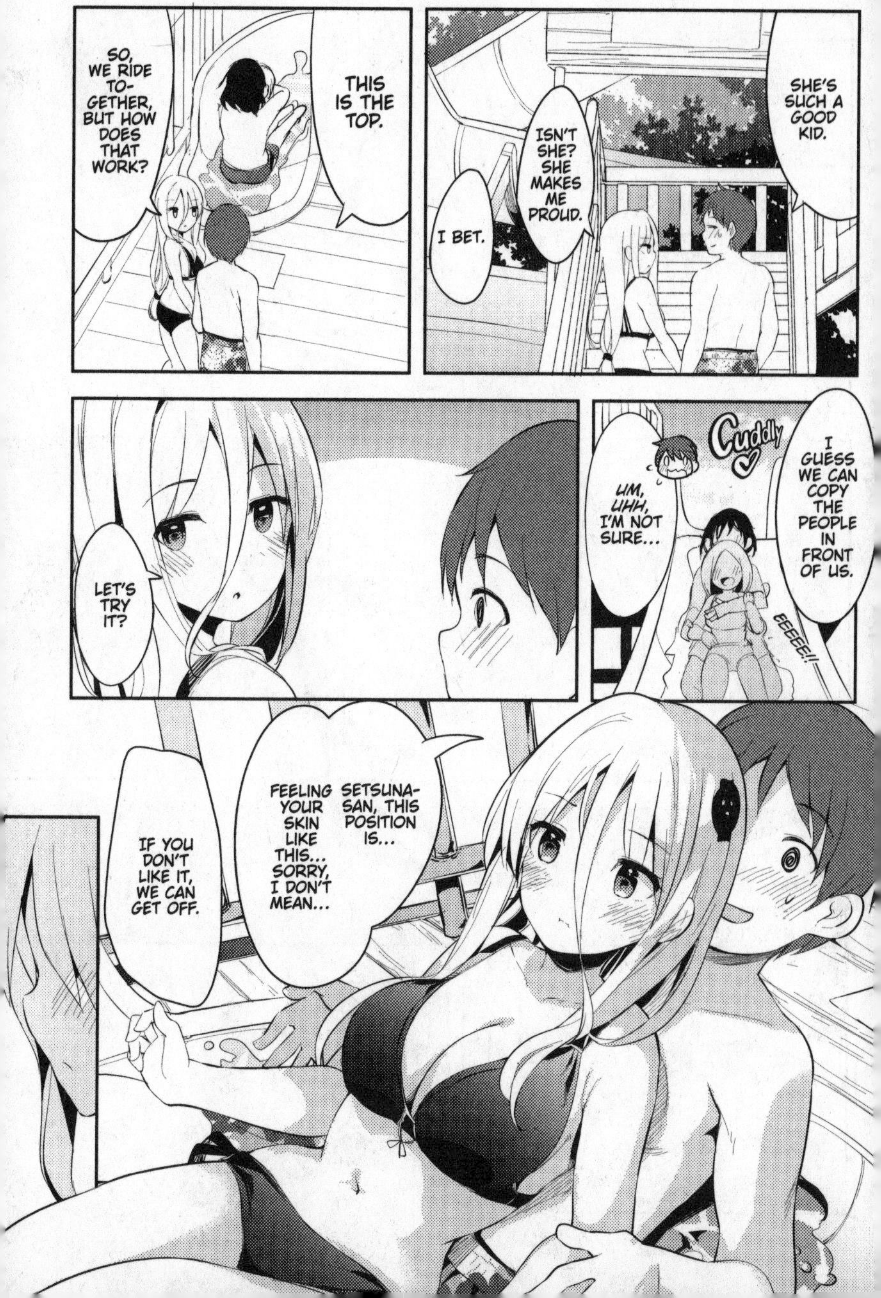
SHE'S SUCH A GOOD KID.
ISN'T SHE? SHE MAKES ME PROUD.
I BET.
THIS IS THE TOP.
SO, WE RIDE TO-GETHER, BUT HOW DOES THAT WORK?
I GUESS WE CAN COPY THE PEOPLE IN FRONT OF US.
Cuddly
UM, UHH, I'M NOT SURE...
EEEEE!!
LET'S TRY IT?
SETSUNA-SAN, THIS POSITION IS...
FEELING YOUR SKIN LIKE THIS... SORRY, I DON'T MEAN...
IF YOU DON'T LIKE IT, WE CAN GET OFF.

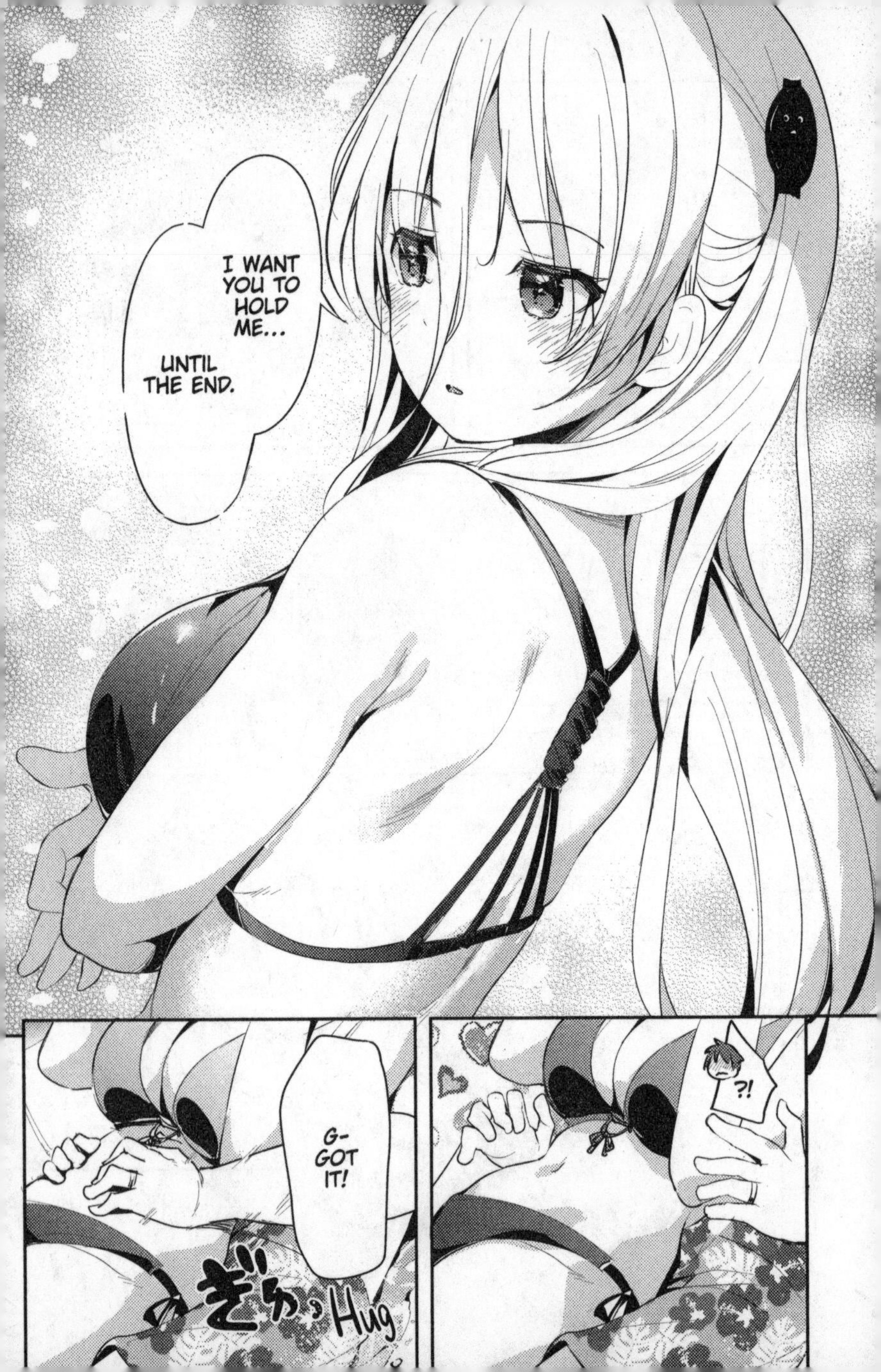
I WANT YOU TO HOLD ME... UNTIL THE END.
?!
G-GOT IT!
ぎゅ Hug

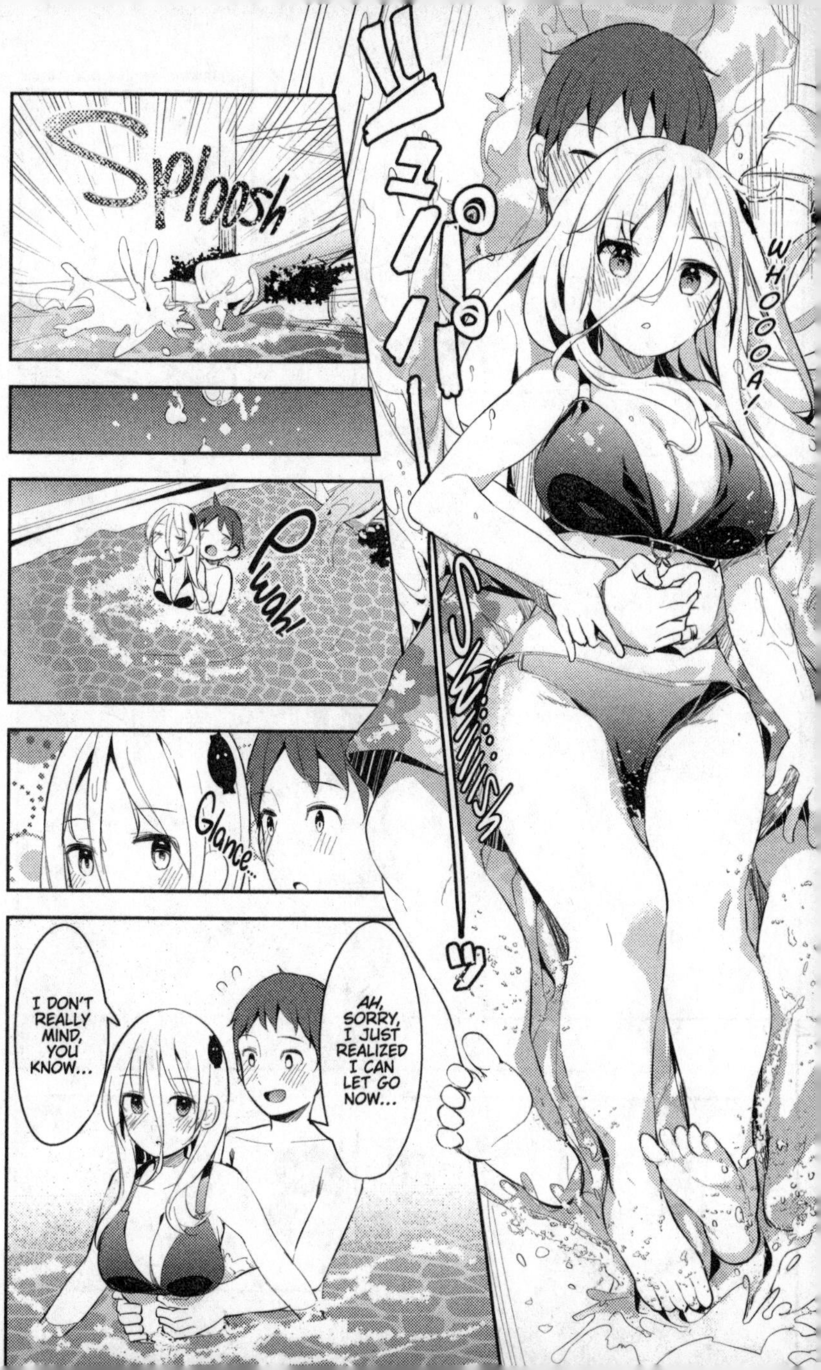
WHOOOOA!
Swish...
Sploosh
Pwah!
Glance...
AH, SORRY, I JUST REALIZED I CAN LET GO NOW...
I DON'T REALLY MIND, YOU KNOW...

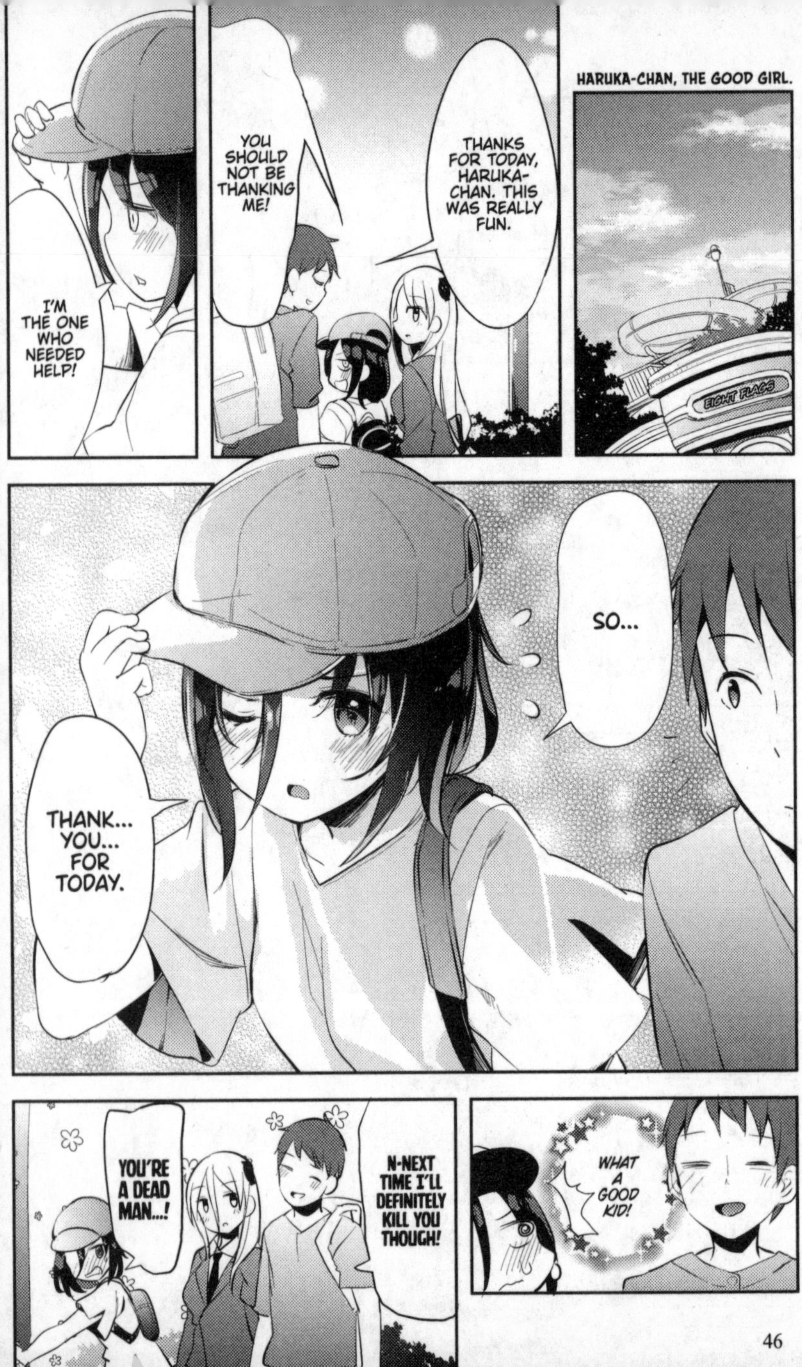
HARUKA-CHAN, THE GOOD GIRL.
THANKS FOR TODAY, HARUKA-CHAN. THIS WAS REALLY FUN.
YOU SHOULD NOT BE THANKING ME!
I'M THE ONE WHO NEEDED HELP!
EIGHT FLAGS
SO...
THANK... YOU... FOR TODAY.
WHAT A GOOD KID!
N-NEXT TIME I'LL DEFINITELY KILL YOU THOUGH!
YOU'RE A DEAD MAN...!

ASSASSIN APPRENTICE STUDY GUIDE

AT THE BOOKSTORE.
Your easy guide to a C-Rank assassin license.
I THINK THAT'S THE TEST HARUKA-CHAN IS PREPARING FOR...
Your easy guide to C-Rank assassin lic
Practice for the Japanese
THIS LOOKS SURPRISINGLY DOABLE IF YOU APPLY YOURSELF... EVEN I COULD MANAGE.
HAPPY HE'S INTERESTED.
C-RANK IS A BEGINNER LICENSE. I COULD TEACH YOU IF YOU WANTED.

MY Lovey-Dovey Wife IS A STONE COLD KILLER

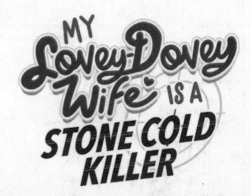

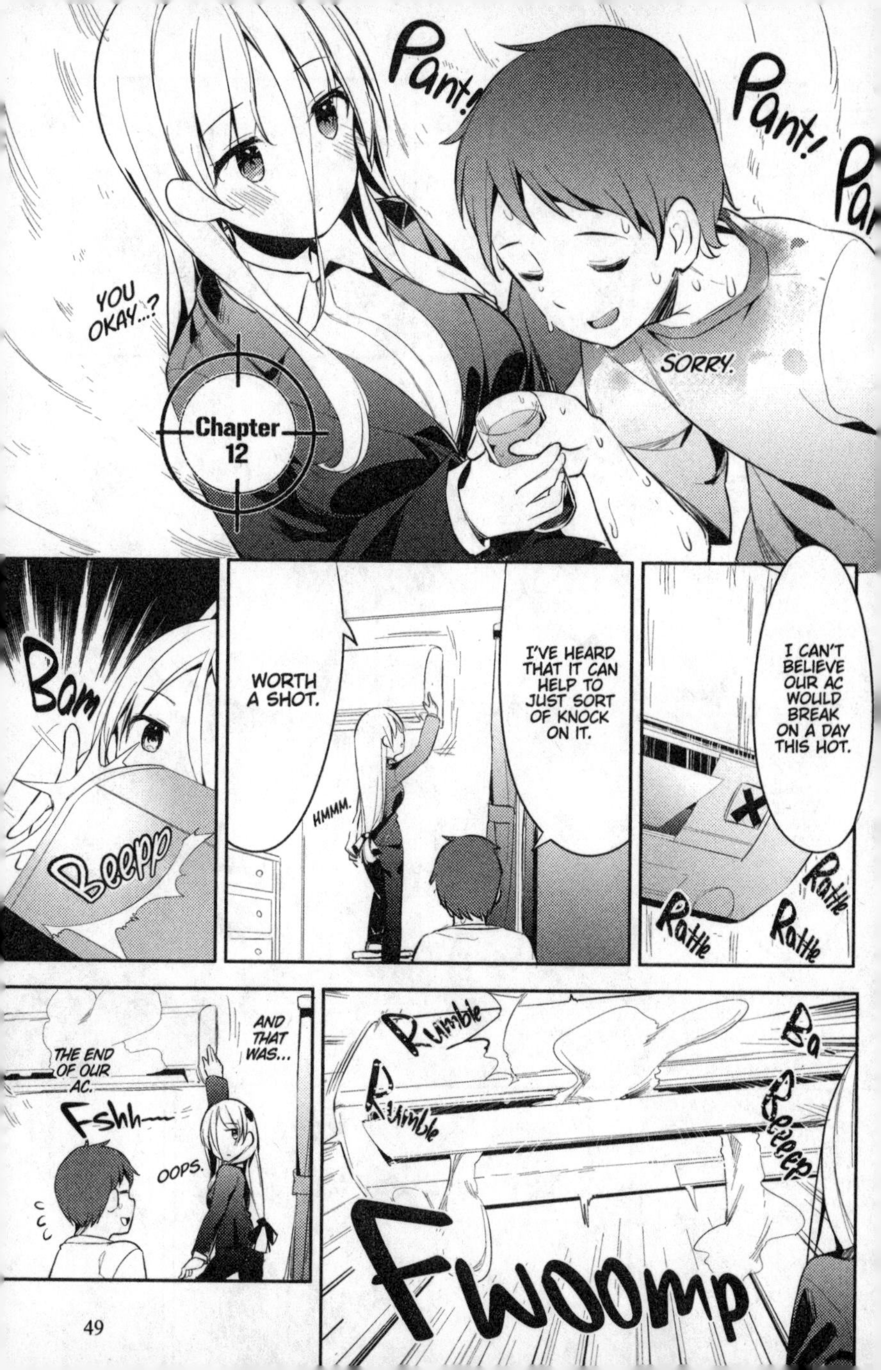
Pant! Pa
Pant!
Pant!
SORRY.
YOU OKAY...?
Chapter 12
I CAN'T BELIEVE OUR AC WOULD BREAK ON A DAY THIS HOT.
Rattle
Rattle
Rattle
I'VE HEARD THAT IT CAN HELP TO JUST SORT OF KNOCK ON IT.
WORTH A SHOT.
HMMM.
Bam
Beepp
Ba Beeep
Rumble
Rumble
Fwoomp
AND THAT WAS...
THE END OF OUR AC.
Fshh
OOPS.

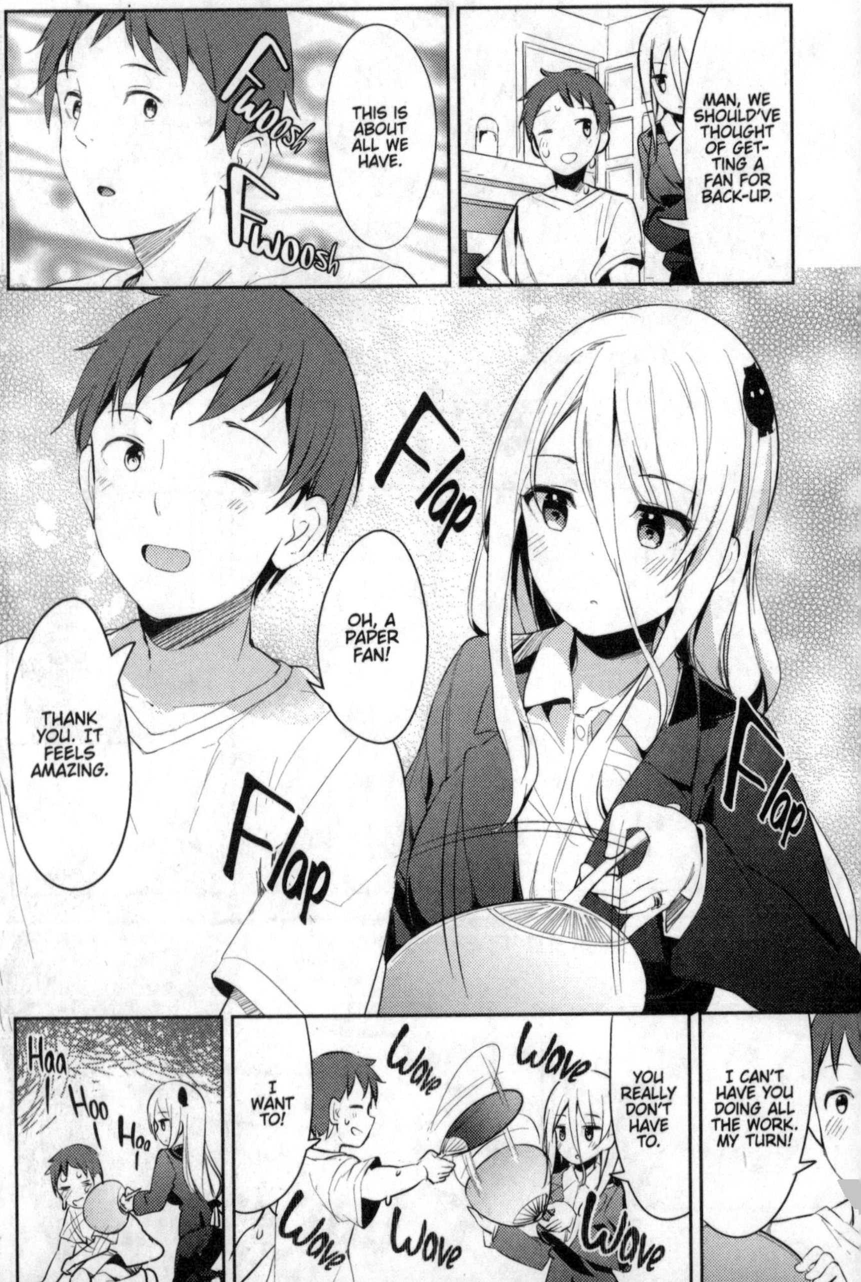
MAN, WE SHOULD'VE THOUGHT OF GET-TING A FAN FOR BACK-UP.
THIS IS ABOUT ALL WE HAVE.
Fwoosh
Fwoosh
Flap
Flap
OH, A PAPER FAN!
THANK YOU. IT FEELS AMAZING.
Flap
I CAN'T HAVE YOU DOING ALL THE WORK. MY TURN!
YOU REALLY DON'T HAVE TO.
Wave
Wave
I WANT TO!
Wave
Wave
Wave
Haa
Hoo
Hoo

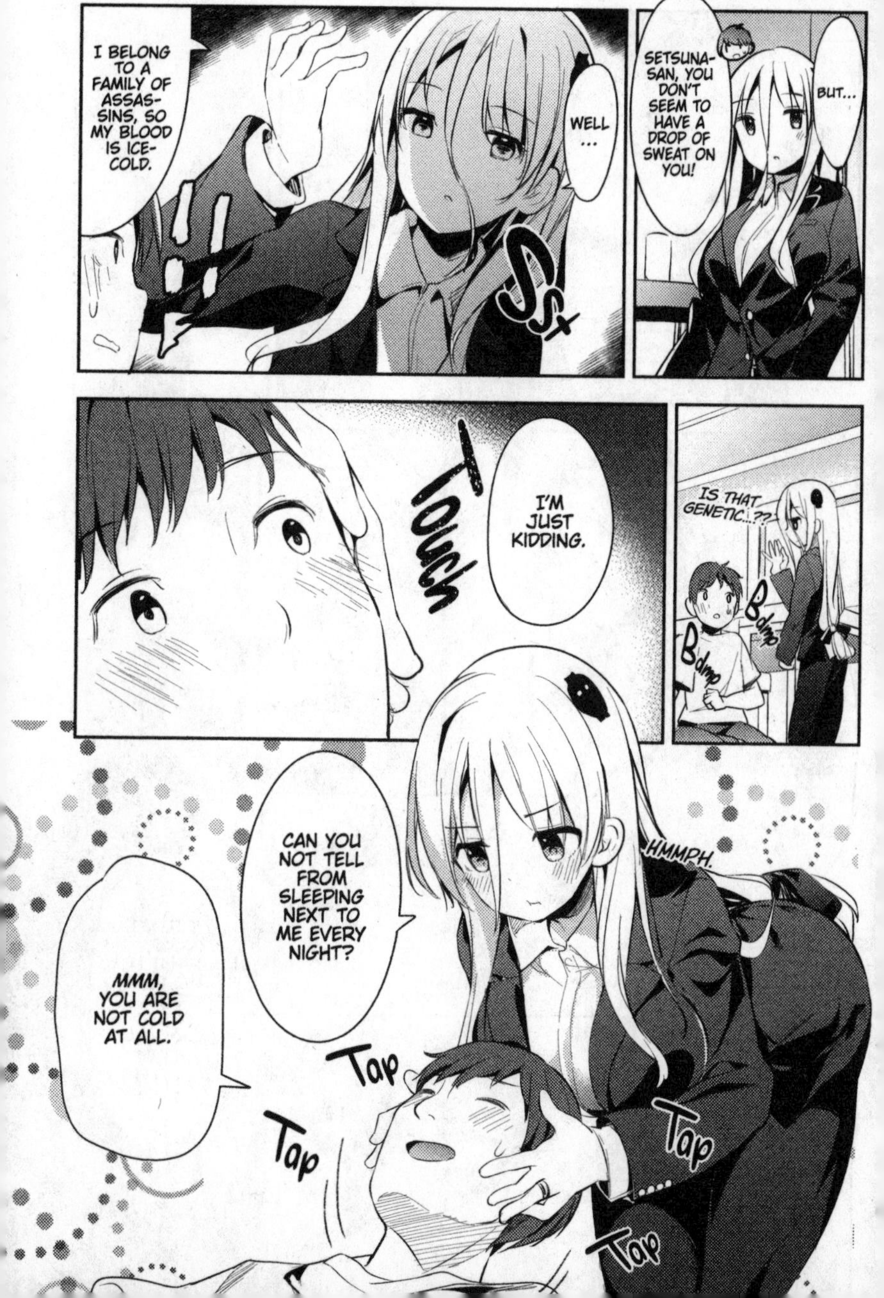
BUT...
SETSUNA-SAN, YOU DON'T SEEM TO HAVE A DROP OF SWEAT ON YOU!
WELL ...
I BELONG TO A FAMILY OF ASSAS-SINS, SO MY BLOOD IS ICE-COLD.
Ssst
IS THAT GENETIC...??
Bdmp
Bdmp
Touch
I'M JUST KIDDING.
HMMPH.
CAN YOU NOT TELL FROM SLEEPING NEXT TO ME EVERY NIGHT?
MMM, YOU ARE NOT COLD AT ALL.
Tap
Tap
Tap
Tap

A CLOTHING SWAP.

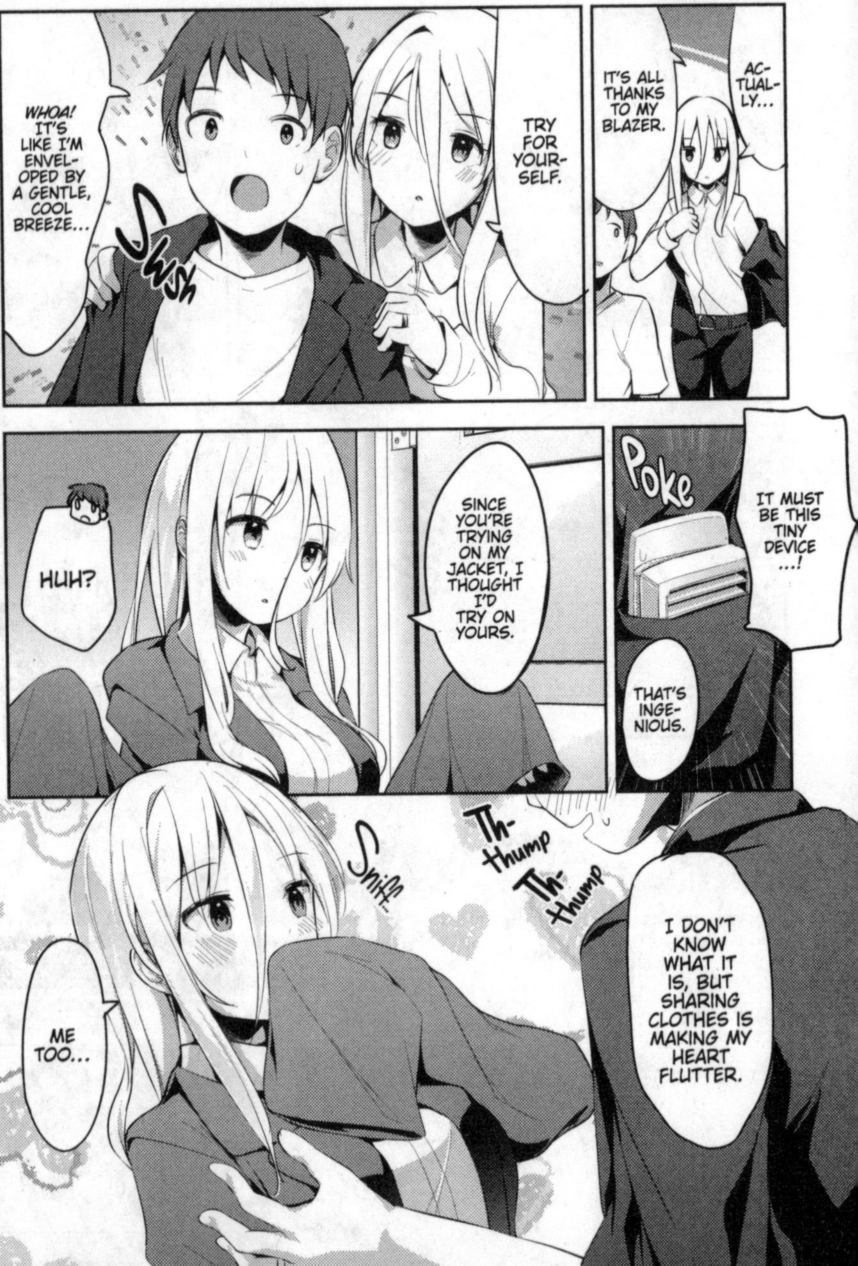
ACTUALLY...
IT'S ALL THANKS TO MY BLAZER.
TRY FOR YOURSELF.
Swsh
WHOA! IT'S LIKE I'M ENVELOPED BY A GENTLE, COOL BREEZE...
Poke
IT MUST BE THIS TINY DEVICE...!
THAT'S INGENIOUS.
SINCE YOU'RE TRYING ON MY JACKET, I THOUGHT I'D TRY ON YOURS.
HUH?
I DON'T KNOW WHAT IT IS, BUT SHARING CLOTHES IS MAKING MY HEART FLUTTER.
Th-thump Th-thump
Sniff...
ME TOO...

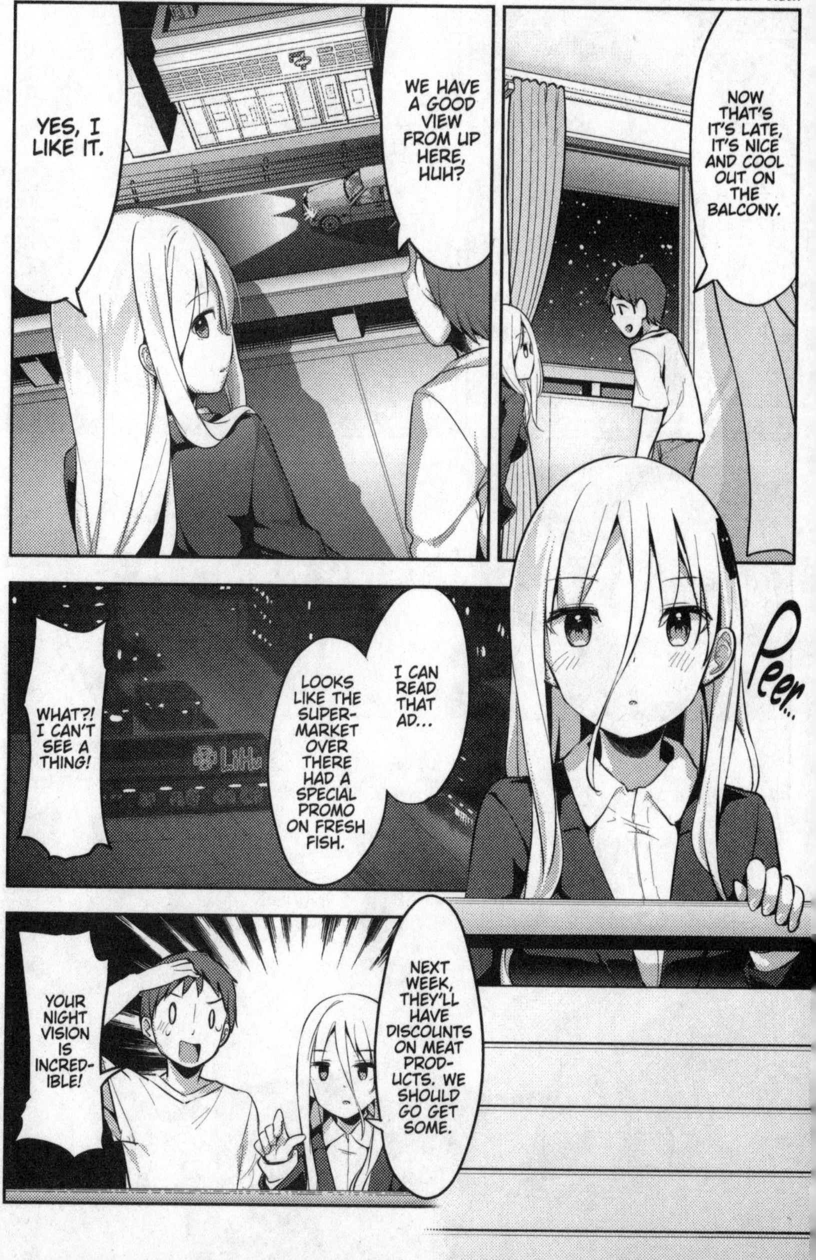
NOW THAT'S IT'S LATE, IT'S NICE AND COOL OUT ON THE BALCONY.
WE HAVE A GOOD VIEW FROM UP HERE, HUH?
YES, I LIKE IT.
Peer...
I CAN READ THAT AD...
LOOKS LIKE THE SUPER-MARKET OVER THERE HAD A SPECIAL PROMO ON FRESH FISH.
WHAT?! I CAN'T SEE A THING!
NEXT WEEK, THEY'LL HAVE DISCOUNTS ON MEAT PROD-UCTS. WE SHOULD GO GET SOME.
YOUR NIGHT VISION IS INCRED-IBLE!

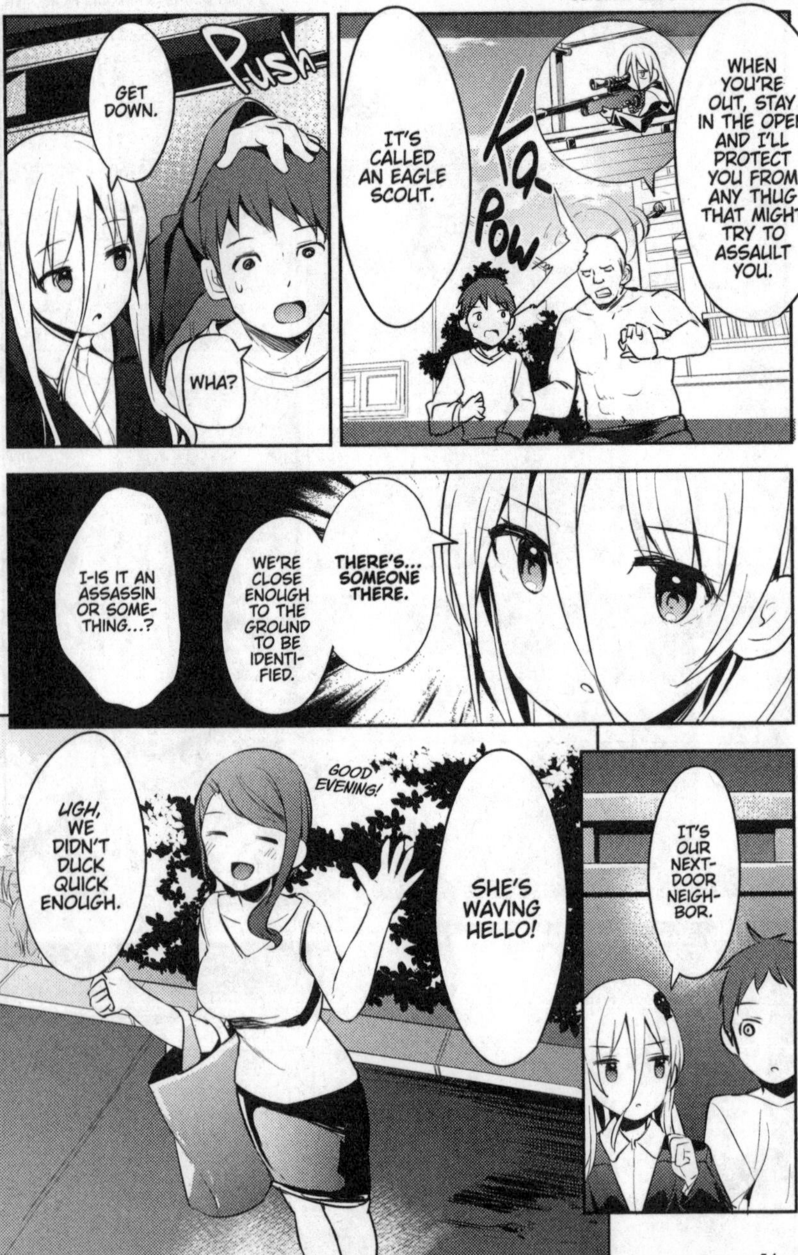
WHEN YOU'RE OUT, STAY IN THE OPEN AND I'LL PROTECT YOU FROM ANY THUG THAT MIGHT TRY TO ASSAULT YOU.
KA-POW
IT'S CALLED AN EAGLE SCOUT.
PUSH
GET DOWN.
WHA?
THERE'S... SOMEONE THERE.
WE'RE CLOSE ENOUGH TO THE GROUND TO BE IDENTIFIED.
I-IS IT AN ASSASSIN OR SOME-THING...?
IT'S OUR NEXT-DOOR NEIGHBOR.
SHE'S WAVING HELLO!
GOOD EVENING!
UGH, WE DIDN'T DUCK QUICK ENOUGH.

A SUMMER TREAT WITH SETSUNA-SAN.

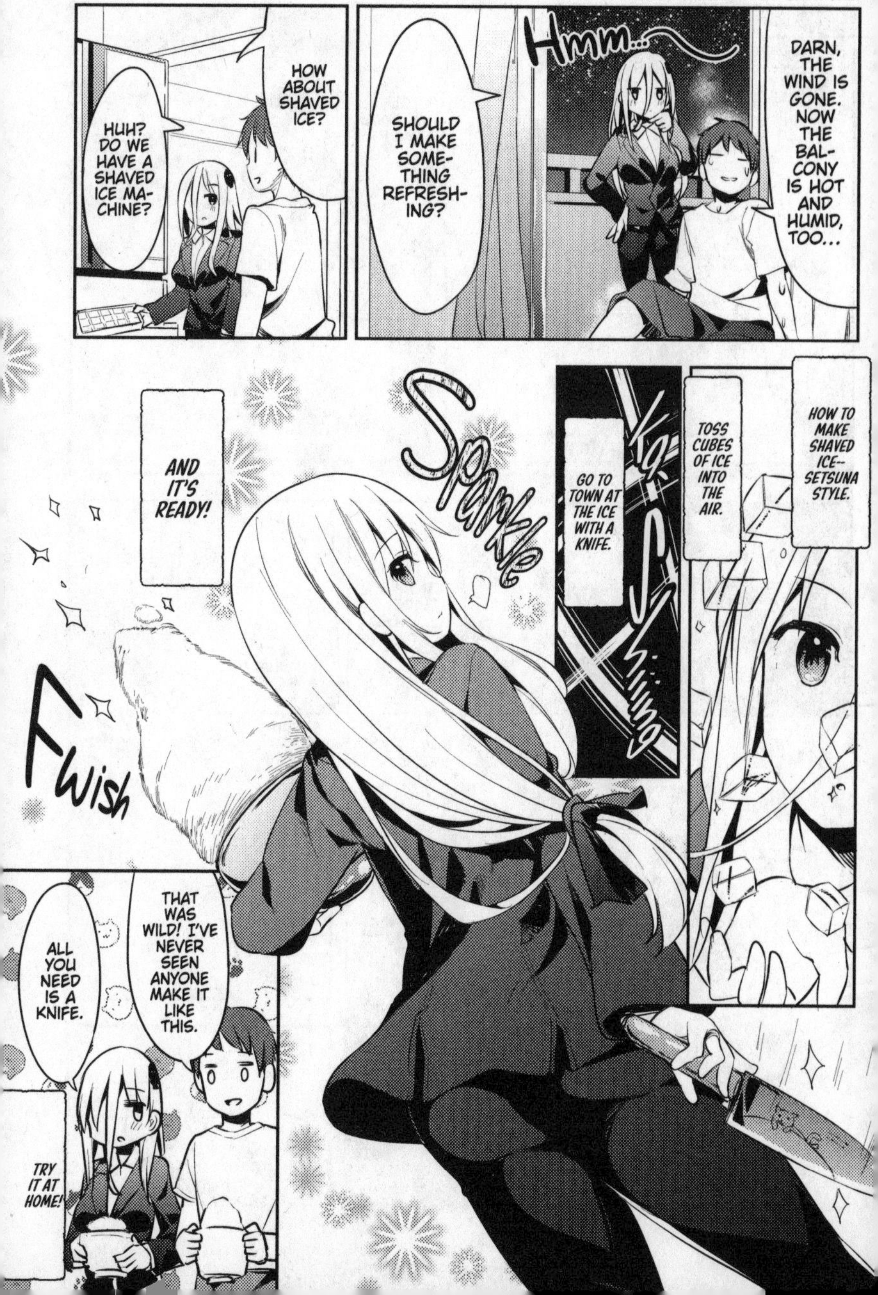
Hmm...
DARN, THE WIND IS GONE. NOW THE BALCONY IS HOT AND HUMID, TOO...
SHOULD I MAKE SOMETHING REFRESHING?
HOW ABOUT SHAVED ICE?
HUH? DO WE HAVE A SHAVED ICE MACHINE?
HOW TO MAKE SHAVED ICE-- SETSUNA STYLE.
TOSS CUBES OF ICE INTO THE AIR.
GO TO TOWN AT THE ICE WITH A KNIFE.
Sparkle
AND IT'S READY!
Fwish
THAT WAS WILD! I'VE NEVER SEEN ANYONE MAKE IT LIKE THIS.
ALL YOU NEED IS A KNIFE.
TRY IT AT HOME!

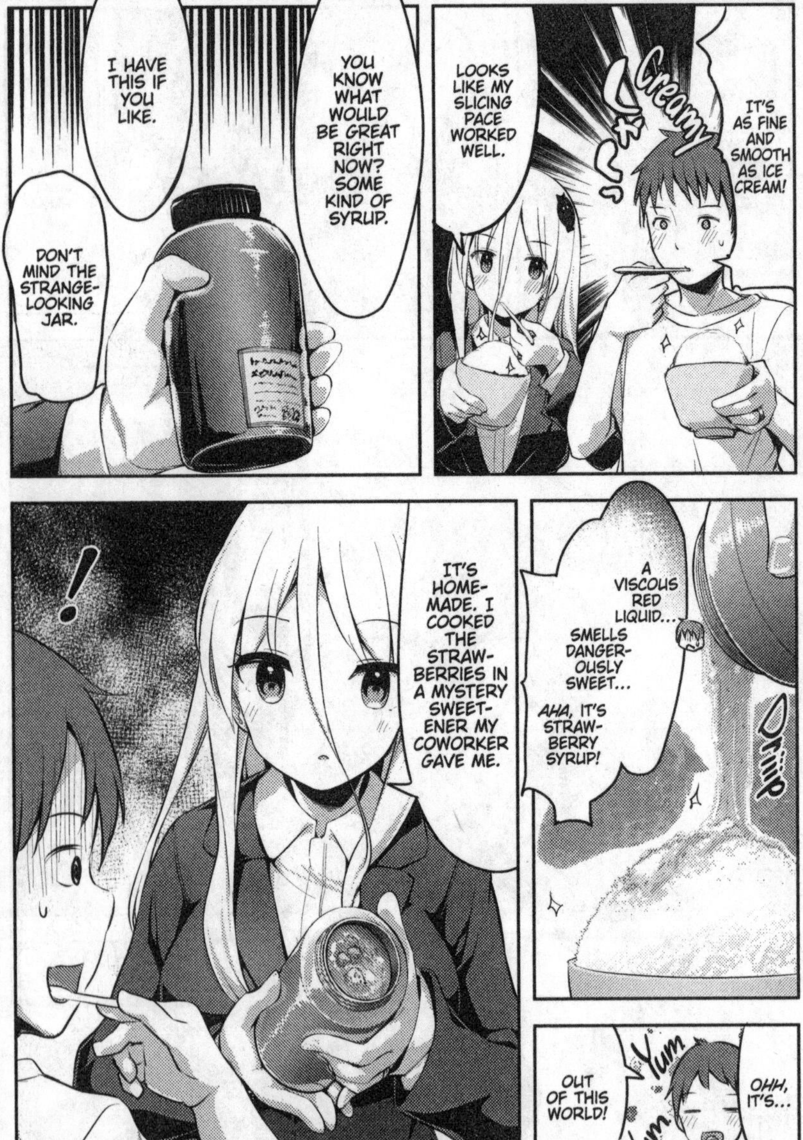
IT'S AS FINE AND SMOOTH AS ICE CREAM!
Creamy
LOOKS LIKE MY SLICING PACE WORKED WELL.
YOU KNOW WHAT WOULD BE GREAT RIGHT NOW? SOME KIND OF SYRUP.
I HAVE THIS IF YOU LIKE.
DON'T MIND THE STRANGE-LOOKING JAR.
A VISCOUS RED LIQUID...
SMELLS DANGEROUSLY SWEET...
AHA, IT'S STRAWBERRY SYRUP!
Driiip
OHH, IT'S...
Yum
Yum
OUT OF THIS WORLD!
!
IT'S HOMEMADE. I COOKED THE STRAWBERRIES IN A MYSTERY SWEETENER MY COWORKER GAVE ME.

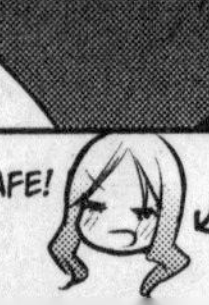
COWORKER
IT'S TOTALLY SAFE!

SHE ONLY EVER NEEDS ONE SHOT.

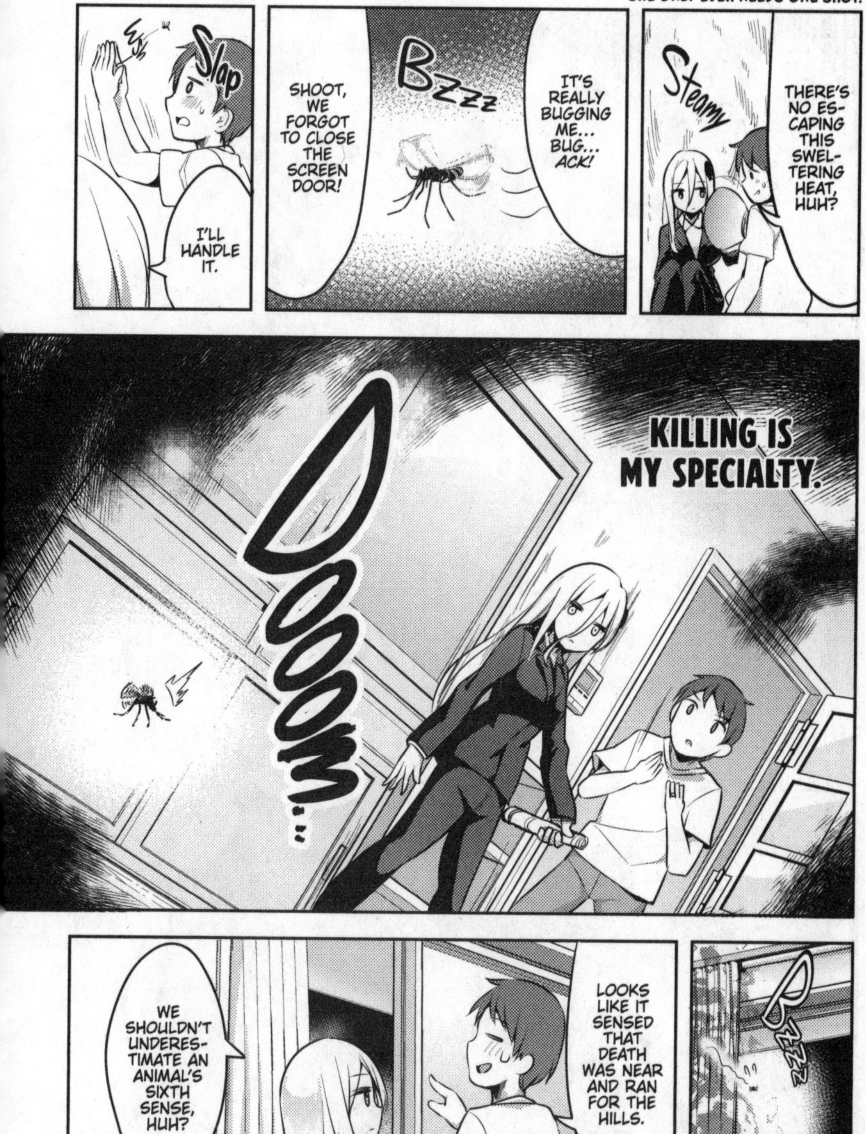
Steamy
THERE'S NO ES-CAPING THIS SWEL-TERING HEAT, HUH?
Bzzz
IT'S REALLY BUGGING ME... BUG... ACK!
SHOOT, WE FORGOT TO CLOSE THE SCREEN DOOR!
Slap
I'LL HANDLE IT.
KILLING IS MY SPECIALTY.
Doooom...
Bzzz
LOOKS LIKE IT SENSED THAT DEATH WAS NEAR AND RAN FOR THE HILLS.
WE SHOULDN'T UNDERES-TIMATE AN ANIMAL'S SIXTH SENSE, HUH?

AN EVENING STROLL WITH SETSUNA-SAN.

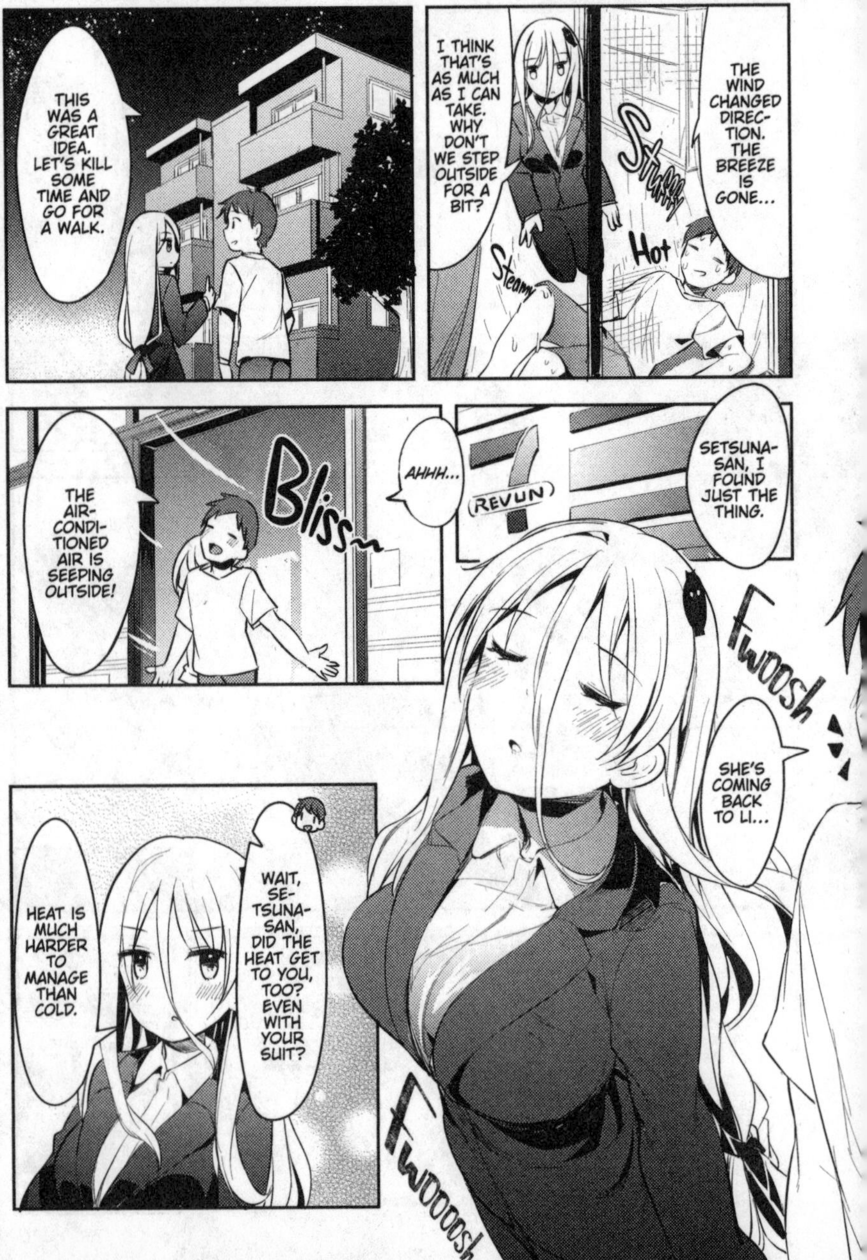
THE WIND CHANGED DIRECTION. THE BREEZE IS GONE...
I THINK THAT'S AS MUCH AS I CAN TAKE. WHY DON'T WE STEP OUTSIDE FOR A BIT?
Stuffy
Hot
Steamy
THIS WAS A GREAT IDEA. LET'S KILL SOME TIME AND GO FOR A WALK.
SETSUNA-SAN, I FOUND JUST THE THING.
REVUN
AHHH...
Bliss~
THE AIR-CONDITIONED AIR IS SEEPING OUTSIDE!
Fwoosh
SHE'S COMING BACK TO LI...
Fwooooosh
WAIT, SETSUNA-SAN, DID THE HEAT GET TO YOU, TOO? EVEN WITH YOUR SUIT?
HEAT IS MUCH HARDER TO MANAGE THAN COLD.

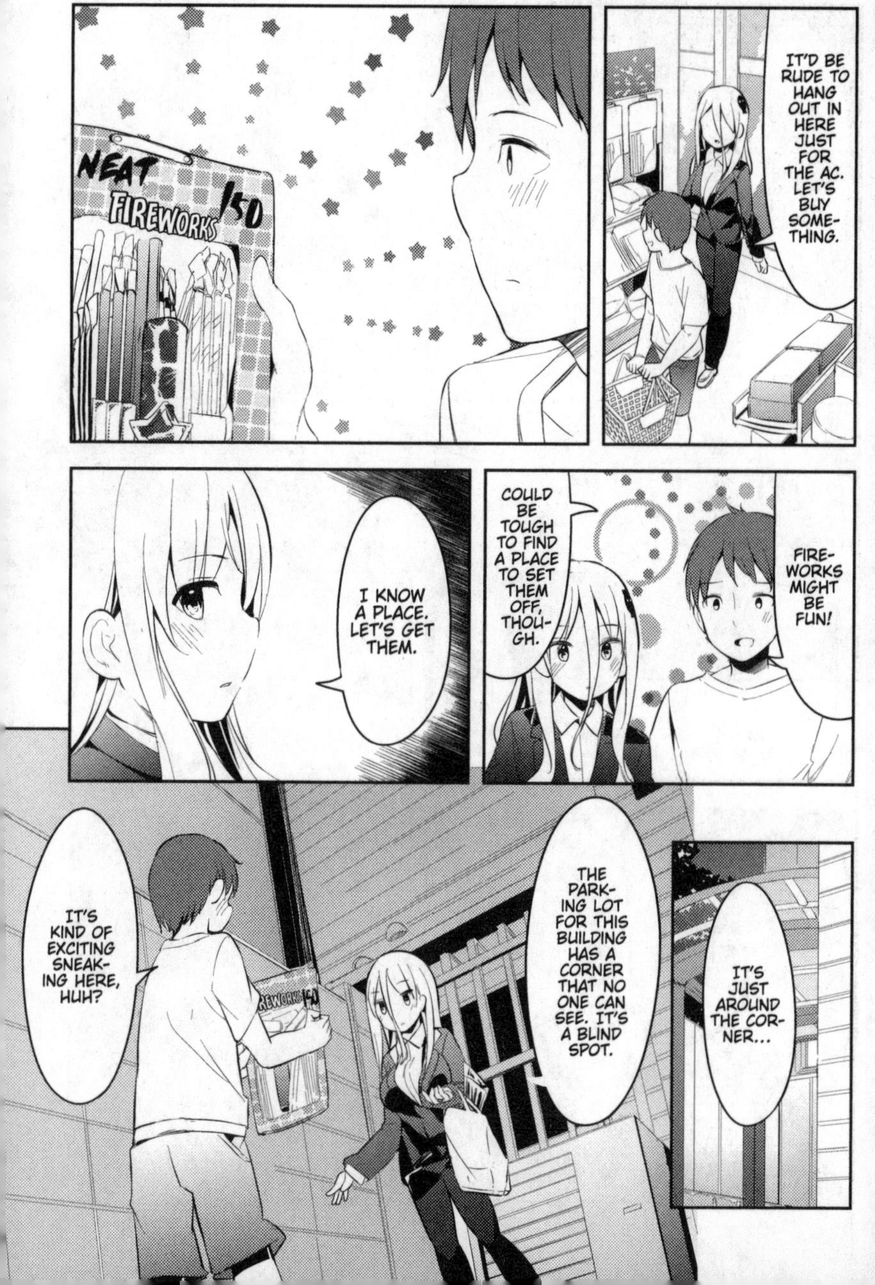
IT'D BE RUDE TO HANG OUT IN HERE JUST FOR THE AC. LET'S BUY SOME-THING.
NEAT
FIREWORKS
150
FIRE-WORKS MIGHT BE FUN!
COULD BE TOUGH TO FIND A PLACE TO SET THEM OFF, THOU-GH.
I KNOW A PLACE. LET'S GET THEM.
IT'S JUST AROUND THE COR-NER...
THE PARK-ING LOT FOR THIS BUILDING HAS A CORNER THAT NO ONE CAN SEE. IT'S A BLIND SPOT.
IT'S KIND OF EXCITING SNEAK-ING HERE, HUH?
FIREWORKS 150

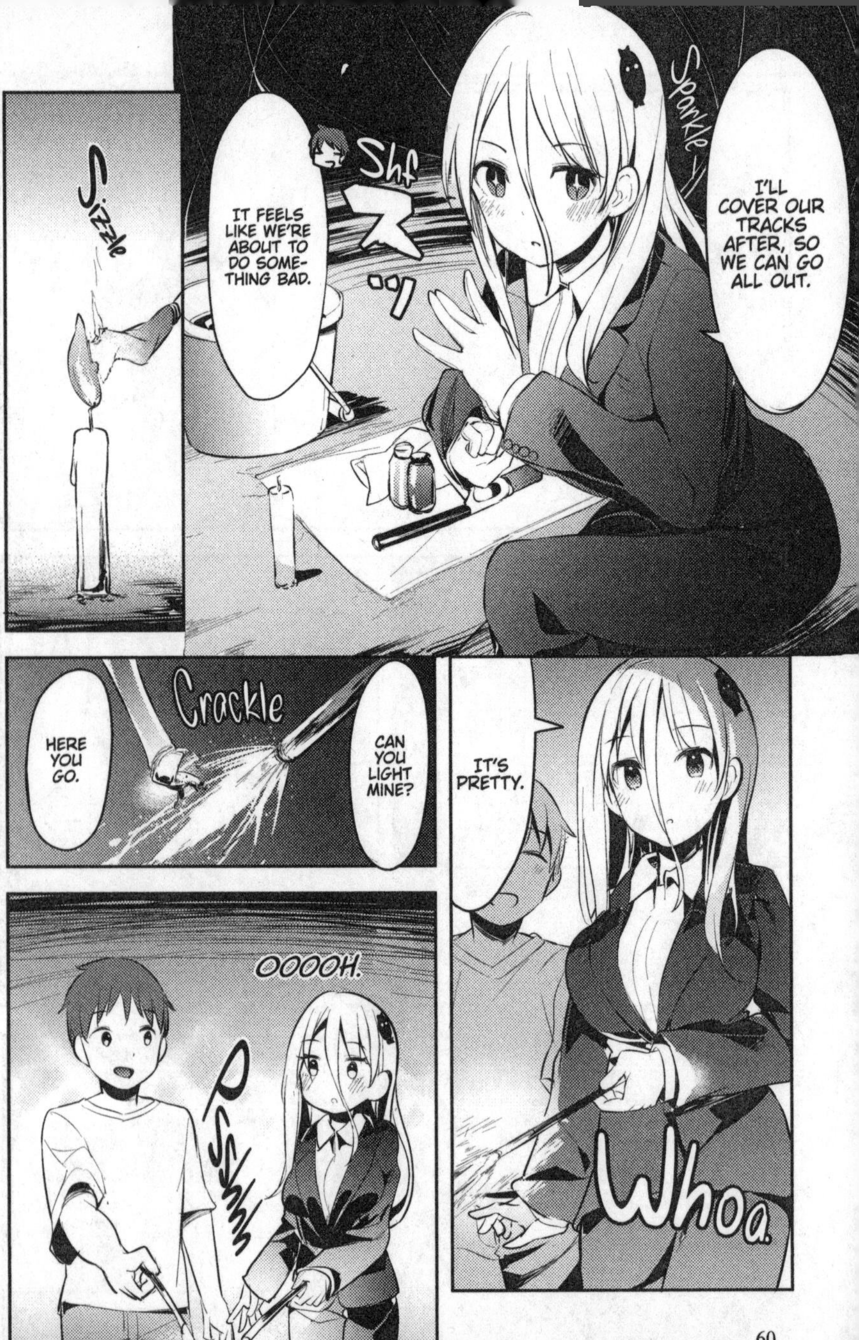
I'LL COVER OUR TRACKS AFTER, SO WE CAN GO ALL OUT.
Sparkle
Shf
IT FEELS LIKE WE'RE ABOUT TO DO SOME-THING BAD.
Sizzle
IT'S PRETTY.
Whoa.
CAN YOU LIGHT MINE?
Crackle
HERE YOU GO.
OOOOH.
Psshhh

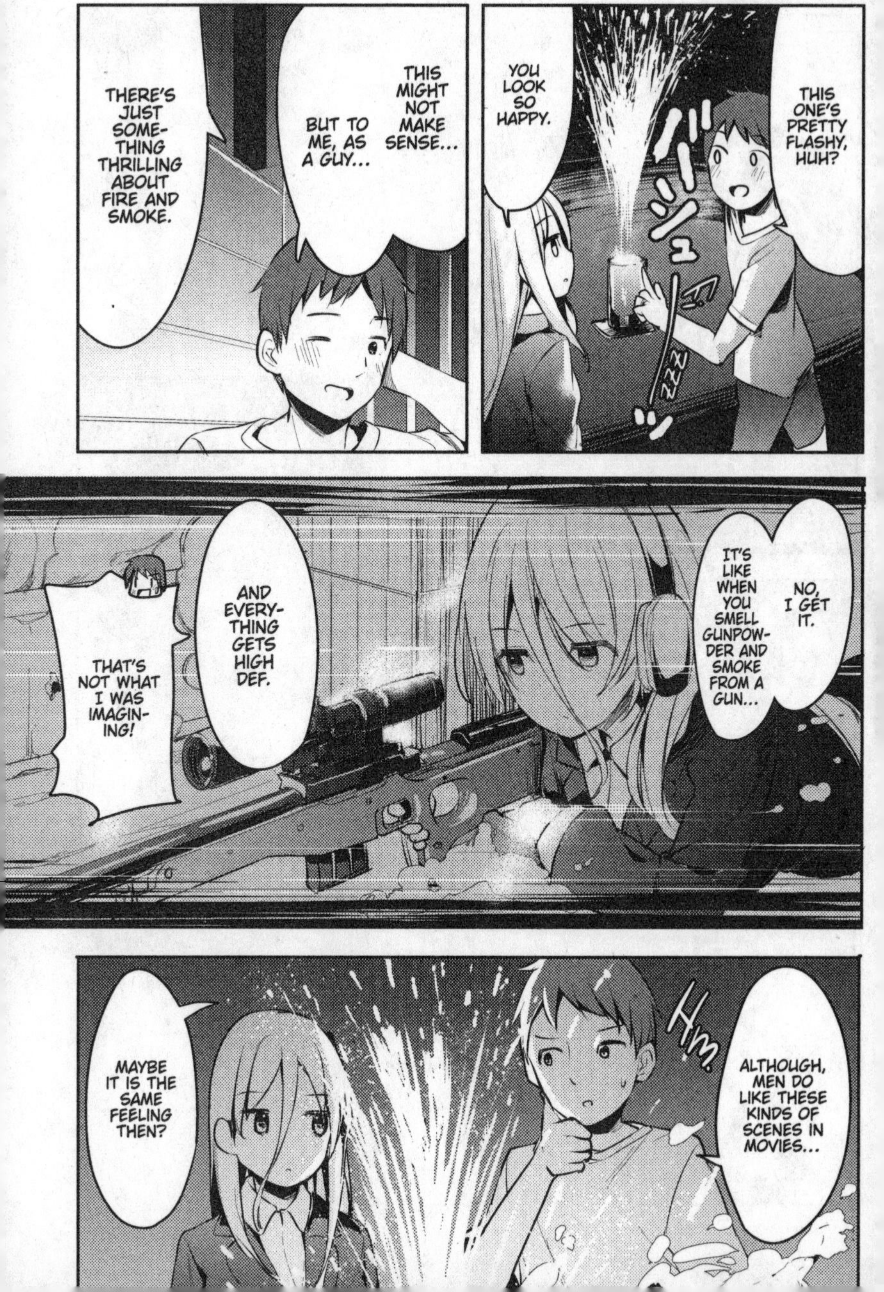
THIS ONE'S PRETTY FLASHY, HUH?
YOU LOOK SO HAPPY.
THIS MIGHT NOT MAKE SENSE...
BUT TO ME, AS A GUY...
THERE'S JUST SOME-THING THRILLING ABOUT FIRE AND SMOKE.
NO, I GET IT.
IT'S LIKE WHEN YOU SMELL GUNPOW-DER AND SMOKE FROM A GUN...
AND EVERY-THING GETS HIGH DEF.
THAT'S NOT WHAT I WAS IMAGIN-ING!
Hm.
ALTHOUGH, MEN DO LIKE THESE KINDS OF SCENES IN MOVIES...
MAYBE IT IS THE SAME FEELING THEN?

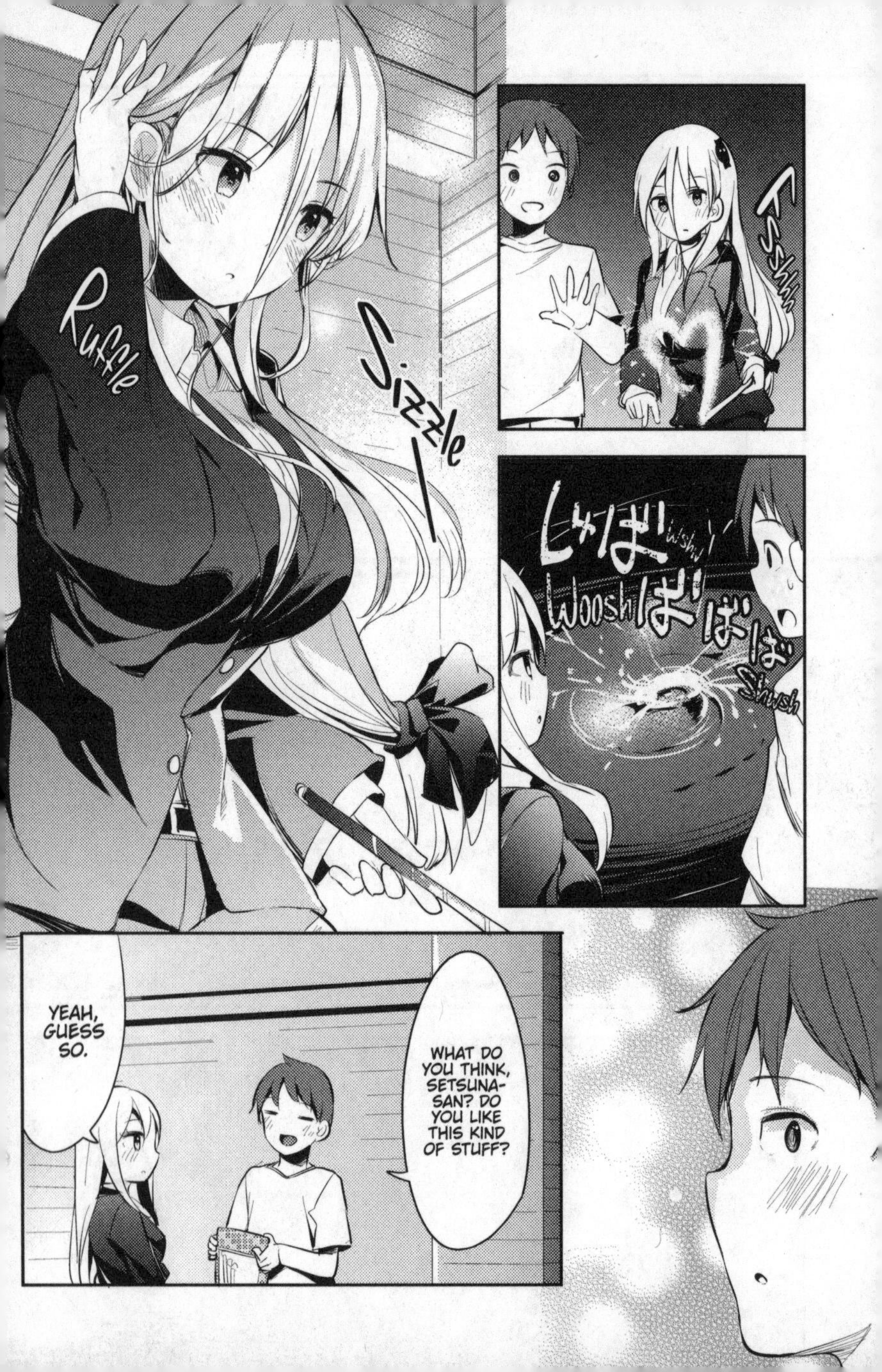
Fsshhh
しゅぱ
Wshu
Woosh
ぱぱぱ
Shwsh
Ruffle
Sizzle
WHAT DO YOU THINK, SETSUNA-SAN? DO YOU LIKE THIS KIND OF STUFF?
YEAH, GUESS SO.

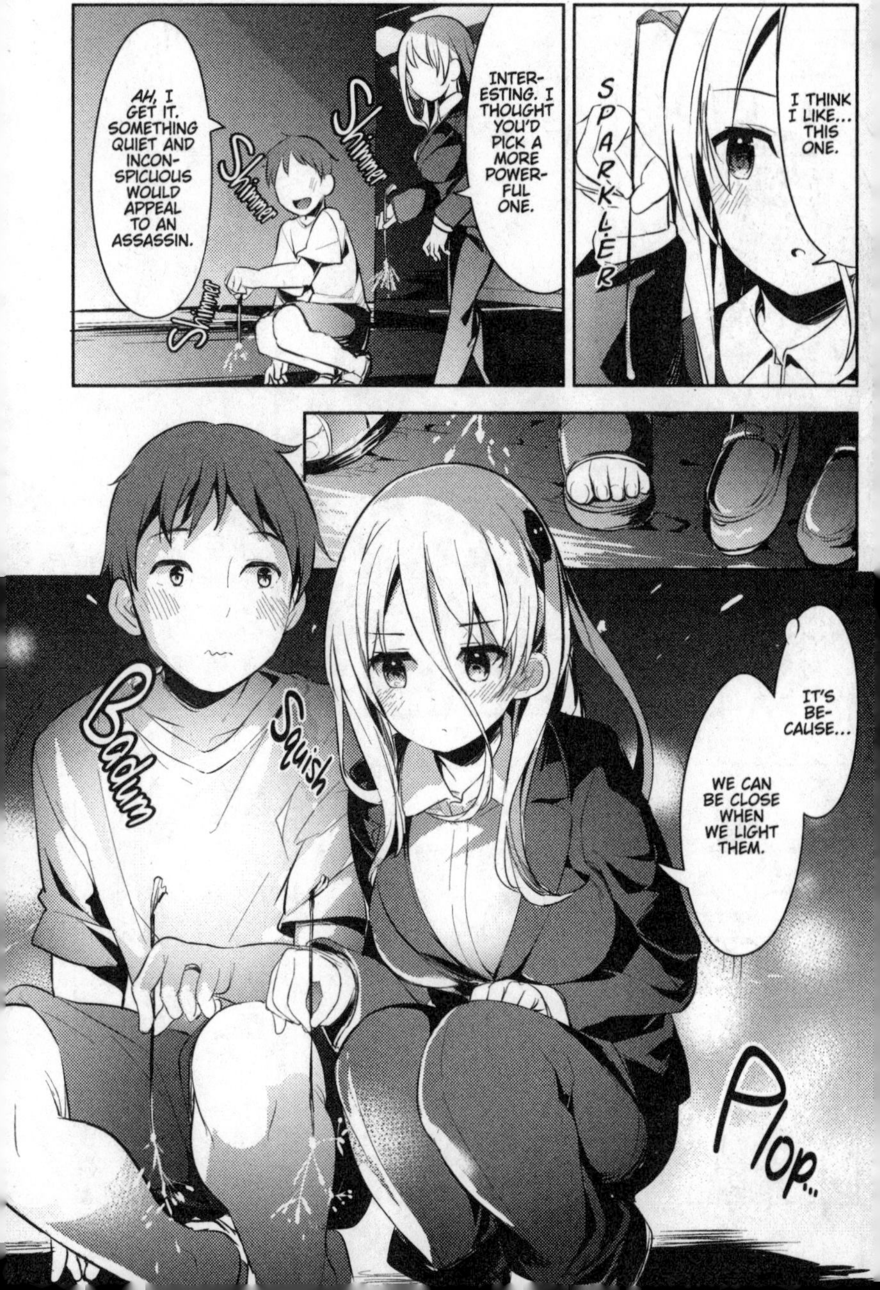
SPARKLER
I THINK I LIKE... THIS ONE.
Shimmer
INTERESTING. I THOUGHT YOU'D PICK A MORE POWERFUL ONE.
AH, I GET IT. SOMETHING QUIET AND INCONSPICUOUS WOULD APPEAL TO AN ASSASSIN.
Shimmer
Shimmer
IT'S BECAUSE...
WE CAN BE CLOSE WHEN WE LIGHT THEM.
Squish
Badum
Plop...

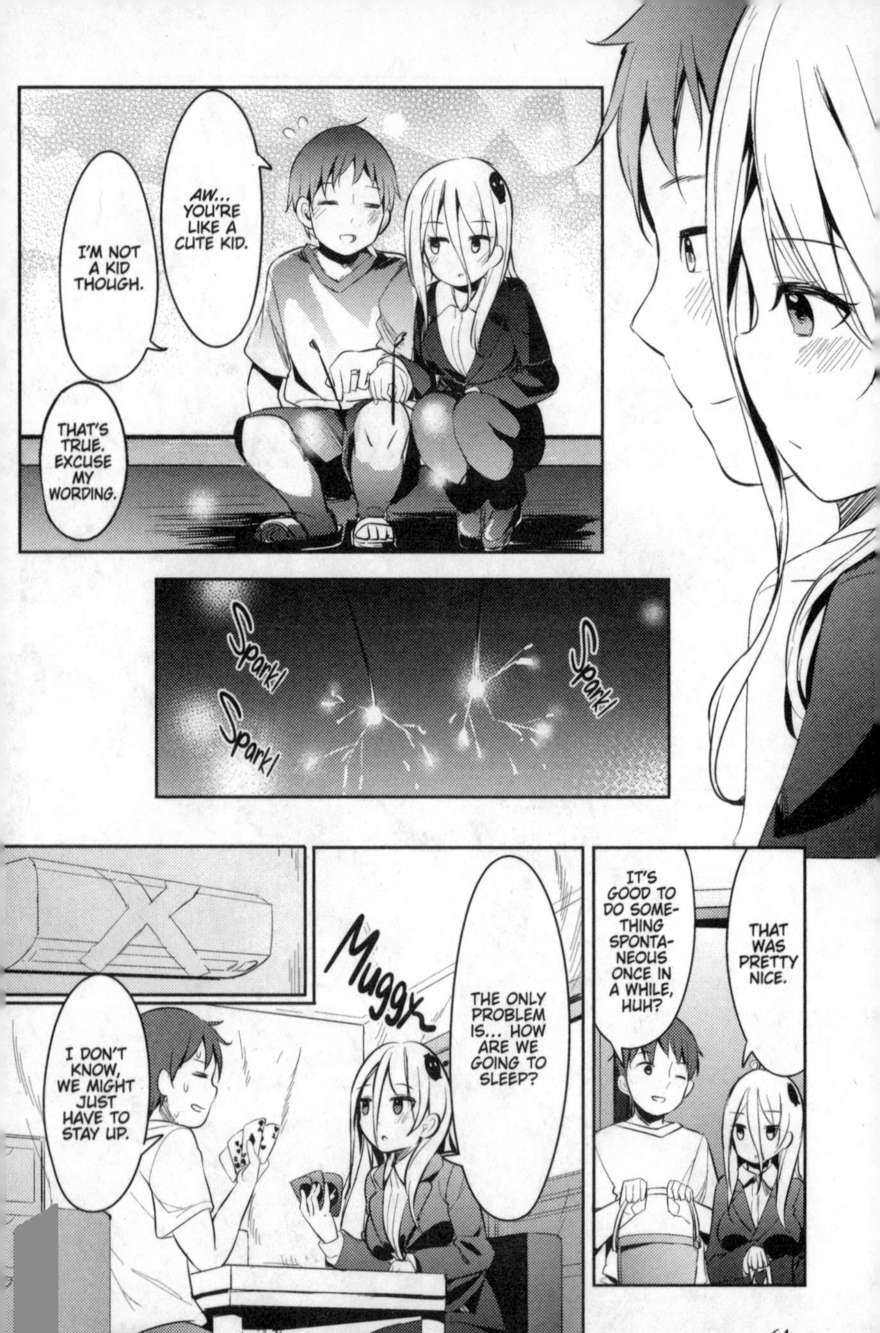
AW... YOU'RE LIKE A CUTE KID.
I'M NOT A KID THOUGH.
THAT'S TRUE. EXCUSE MY WORDING.
Spark!
Spark!
Spark!
THAT WAS PRETTY NICE.
IT'S GOOD TO DO SOME-THING SPONTA-NEOUS ONCE IN A WHILE, HUH?
Muggy
THE ONLY PROBLEM IS... HOW ARE WE GOING TO SLEEP?
I DON'T KNOW, WE MIGHT JUST HAVE TO STAY UP.

SETSUNA-SAN AND MORTAR FIREWORKS.

I'M THINKING...
NEXT TIME, IT'D BE FUN TO LAUNCH SOME FIREWORKS TOGETHER.
THE MORTAR ONES? SOUNDS GREAT.
WELL, GETTING GUNPOWDER IS NO PROBLEM, SO WE WOULD JUST NEED TO FIND A MORTAR OR TWO AND A PLACE TO SET THEM OFF.
I WANNA LIGHT IT!

MY Lovey-Dovey Wife IS A STONE COLD KILLER

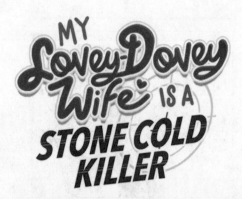

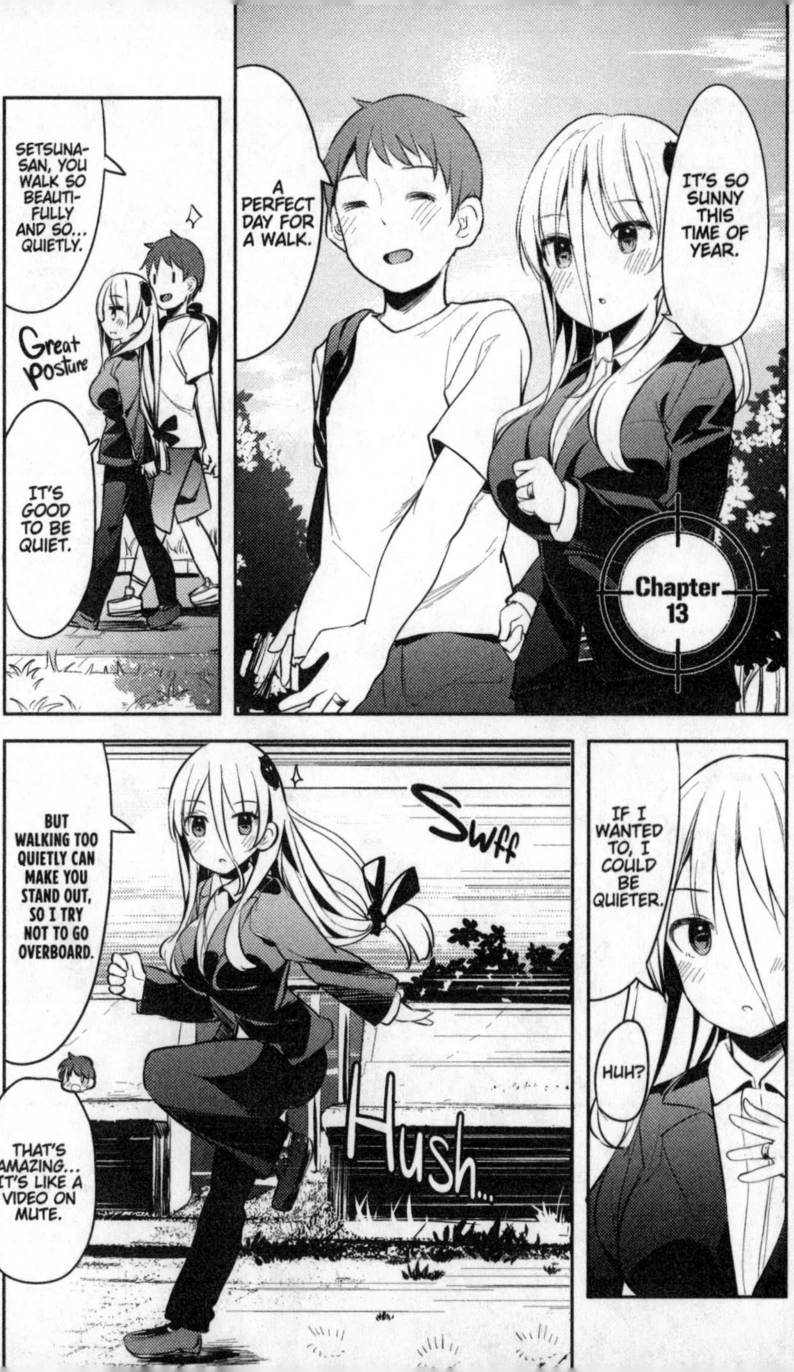
IT'S SO SUNNY THIS TIME OF YEAR.
A PERFECT DAY FOR A WALK.
Chapter 13
SETSUNA-SAN, YOU WALK SO BEAUTIFULLY AND SO... QUIETLY.
Great posture
IT'S GOOD TO BE QUIET.
IF I WANTED TO, I COULD BE QUIETER.
HUH?
Swff
BUT WALKING TOO QUIETLY CAN MAKE YOU STAND OUT, SO I TRY NOT TO GO OVERBOARD.
Hush...
THAT'S AMAZING... IT'S LIKE A VIDEO ON MUTE.

AT THE PARK WITH SETSUNA-SAN.

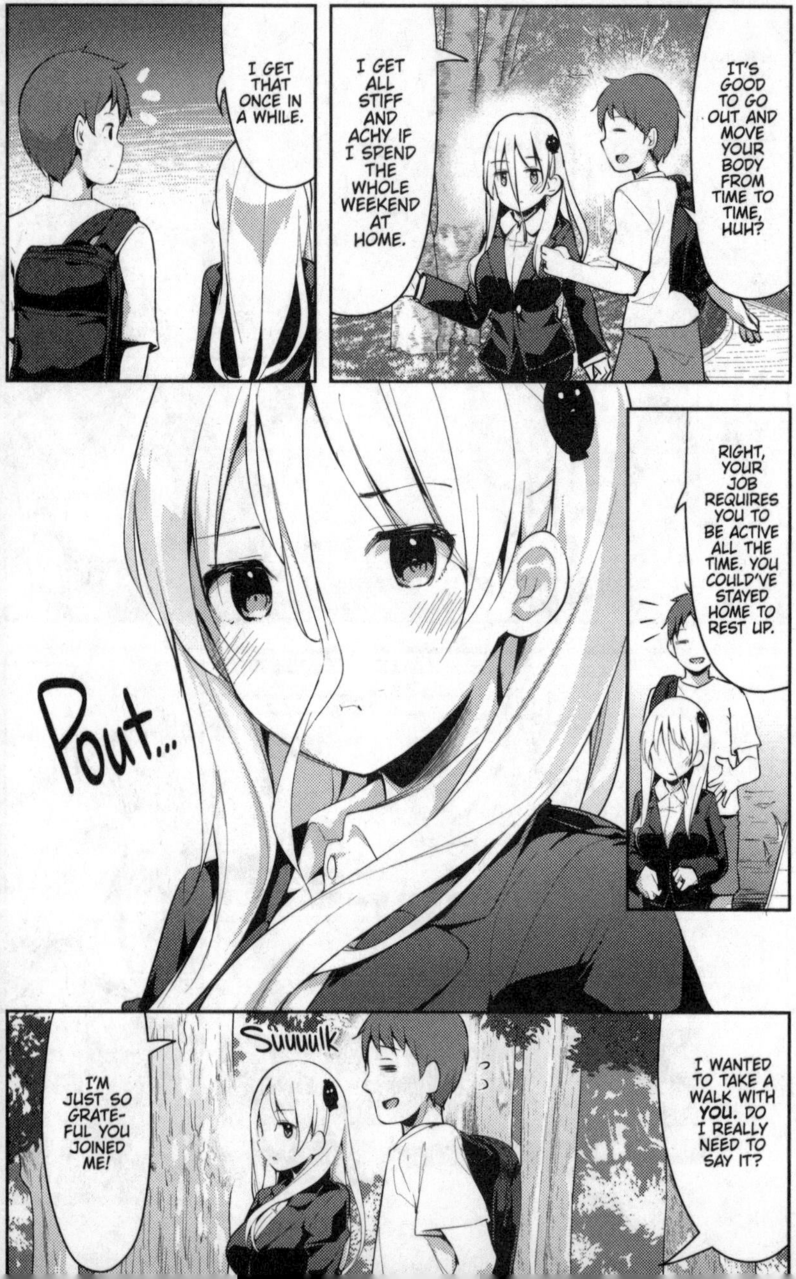

IT'S GOOD TO GO OUT AND MOVE YOUR BODY FROM TIME TO TIME, HUH?
I GET ALL STIFF AND ACHY IF I SPEND THE WHOLE WEEKEND AT HOME.
I GET THAT ONCE IN A WHILE.
RIGHT, YOUR JOB REQUIRES YOU TO BE ACTIVE ALL THE TIME. YOU COULD'VE STAYED HOME TO REST UP.
Pout...
I WANTED TO TAKE A WALK WITH **YOU**. DO I REALLY NEED TO SAY IT?
Suuuulk
I'M JUST SO GRATE-FUL YOU JOINED ME!

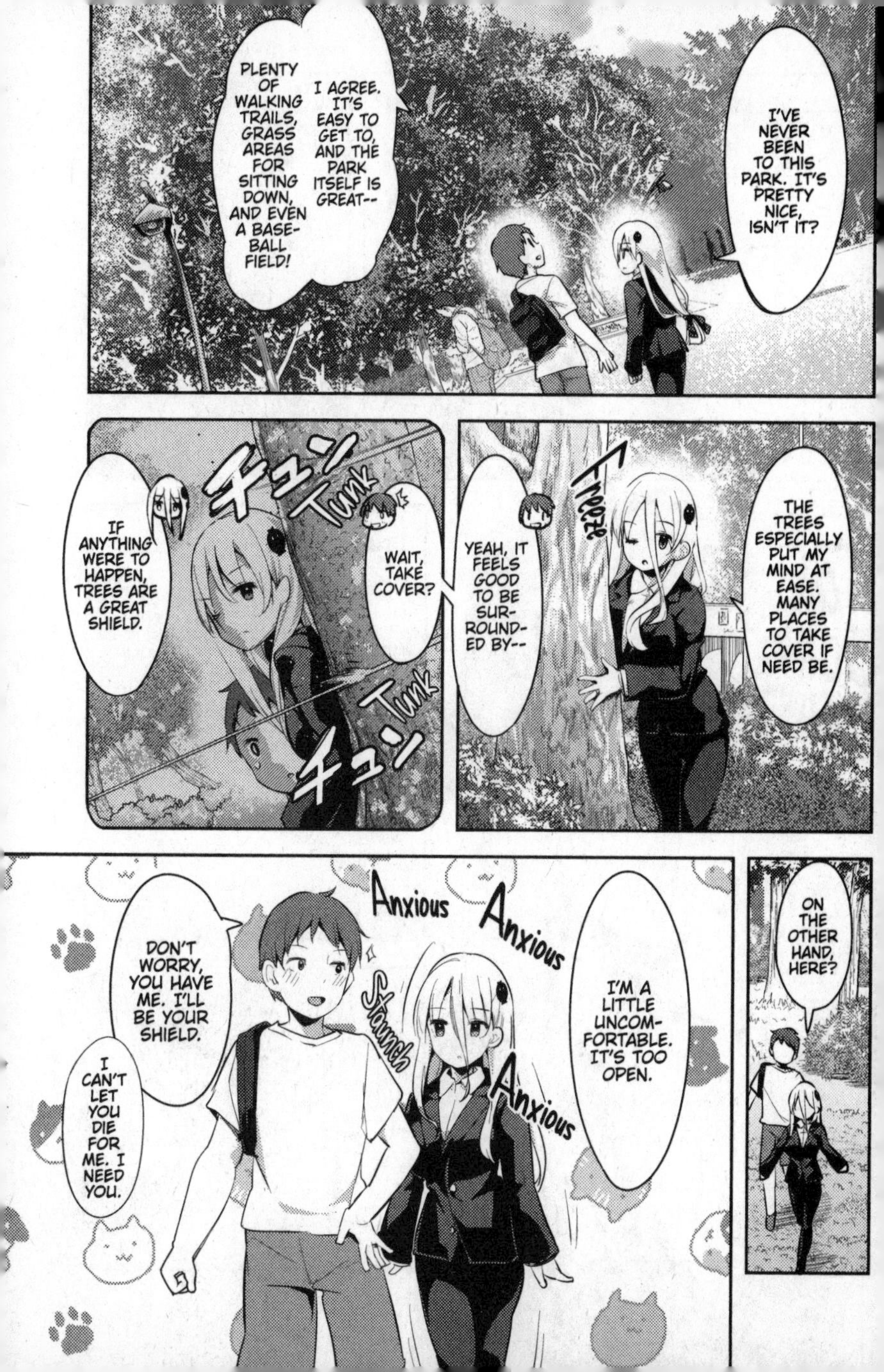
I'VE NEVER BEEN TO THIS PARK. IT'S PRETTY NICE, ISN'T IT?
I AGREE. IT'S EASY TO GET TO, AND THE PARK ITSELF IS GREAT--
PLENTY OF WALKING TRAILS, GRASS AREAS FOR SITTING DOWN, AND EVEN A BASE-BALL FIELD!
THE TREES ESPECIALLY PUT MY MIND AT EASE. MANY PLACES TO TAKE COVER IF NEED BE.
Freeze
YEAH, IT FEELS GOOD TO BE SUR-ROUND-ED BY--
WAIT, TAKE COVER?
チュン Tunk
チュン Tunk
IF ANYTHING WERE TO HAPPEN, TREES ARE A GREAT SHIELD.
ON THE OTHER HAND, HERE?
I'M A LITTLE UNCOM-FORTABLE. IT'S TOO OPEN.
Anxious
Anxious
Anxious
Staunch
DON'T WORRY, YOU HAVE ME. I'LL BE YOUR SHIELD.
I CAN'T LET YOU DIE FOR ME. I NEED YOU.

SETSUNA-SAN'S SUNHAT.

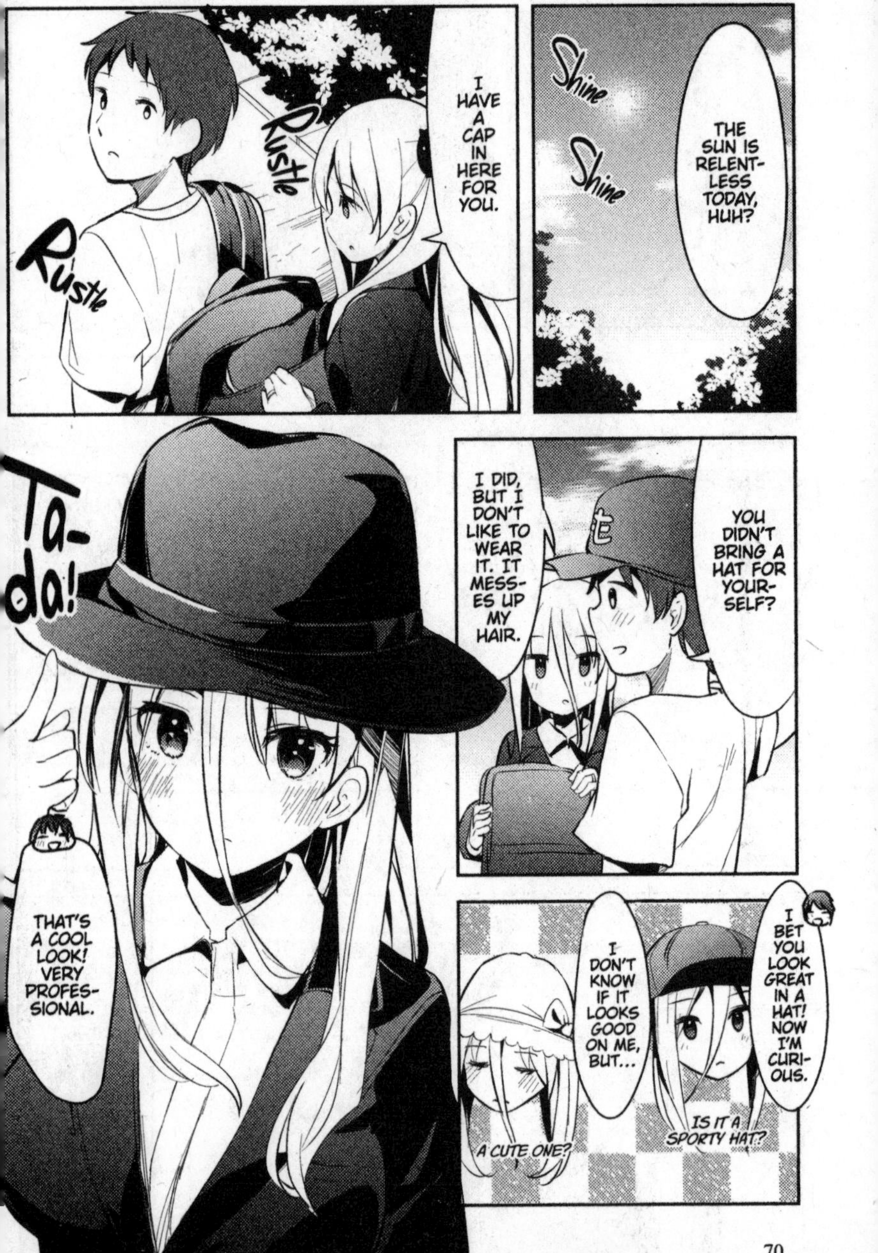
Shine
Shine
THE SUN IS RELENTLESS TODAY, HUH?
I HAVE A CAP IN HERE FOR YOU.
Rustle
Rustle
YOU DIDN'T BRING A HAT FOR YOURSELF?
I DID, BUT I DON'T LIKE TO WEAR IT. IT MESSES UP MY HAIR.
I BET YOU LOOK GREAT IN A HAT! NOW I'M CURIOUS.
I DON'T KNOW IF IT LOOKS GOOD ON ME, BUT...
IS IT A SPORTY HAT?
A CUTE ONE?
Ta-da!
THAT'S A COOL LOOK! VERY PROFESSIONAL.

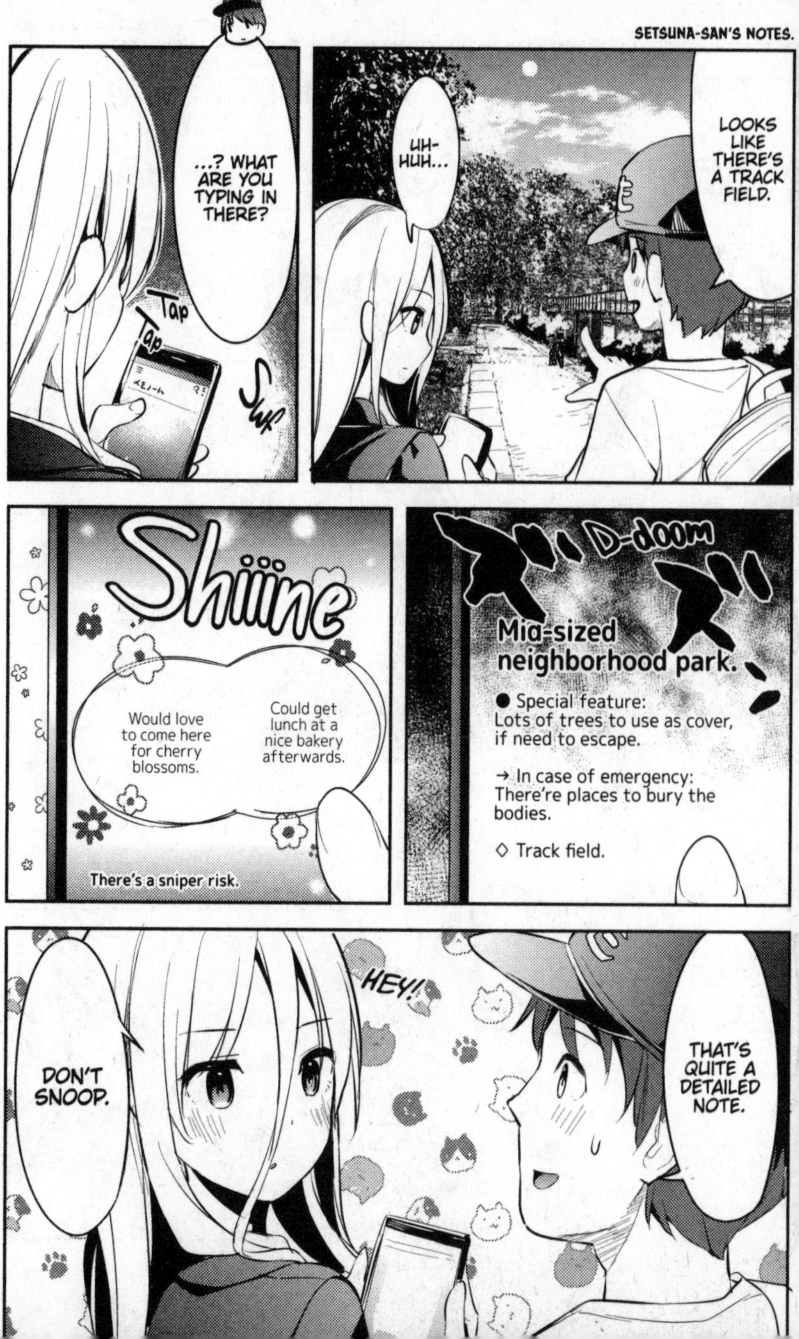
LOOKS LIKE THERE'S A TRACK FIELD.
UH-HUH...
...? WHAT ARE YOU TYPING IN THERE?
Tap
Tap
Shuf
D-doom
Mia-sized neighborhood park.
● Special feature:
Lots of trees to use as cover, if need to escape.
→ In case of emergency:
There're places to bury the bodies.
◇ Track field.
Shiine
Could get lunch at a nice bakery afterwards.
Would love to come here for cherry blossoms.
There's a sniper risk.
THAT'S QUITE A DETAILED NOTE.
HEY!
DON'T SNOOP.

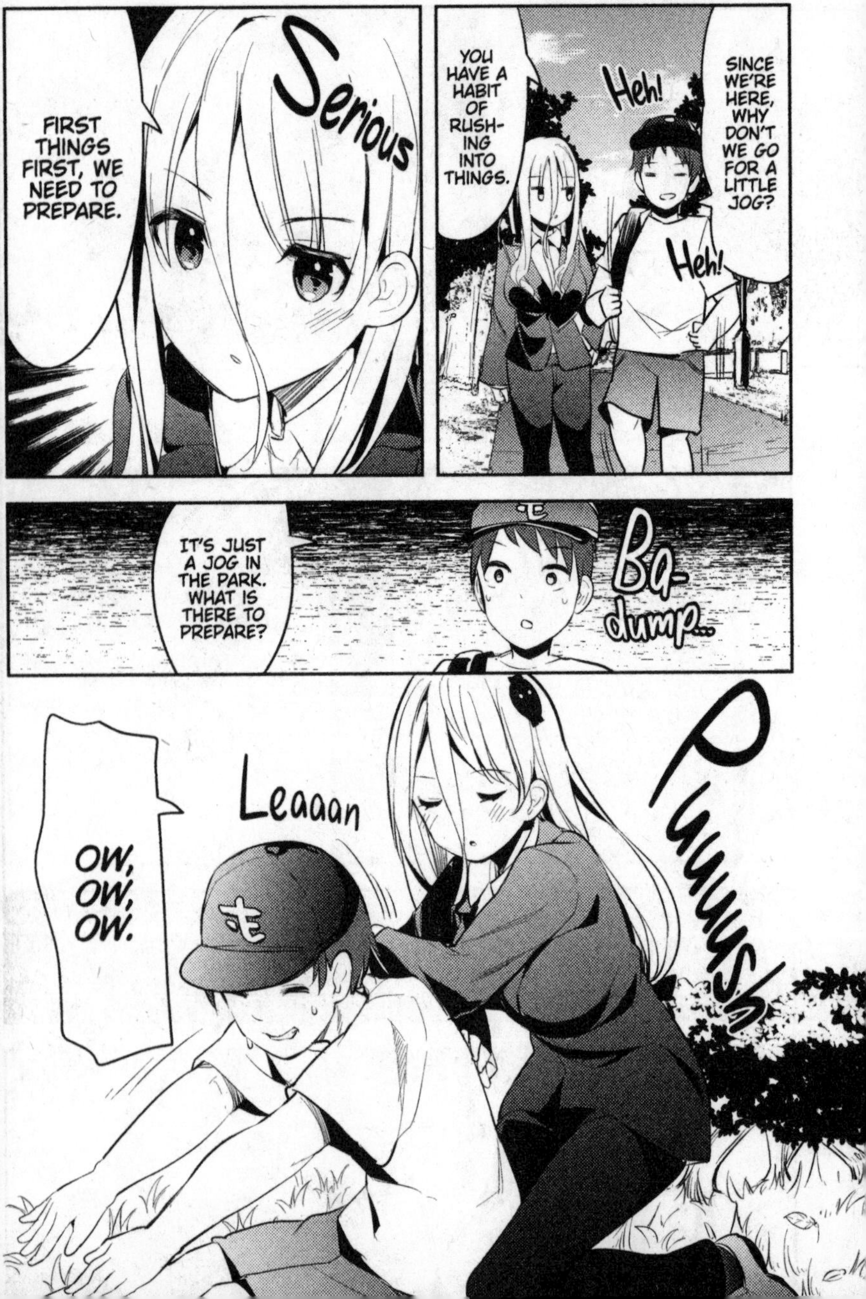
SINCE WE'RE HERE, WHY DON'T WE GO FOR A LITTLE JOG?
Heh!
Heh!
YOU HAVE A HABIT OF RUSH-ING INTO THINGS.
Serious
FIRST THINGS FIRST, WE NEED TO PREPARE.
Ba-dump...
IT'S JUST A JOG IN THE PARK. WHAT IS THERE TO PREPARE?
Puuuush
Leaaan
OW, OW, OW.

STRETCHING WITH SETSUNA-SAN.

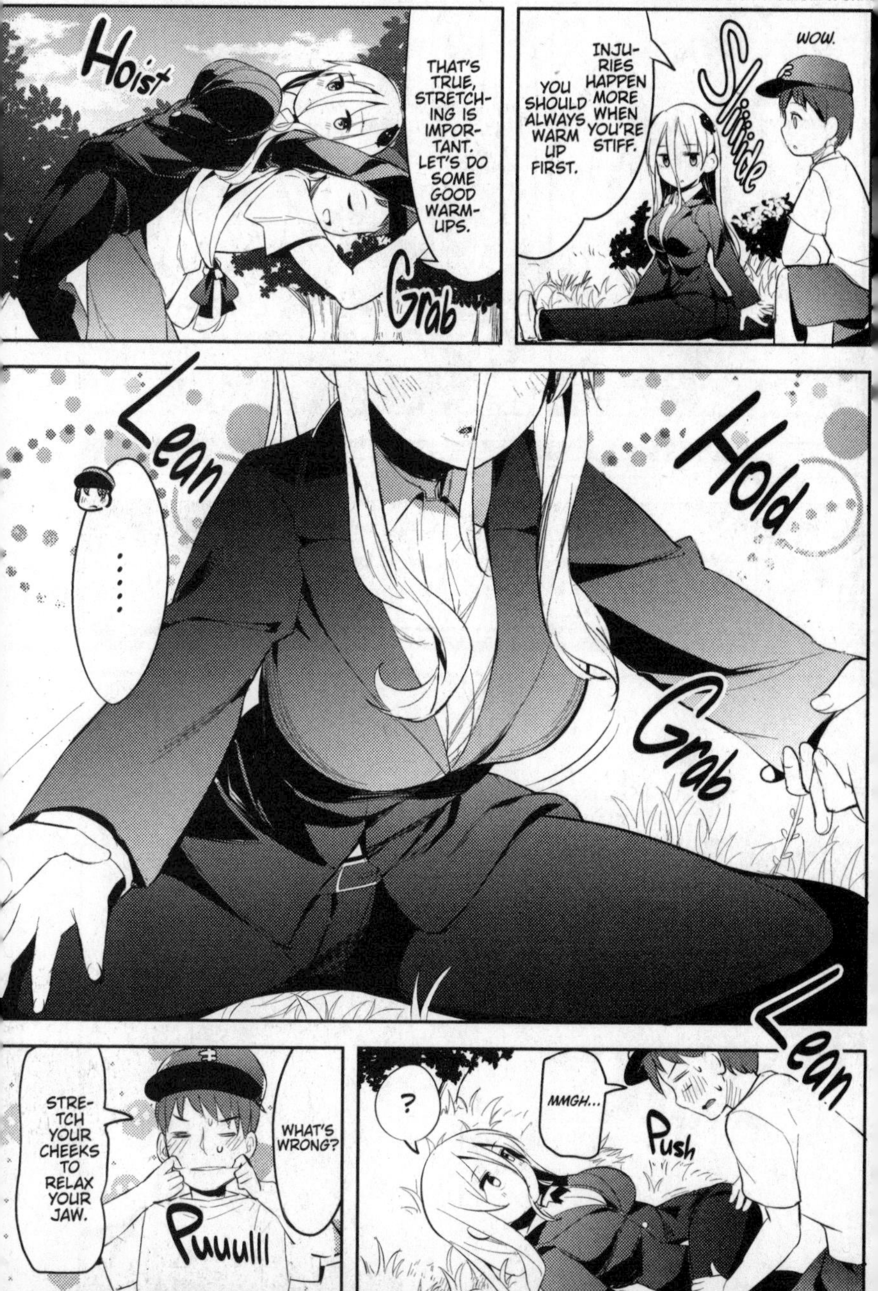

WOW.
Sliiide
INJURIES HAPPEN MORE WHEN YOU'RE STIFF.
YOU SHOULD ALWAYS WARM UP FIRST.
THAT'S TRUE, STRETCHING IS IMPORTANT. LET'S DO SOME GOOD WARM-UPS.
Hoist
Grab
Hold
Lean
.....
Grab
Lean
MMGH...
Push
?
WHAT'S WRONG?
STRETCH YOUR CHEEKS TO RELAX YOUR JAW.
Puuulll

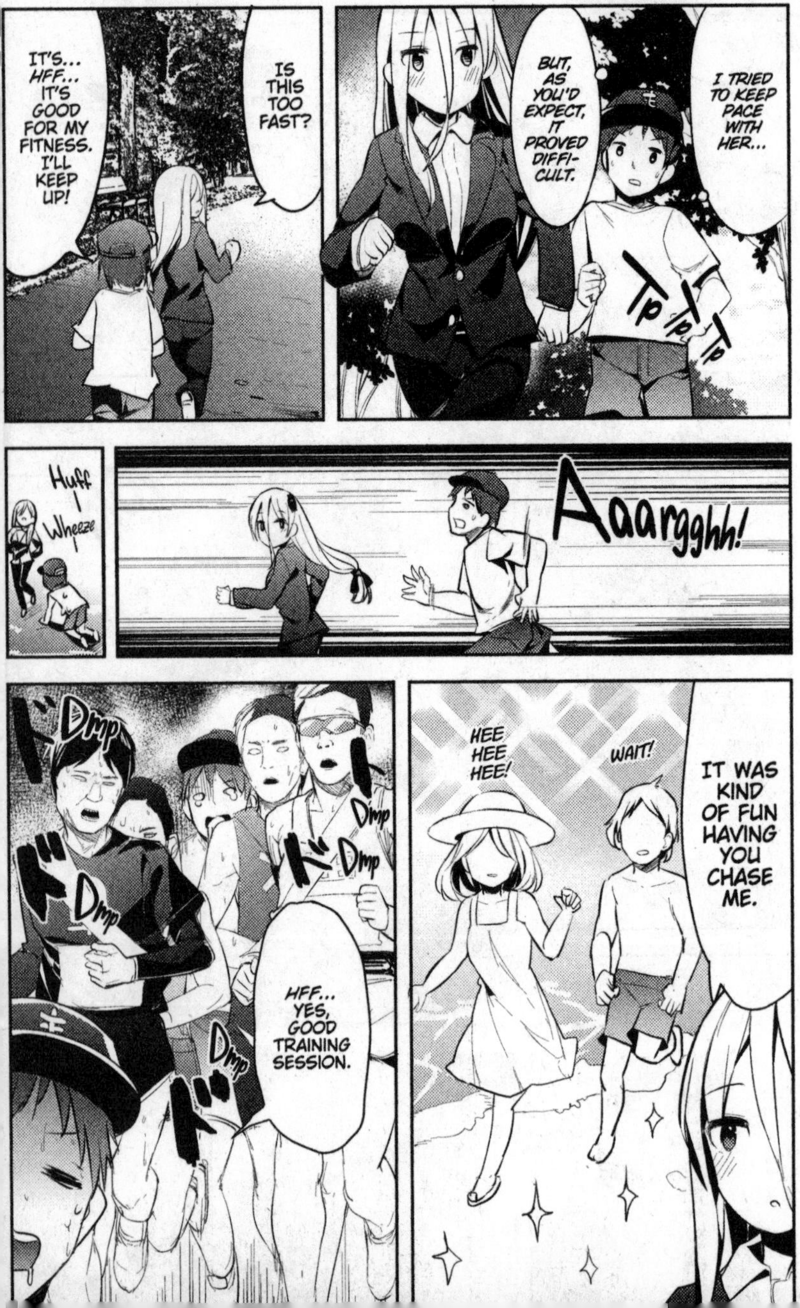
I TRIED TO KEEP PACE WITH HER...
BUT, AS YOU'D EXPECT, IT PROVED DIFFICULT.
Tp Tp Tp
IS THIS TOO FAST?
IT'S... HFF... IT'S GOOD FOR MY FITNESS. I'LL KEEP UP!
Aaargghh!
Huff
Wheeze
IT WAS KIND OF FUN HAVING YOU CHASE ME.
WAIT!
HEE HEE HEE!
Dmp
Dmp
Dmp
Dmp
Dmp
HFF... YES, GOOD TRAINING SESSION.

AN INDIRECT KISS...?

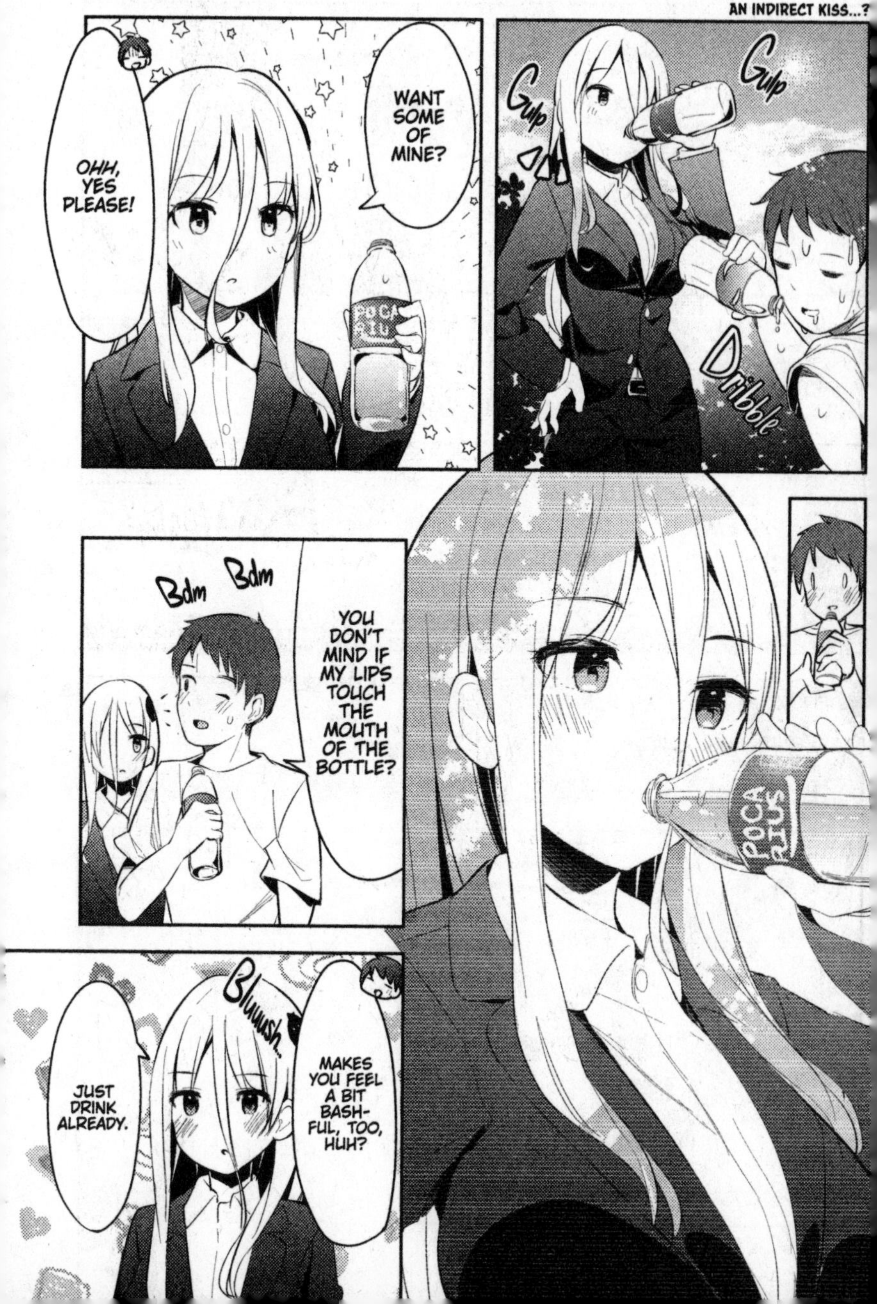
Gulp
Gulp
Dribble
WANT SOME OF MINE?
OHH, YES PLEASE!
Bdm Bdm
YOU DON'T MIND IF MY LIPS TOUCH THE MOUTH OF THE BOTTLE?
Bluuush...
MAKES YOU FEEL A BIT BASH-FUL, TOO, HUH?
JUST DRINK ALREADY.

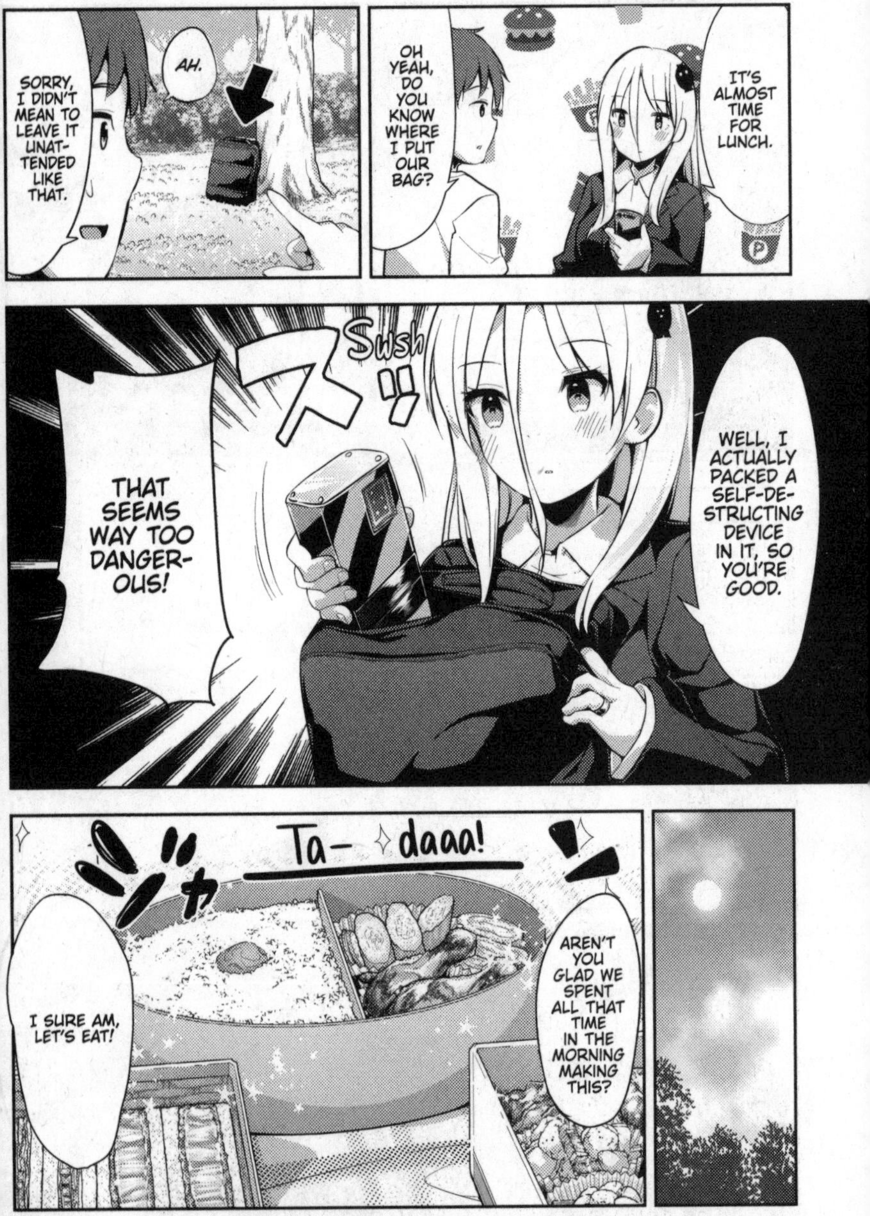
IT'S ALMOST TIME FOR LUNCH.
OH YEAH, DO YOU KNOW WHERE I PUT OUR BAG?
AH.
SORRY, I DIDN'T MEAN TO LEAVE IT UNATTENDED LIKE THAT.
Swsh
WELL, I ACTUALLY PACKED A SELF-DESTRUCTING DEVICE IN IT, SO YOU'RE GOOD.
THAT SEEMS WAY TOO DANGEROUS!
Ta-daaa!
AREN'T YOU GLAD WE SPENT ALL THAT TIME IN THE MORNING MAKING THIS?
I SURE AM, LET'S EAT!

THE MASSACRE.

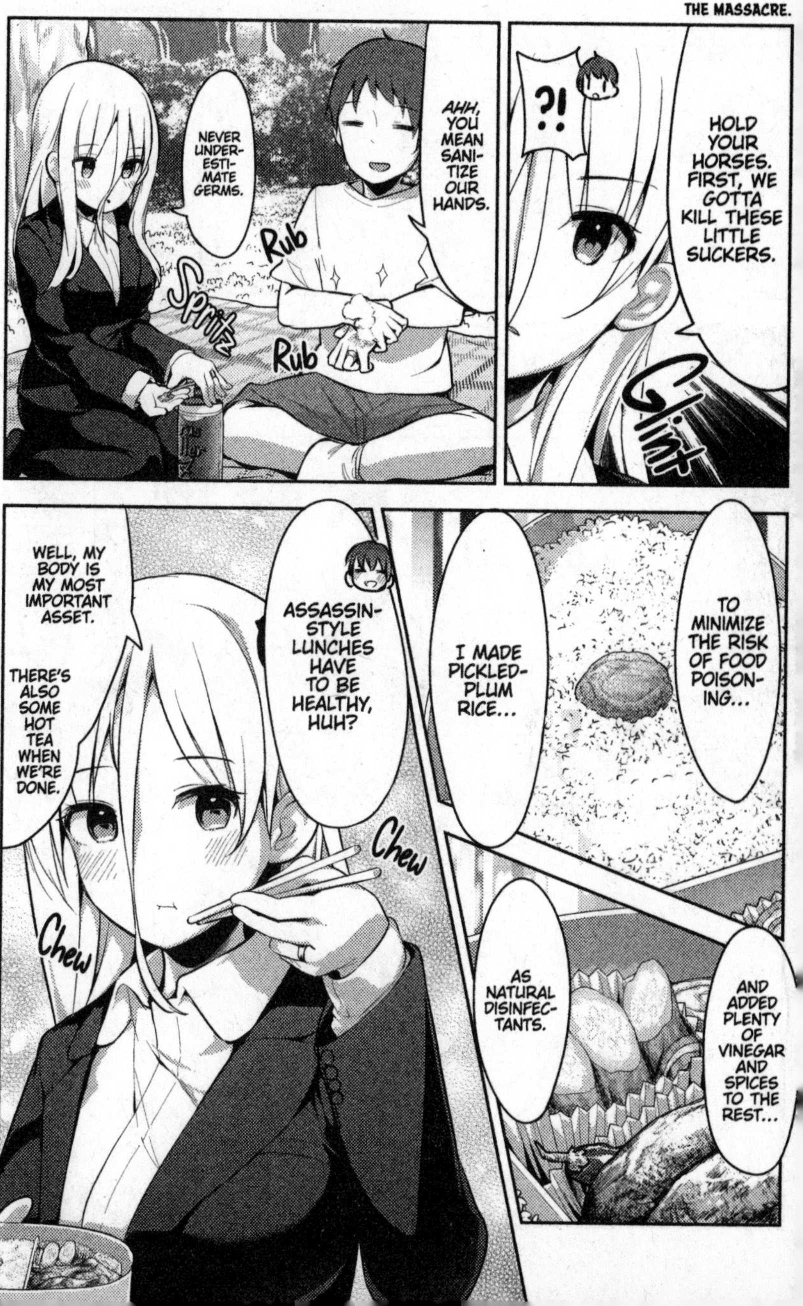
?!
HOLD YOUR HORSES. FIRST, WE GOTTA KILL THESE LITTLE SUCKERS.
Glint
AHH, YOU MEAN SANITIZE OUR HANDS.
NEVER UNDERESTIMATE GERMS.
Rub
Spritz
Rub
TO MINIMIZE THE RISK OF FOOD POISONING...
I MADE PICKLED-PLUM RICE...
AND ADDED PLENTY OF VINEGAR AND SPICES TO THE REST...
AS NATURAL DISINFECTANTS.
ASSASSIN-STYLE LUNCHES HAVE TO BE HEALTHY, HUH?
WELL, MY BODY IS MY MOST IMPORTANT ASSET.
THERE'S ALSO SOME HOT TEA WHEN WE'RE DONE.
Chew
Chew

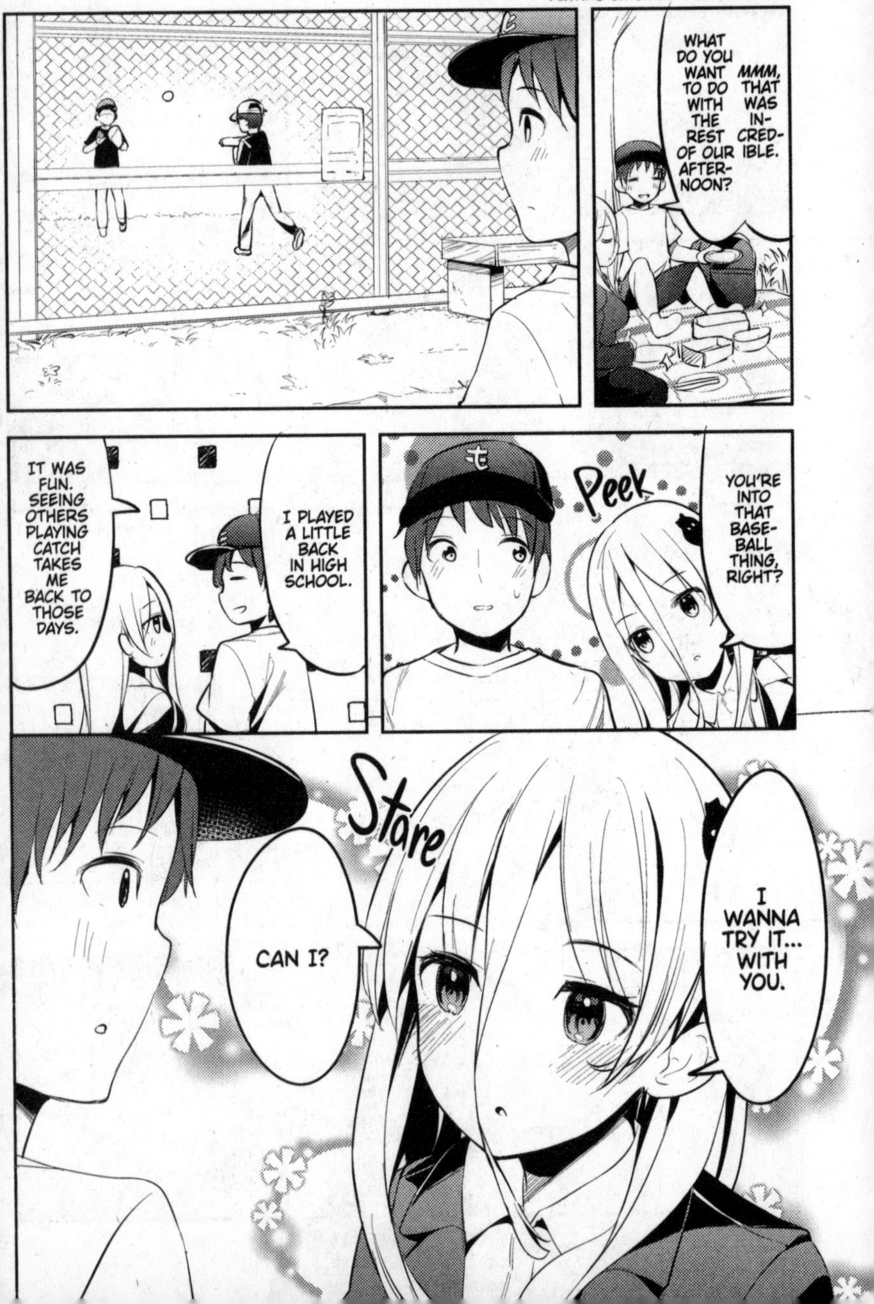
MMM, THAT WAS IN-CREDIBLE.
WHAT DO YOU WANT TO DO WITH THE REST OF OUR AFTER-NOON?
YOU'RE INTO THAT BASE-BALL THING, RIGHT?
Peek
I PLAYED A LITTLE BACK IN HIGH SCHOOL.
IT WAS FUN. SEEING OTHERS PLAYING CATCH TAKES ME BACK TO THOSE DAYS.
I WANNA TRY IT... WITH YOU.
Stare
CAN I?

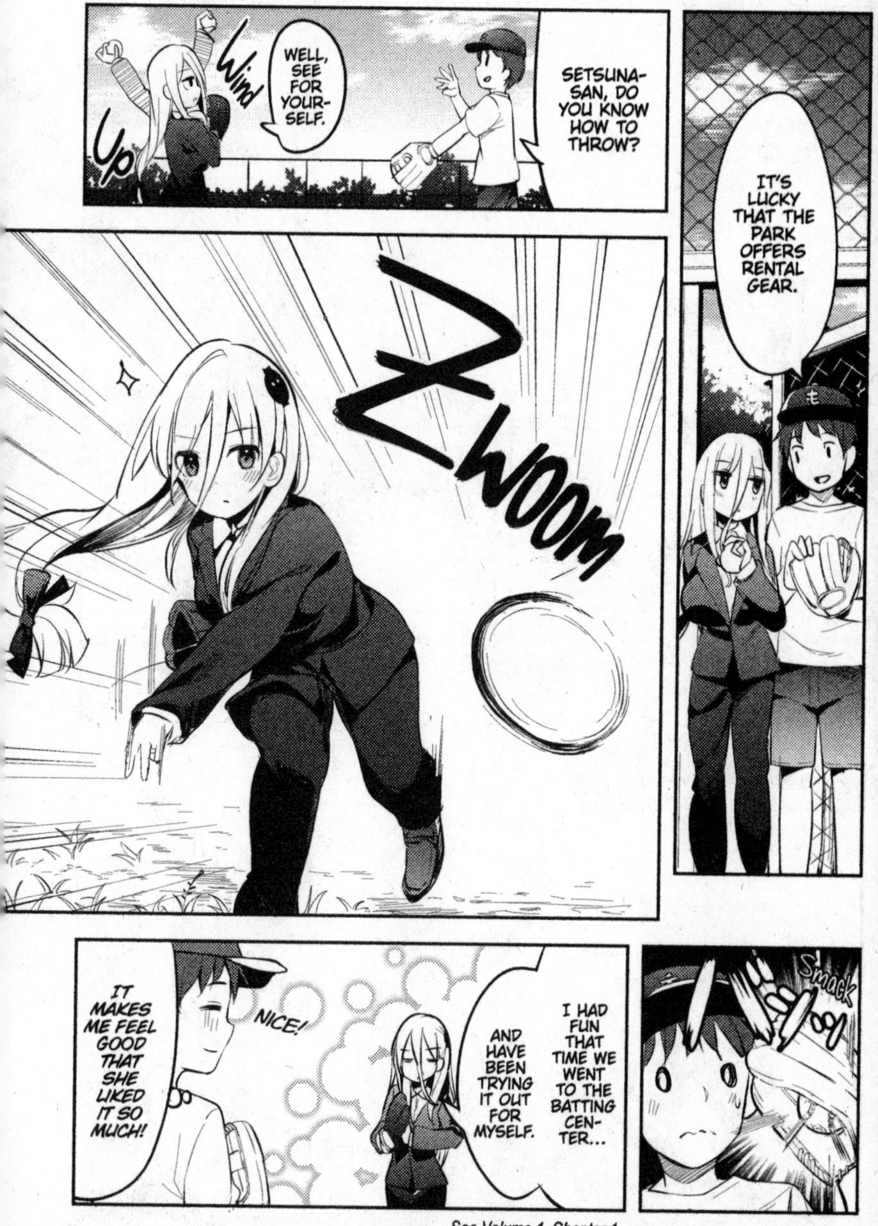
IT'S LUCKY THAT THE PARK OFFERS RENTAL GEAR.
SETSUNA-SAN, DO YOU KNOW HOW TO THROW?
WELL, SEE FOR YOURSELF.
Wind Up
ZWOOM
Smack
I HAD FUN THAT TIME WE WENT TO THE BATTING CENTER...
AND HAVE BEEN TRYING IT OUT FOR MYSELF.
NICE!
IT MAKES ME FEEL GOOD THAT SHE LIKED IT SO MUCH!

See Volume 1, Chapter 1.

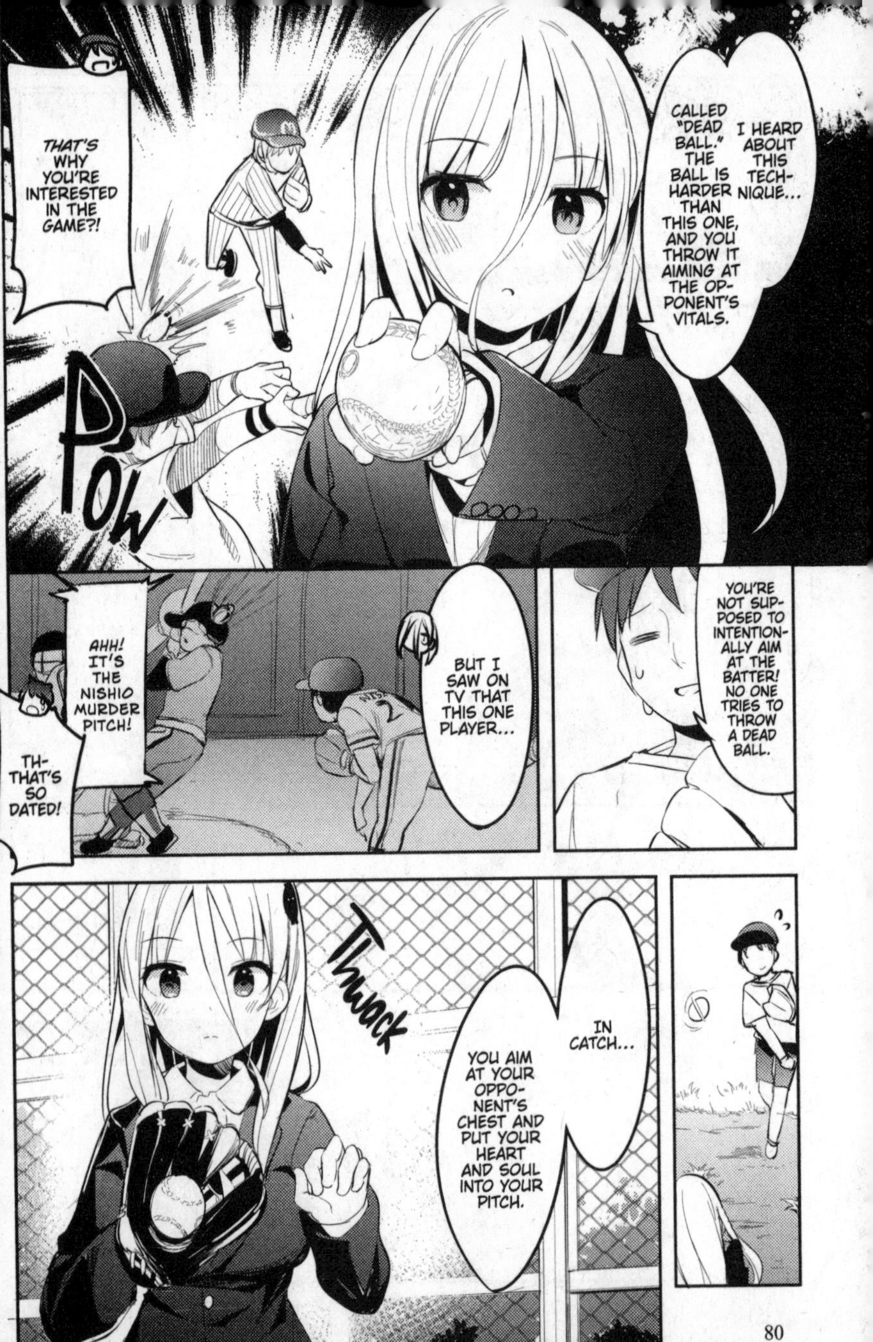
I HEARD ABOUT THIS TECHNIQUE...
CALLED "DEAD BALL." THE BALL IS HARDER THAN THIS ONE, AND YOU THROW IT AIMING AT THE OPPONENT'S VITALS.
THAT'S WHY YOU'RE INTERESTED IN THE GAME?!
POW
YOU'RE NOT SUPPOSED TO INTENTIONALLY AIM AT THE BATTER! NO ONE TRIES TO THROW A DEAD BALL.
BUT I SAW ON TV THAT THIS ONE PLAYER...
AHH! IT'S THE NISHIO MURDER PITCH!
TH-THAT'S SO DATED!
IN CATCH...
YOU AIM AT YOUR OPPONENT'S CHEST AND PUT YOUR HEART AND SOUL INTO YOUR PITCH.
THWACK

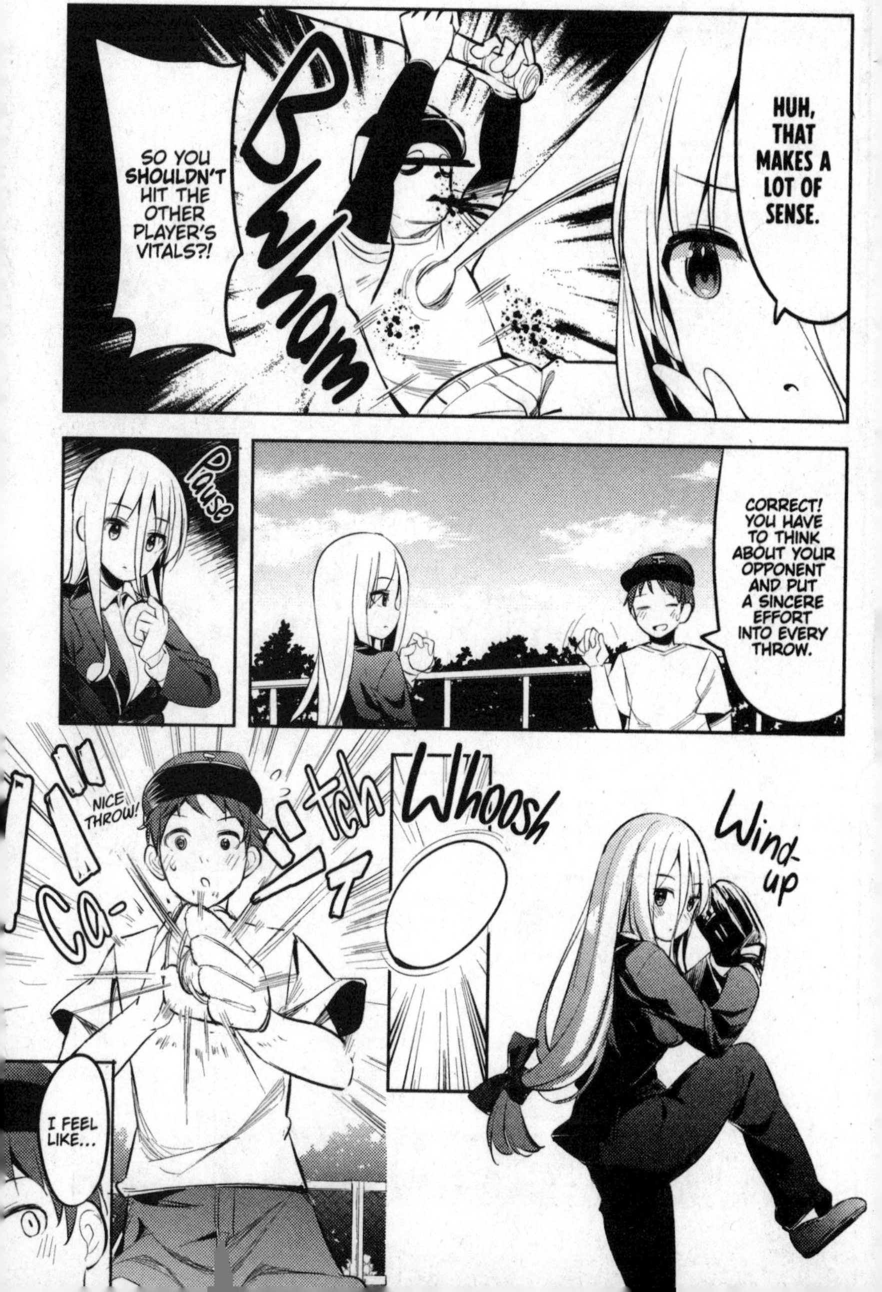
HUH, THAT MAKES A LOT OF SENSE.
BWham
SO YOU SHOULDN'T HIT THE OTHER PLAYER'S VITALS?!
CORRECT! YOU HAVE TO THINK ABOUT YOUR OPPONENT AND PUT A SINCERE EFFORT INTO EVERY THROW.
Pause
Wind-up
Whoosh
Ca-tch
NICE THROW!
I FEEL LIKE...

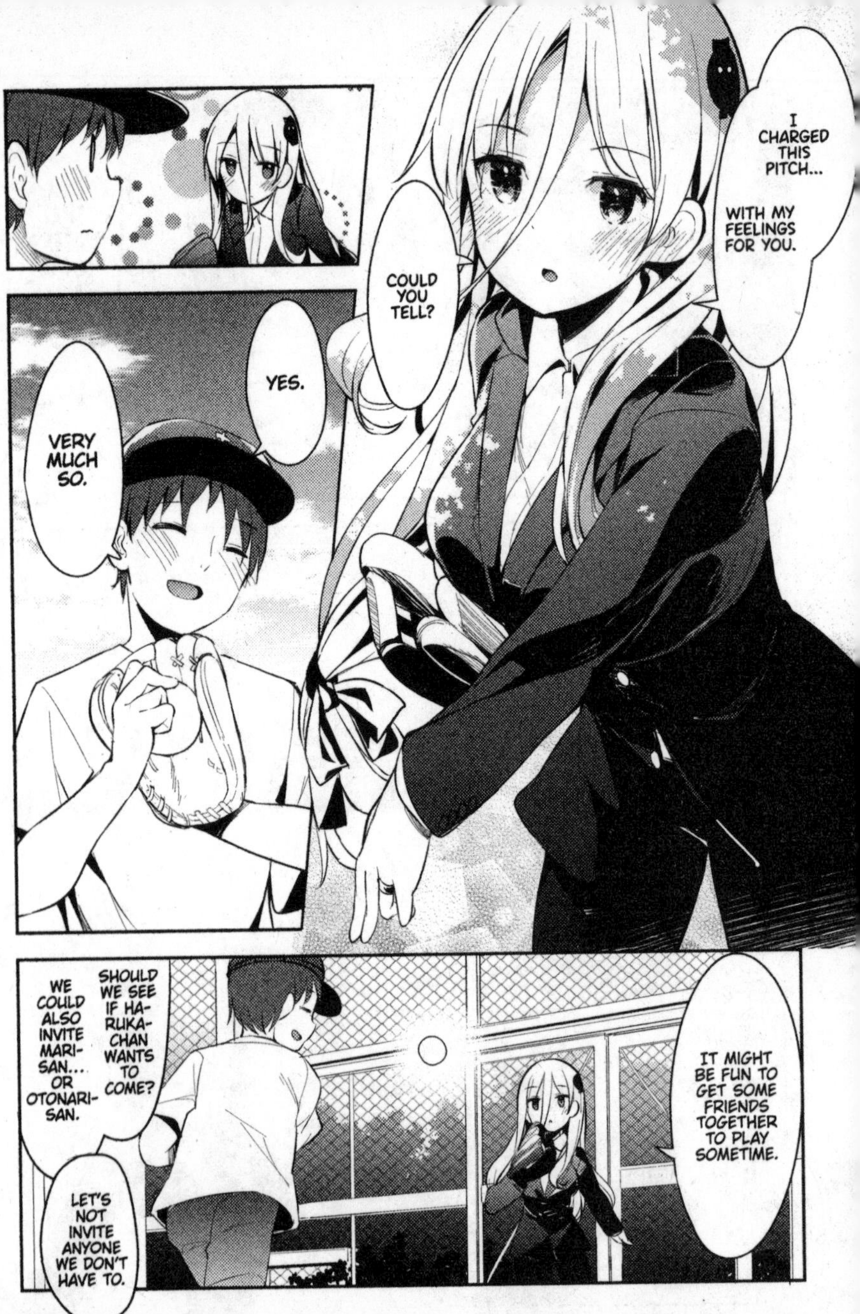
I CHARGED THIS PITCH...
WITH MY FEELINGS FOR YOU.
COULD YOU TELL?
YES.
VERY MUCH SO.
IT MIGHT BE FUN TO GET SOME FRIENDS TOGETHER TO PLAY SOMETIME.
SHOULD WE SEE IF HARUKA-CHAN WANTS TO COME?
WE COULD ALSO INVITE MARI-SAN... OR OTONARI-SAN.
LET'S NOT INVITE ANYONE WE DON'T HAVE TO.

BASEBALL LINGO THROUGH THE EYES OF AN ASSASSIN.

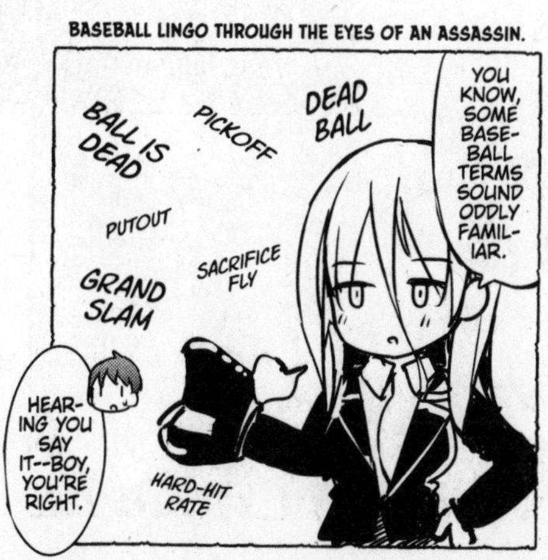
YOU KNOW, SOME BASE-BALL TERMS SOUND ODDLY FAMIL-IAR.
DEAD BALL
PICKOFF
BALL IS DEAD
PUTOUT
SACRIFICE FLY
GRAND SLAM
HARD-HIT RATE
HEAR-ING YOU SAY IT--BOY, YOU'RE RIGHT.

MY Lovey-Dovey Wife IS A STONE COLD KILLER

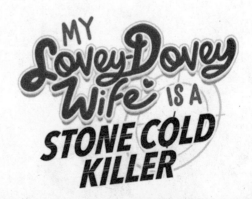

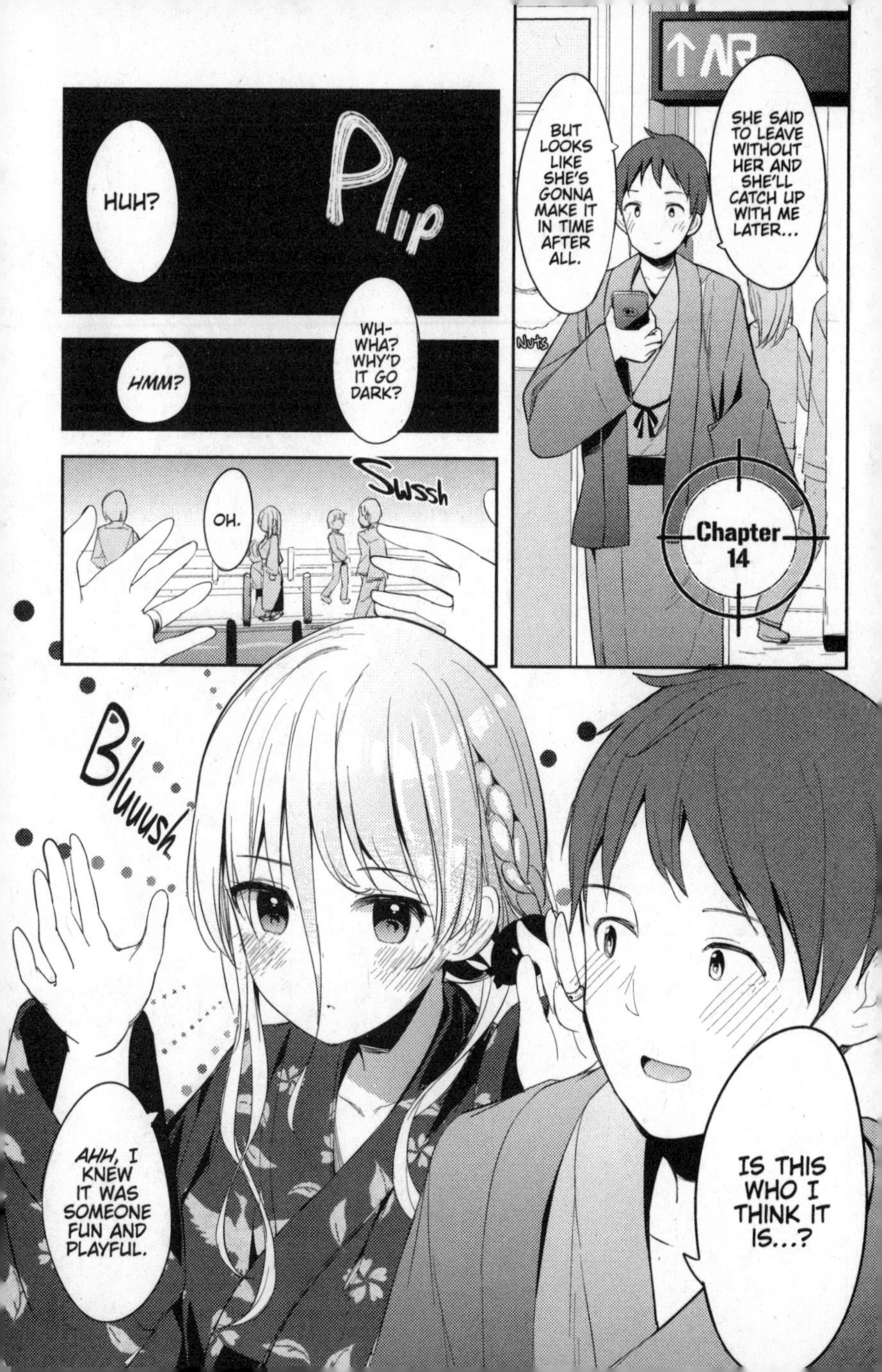
SHE SAID TO LEAVE WITHOUT HER AND SHE'LL CATCH UP WITH ME LATER...
BUT LOOKS LIKE SHE'S GONNA MAKE IT IN TIME AFTER ALL.
Nuts
Chapter 14
Plip
HUH?
WH-WHA? WHY'D IT GO DARK?
HMM?
Swssh
OH.
IS THIS WHO I THINK IT IS...?
Bluuush
AHH, I KNEW IT WAS SOMEONE FUN AND PLAYFUL.

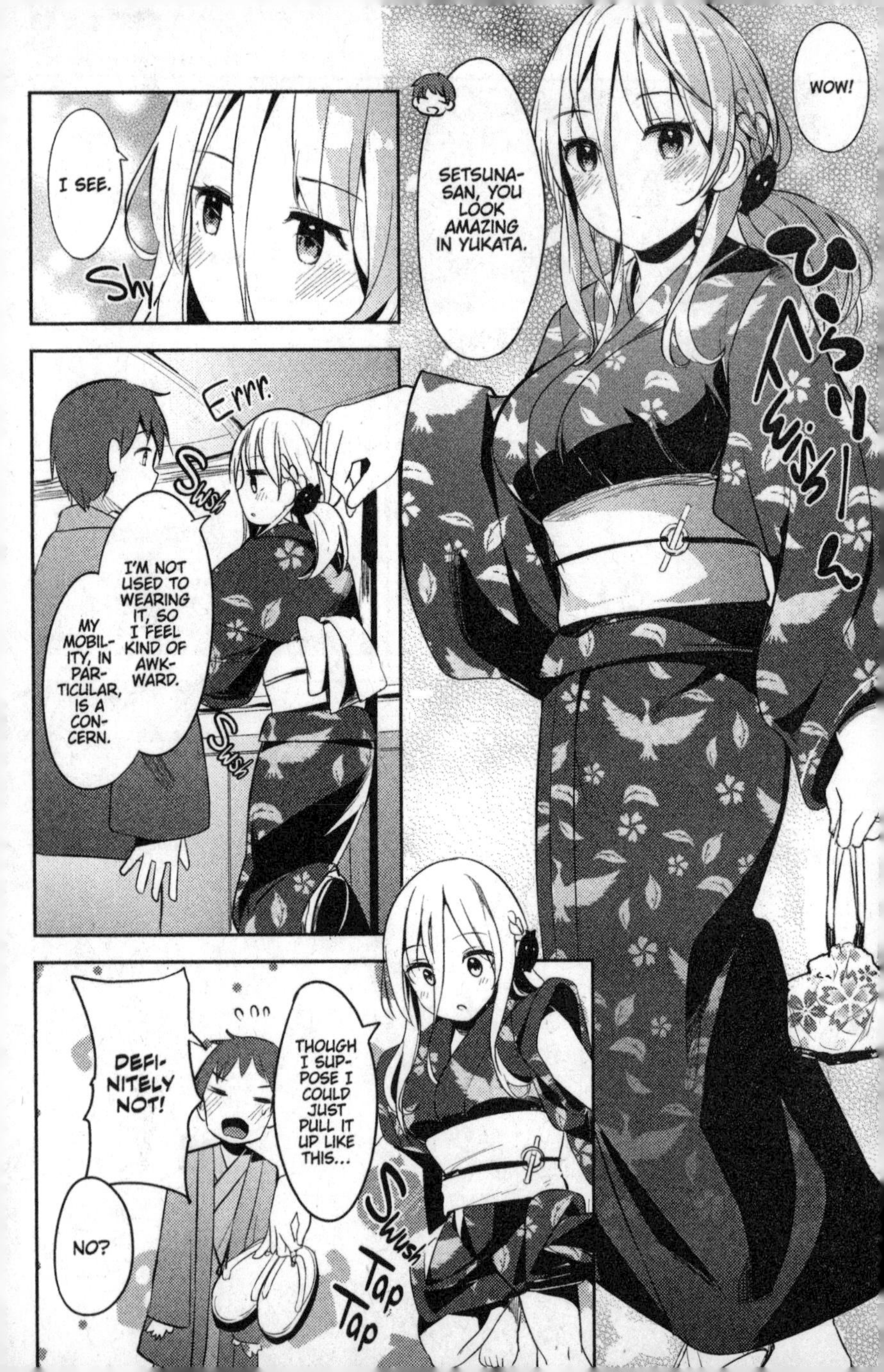
WOW!
SETSUNA-SAN, YOU LOOK AMAZING IN YUKATA.
ひらーん
Fwish
I SEE.
Shy
Errr.
Swush
I'M NOT USED TO WEARING IT, SO I FEEL KIND OF AWKWARD.
MY MOBILITY, IN PARTICULAR, IS A CONCERN.
Swush
THOUGH I SUPPOSE I COULD JUST PULL IT UP LIKE THIS...
Swush
Tap
Tap
DEFINITELY NOT!
NO?

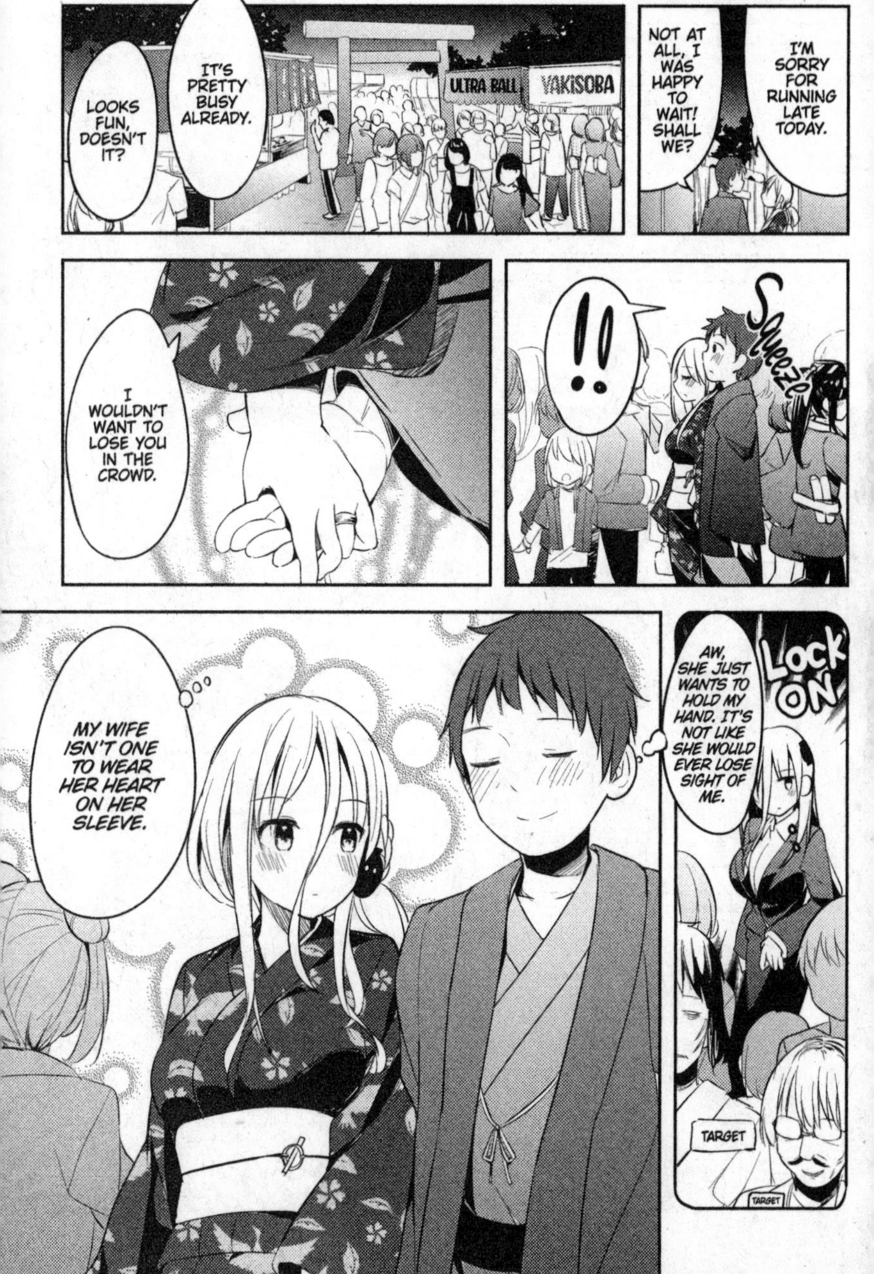
I'M SORRY FOR RUNNING LATE TODAY.
NOT AT ALL, I WAS HAPPY TO WAIT! SHALL WE?
YAKISOBA
ULTRA BALL
IT'S PRETTY BUSY ALREADY.
LOOKS FUN, DOESN'T IT?
SQUEEZE
!!
I WOULDN'T WANT TO LOSE YOU IN THE CROWD.
LOCK ON
AW, SHE JUST WANTS TO HOLD MY HAND. IT'S NOT LIKE SHE WOULD EVER LOSE SIGHT OF ME.
TARGET
TARGET
MY WIFE ISN'T ONE TO WEAR HER HEART ON HER SLEEVE.

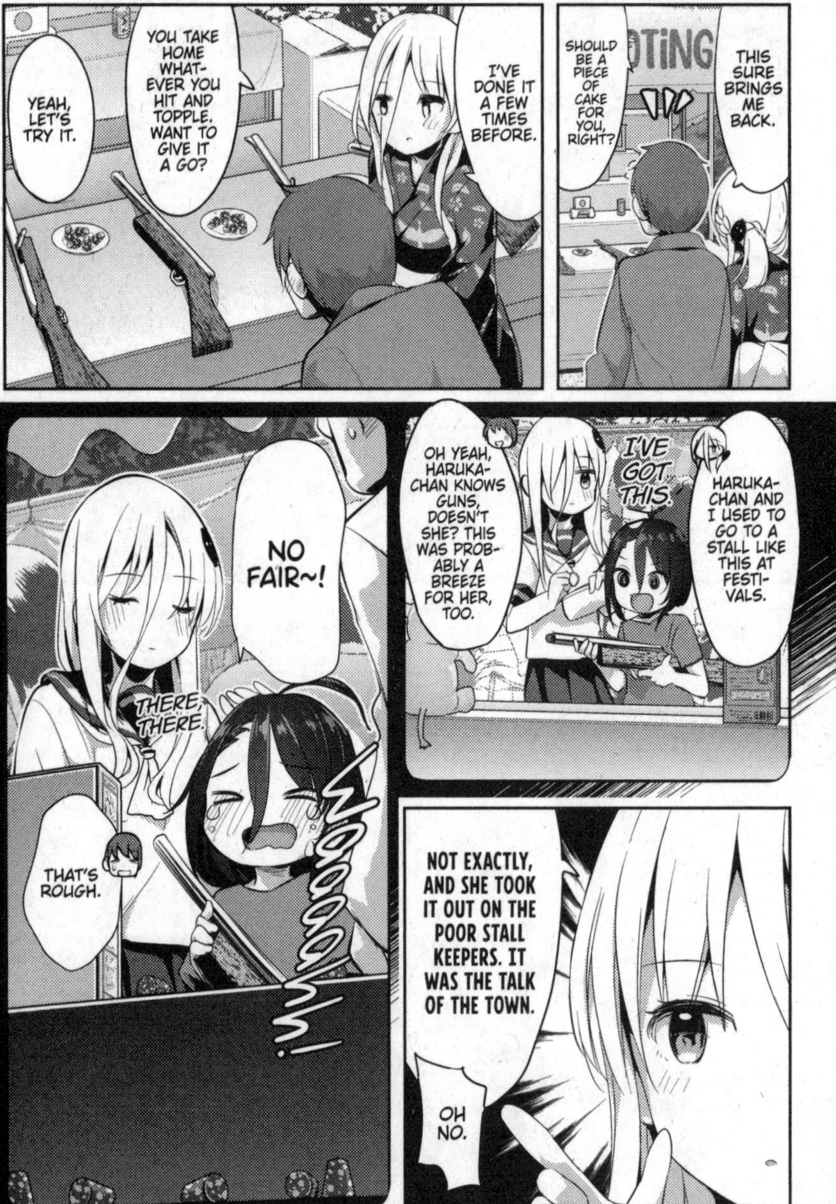
THIS SURE BRINGS ME BACK.
SHOULD BE A PIECE OF CAKE FOR YOU, RIGHT?
I'VE DONE IT A FEW TIMES BEFORE.
YOU TAKE HOME WHATEVER YOU HIT AND TOPPLE. WANT TO GIVE IT A GO?
YEAH, LET'S TRY IT.
HARUKA-CHAN AND I USED TO GO TO A STALL LIKE THIS AT FESTIVALS.
I'VE GOT THIS.
OH YEAH, HARUKA-CHAN KNOWS GUNS, DOESN'T SHE? THIS WAS PROBABLY A BREEZE FOR HER, TOO.
NOT EXACTLY, AND SHE TOOK IT OUT ON THE POOR STALL KEEPERS. IT WAS THE TALK OF THE TOWN.
OH NO.
NO FAIR~!
THERE, THERE.
Waaaaahh!
THAT'S ROUGH.

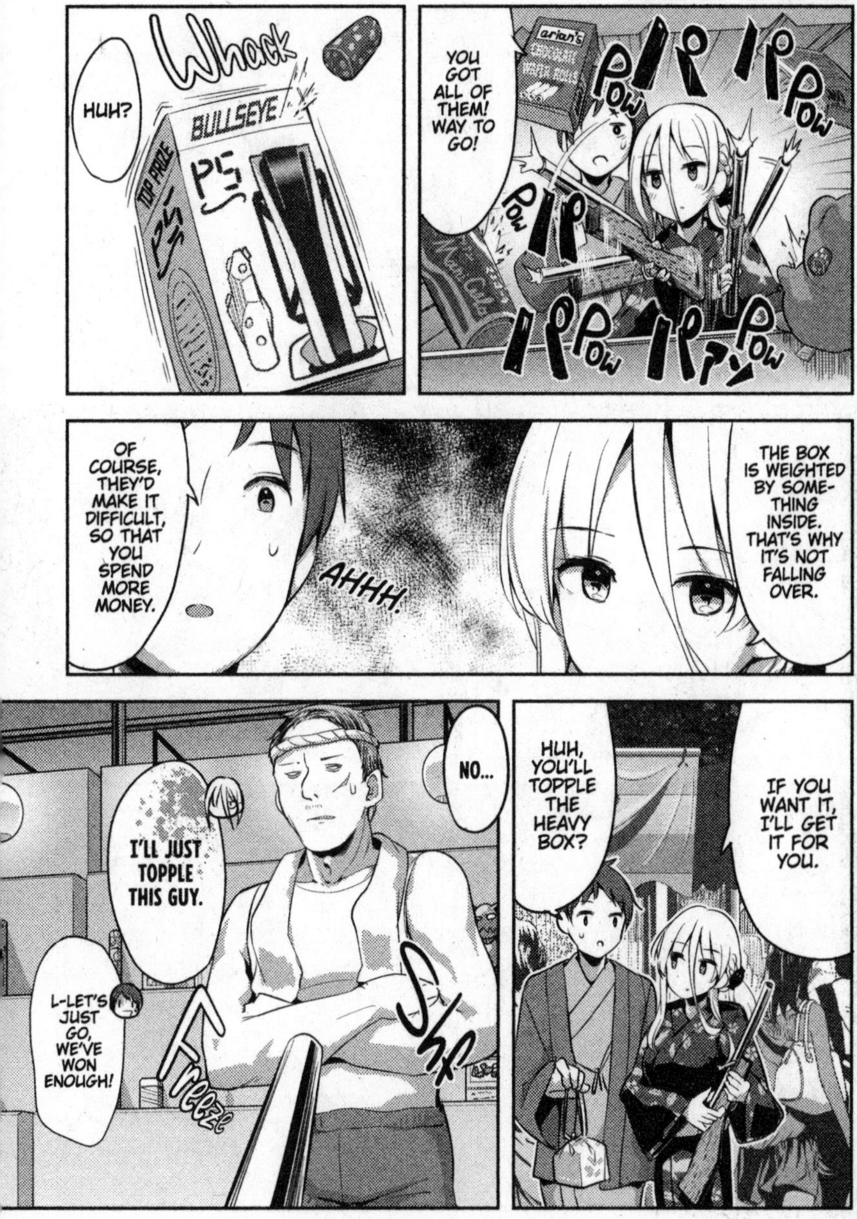
YOU GOT ALL OF THEM! WAY TO GO!
POW POW POW POW POW
HUH?
Whack
BULLSEYE
TOP PRIZE
PS
THE BOX IS WEIGHTED BY SOMETHING INSIDE. THAT'S WHY IT'S NOT FALLING OVER.
AHHHH.
OF COURSE, THEY'D MAKE IT DIFFICULT, SO THAT YOU SPEND MORE MONEY.
IF YOU WANT IT, I'LL GET IT FOR YOU.
HUH, YOU'LL TOPPLE THE HEAVY BOX?
NO...
I'LL JUST TOPPLE THIS GUY.
Shf
Freeze
L-LET'S JUST GO, WE'VE WON ENOUGH!

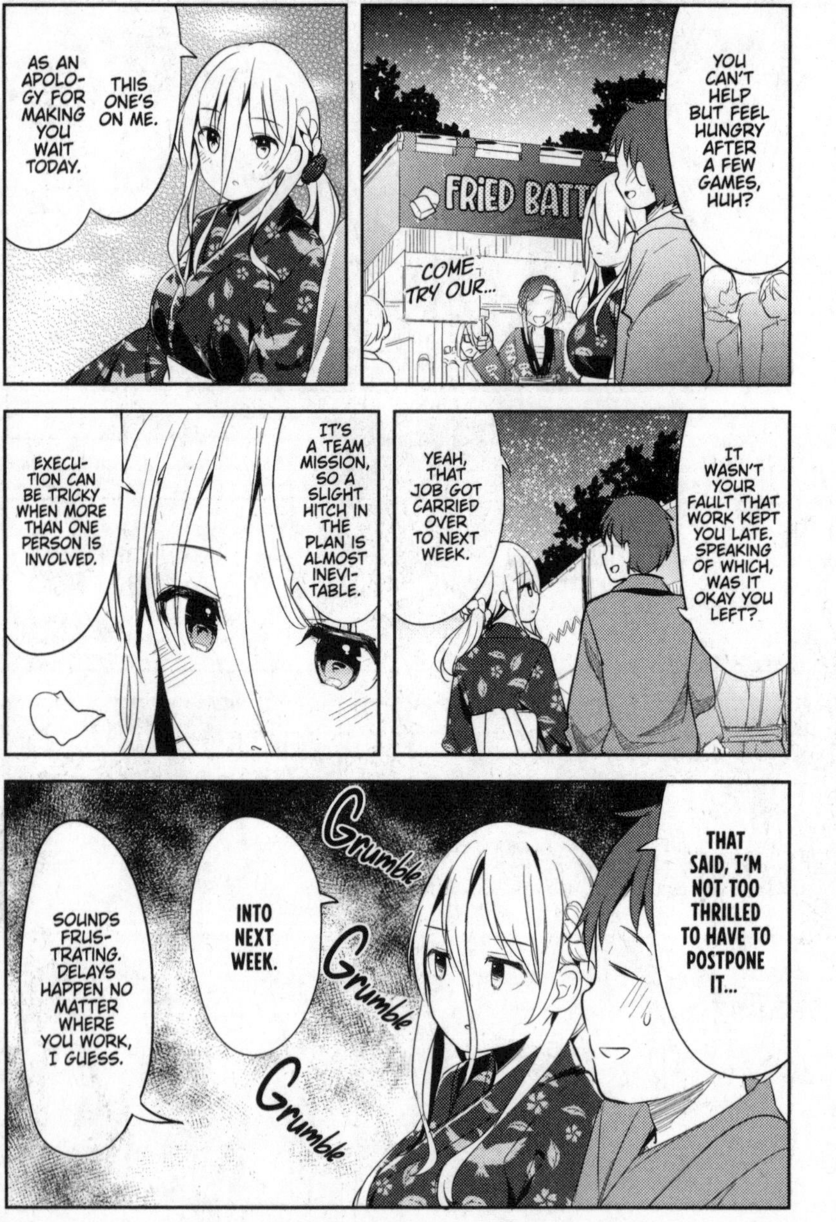
YOU CAN'T HELP BUT FEEL HUNGRY AFTER A FEW GAMES, HUH?
FRiED BATT
COME TRY OUR...
AS AN APOLOGY FOR MAKING YOU WAIT TODAY.
THIS ONE'S ON ME.
IT WASN'T YOUR FAULT THAT WORK KEPT YOU LATE. SPEAKING OF WHICH, WAS IT OKAY YOU LEFT?
YEAH, THAT JOB GOT CARRIED OVER TO NEXT WEEK.
IT'S A TEAM MISSION, SO A SLIGHT HITCH IN THE PLAN IS ALMOST INEVITABLE.
EXECUTION CAN BE TRICKY WHEN MORE THAN ONE PERSON IS INVOLVED.
THAT SAID, I'M NOT TOO THRILLED TO HAVE TO POSTPONE IT...
Grumble
Grumble
Grumble
INTO NEXT WEEK.
SOUNDS FRUSTRATING. DELAYS HAPPEN NO MATTER WHERE YOU WORK, I GUESS.

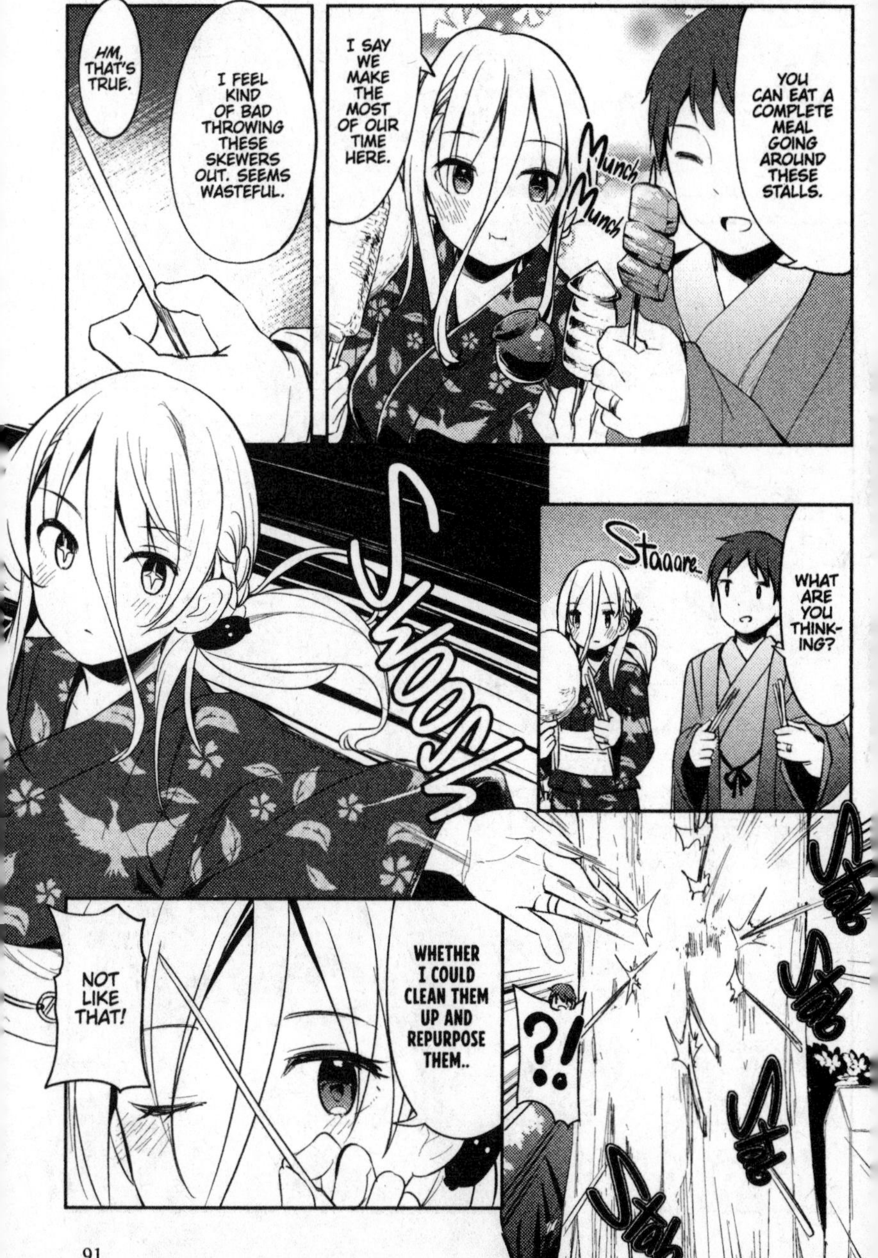
YOU CAN EAT A COMPLETE MEAL GOING AROUND THESE STALLS.
Munch Munch
I SAY WE MAKE THE MOST OF OUR TIME HERE.
I FEEL KIND OF BAD THROWING THESE SKEWERS OUT. SEEMS WASTEFUL.
HM, THAT'S TRUE.
Staaare
WHAT ARE YOU THINKING?
SWOOSH
Stab Stab Stab Stab Stab
?!
WHETHER I COULD CLEAN THEM UP AND REPURPOSE THEM..
NOT LIKE THAT!

FESTIVAL SHOPPING WITH SETSUNA-SAN.

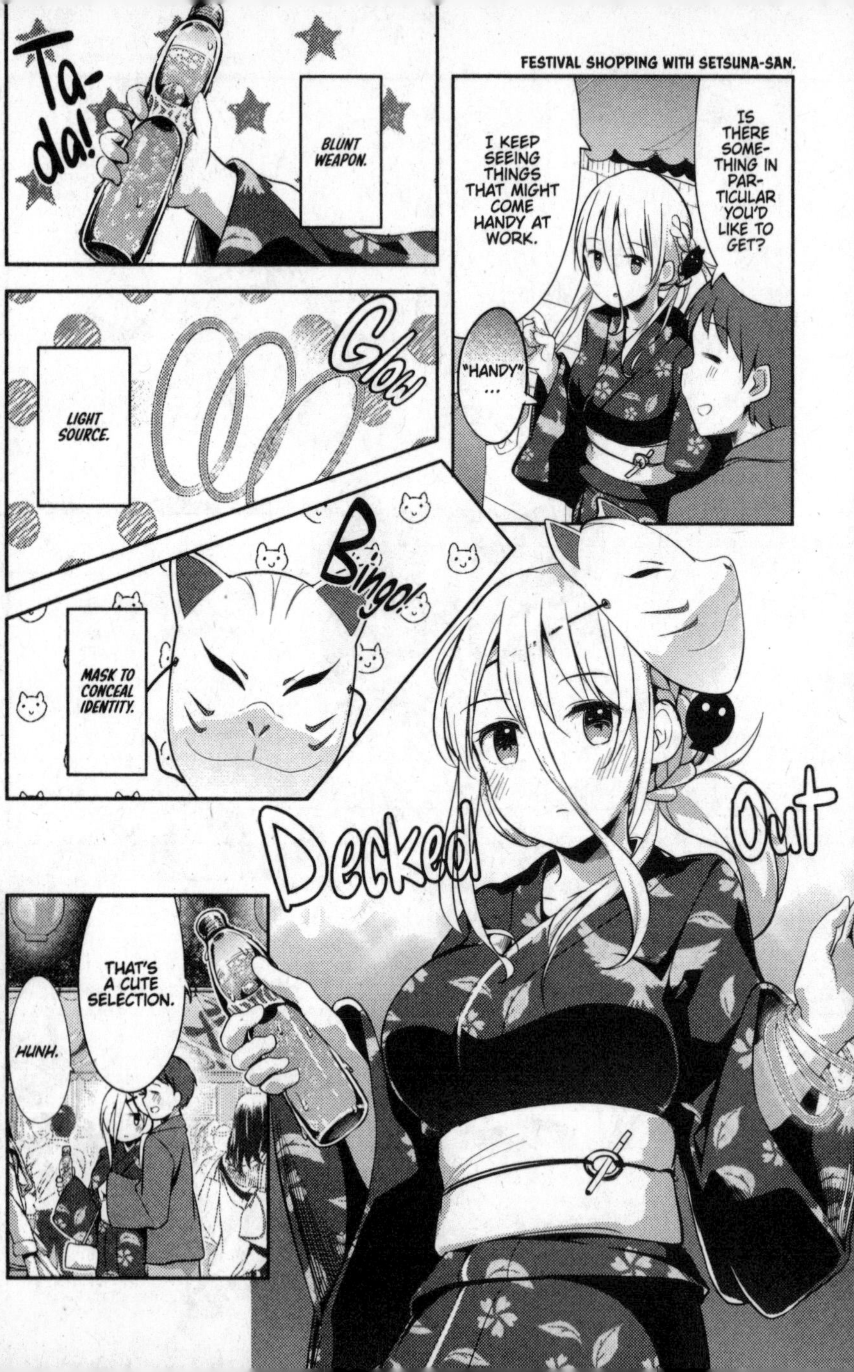
IS THERE SOMETHING IN PARTICULAR YOU'D LIKE TO GET?
I KEEP SEEING THINGS THAT MIGHT COME HANDY AT WORK.
"HANDY"...
Ta-da!
BLUNT WEAPON.
Glow
LIGHT SOURCE.
Bingo!
MASK TO CONCEAL IDENTITY.
Decked Out
THAT'S A CUTE SELECTION.
HUNH.

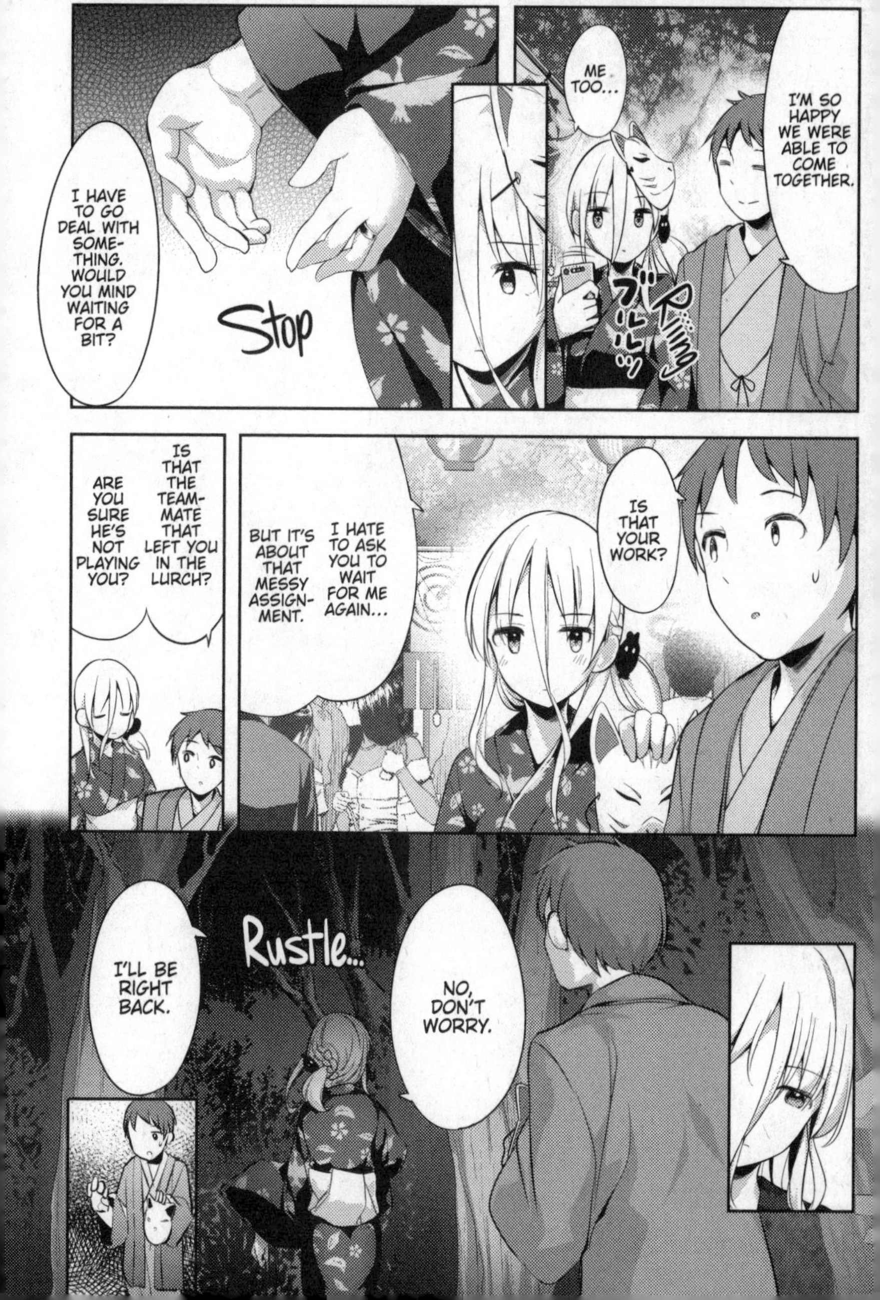
I'M SO HAPPY WE WERE ABLE TO COME TOGETHER.
ME TOO...
ブルルッ
Ring
Stop
I HAVE TO GO DEAL WITH SOME-THING. WOULD YOU MIND WAITING FOR A BIT?
IS THAT YOUR WORK?
I HATE TO ASK YOU TO WAIT FOR ME AGAIN...
BUT IT'S ABOUT THAT MESSY ASSIGN-MENT.
IS THAT THE TEAM-MATE THAT LEFT YOU IN THE LURCH?
ARE YOU SURE HE'S NOT PLAYING YOU?
NO, DON'T WORRY.
Rustle...
I'LL BE RIGHT BACK.

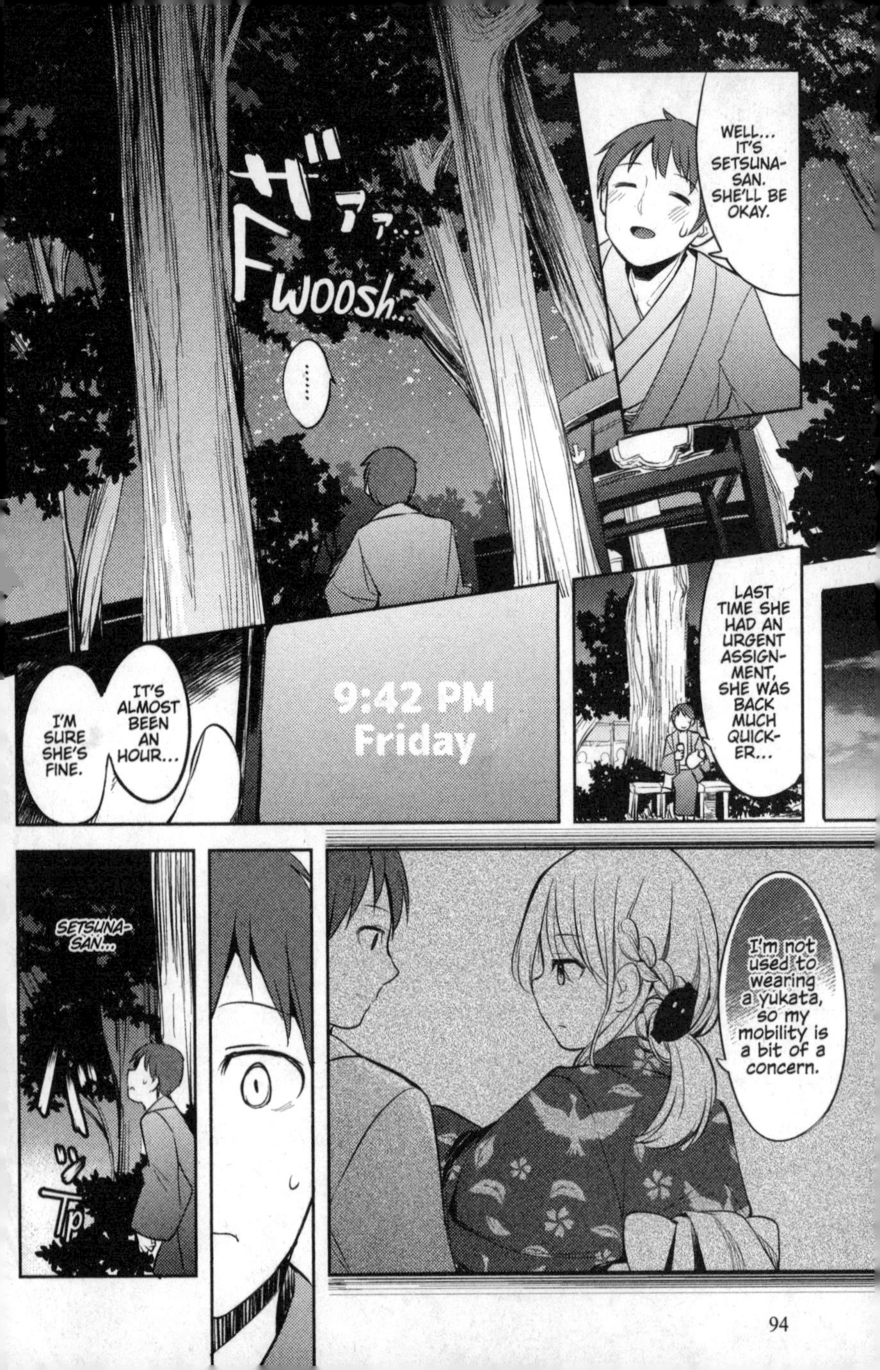
WELL... IT'S SETSUNA-SAN. SHE'LL BE OKAY.
Fwoosh...
......
LAST TIME SHE HAD AN URGENT ASSIGNMENT, SHE WAS BACK MUCH QUICKER...
9:42 PM Friday
IT'S ALMOST BEEN AN HOUR...
I'M SURE SHE'S FINE.
I'm not used to wearing a yukata, so my mobility is a bit of a concern.
SETSUNA-SAN...
Tp

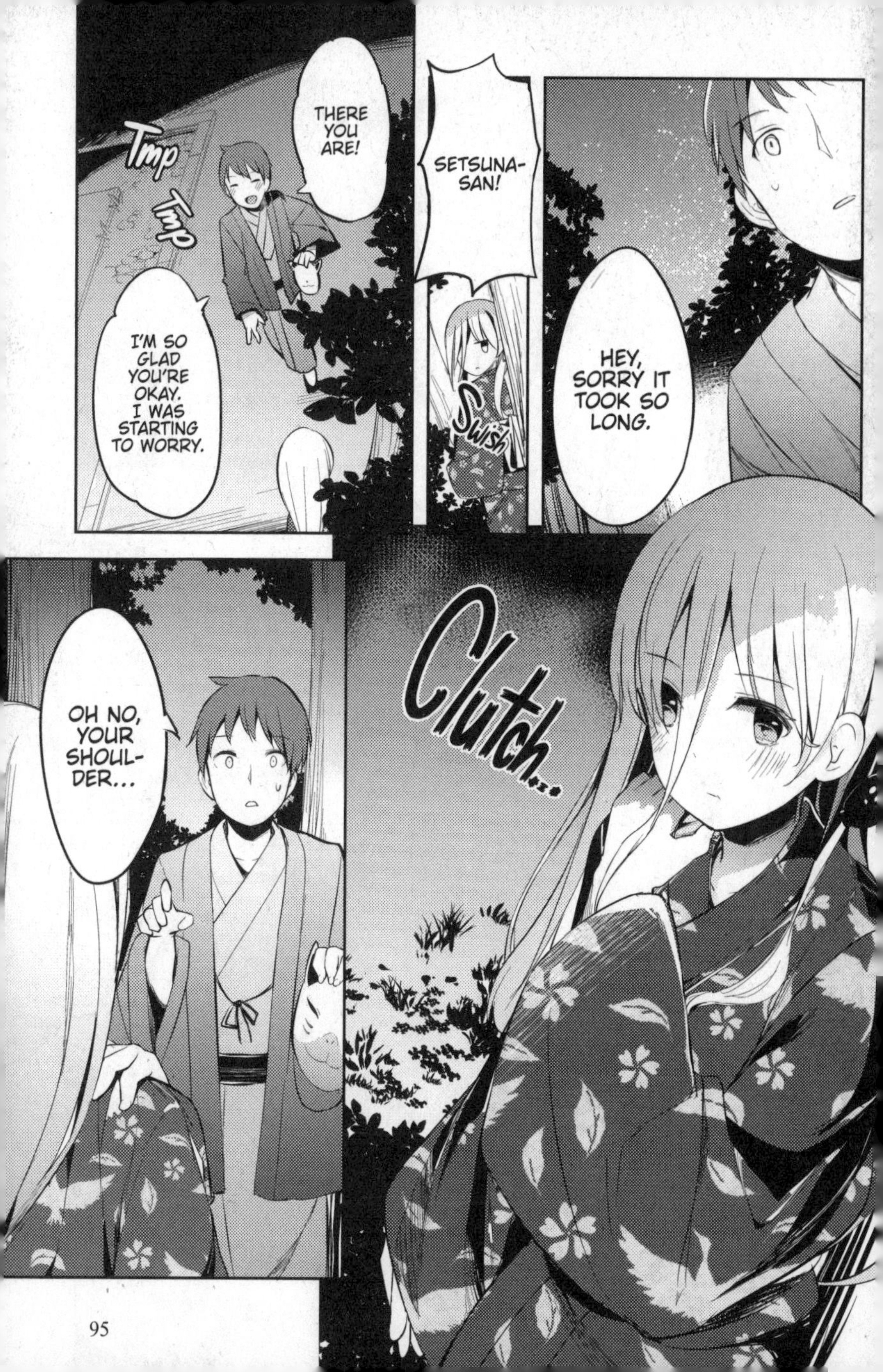
HEY, SORRY IT TOOK SO LONG.
SETSUNA-SAN!
Swish
THERE YOU ARE!
Tmp Tmp
I'M SO GLAD YOU'RE OKAY. I WAS STARTING TO WORRY.
Clutch...
OH NO, YOUR SHOULDER...

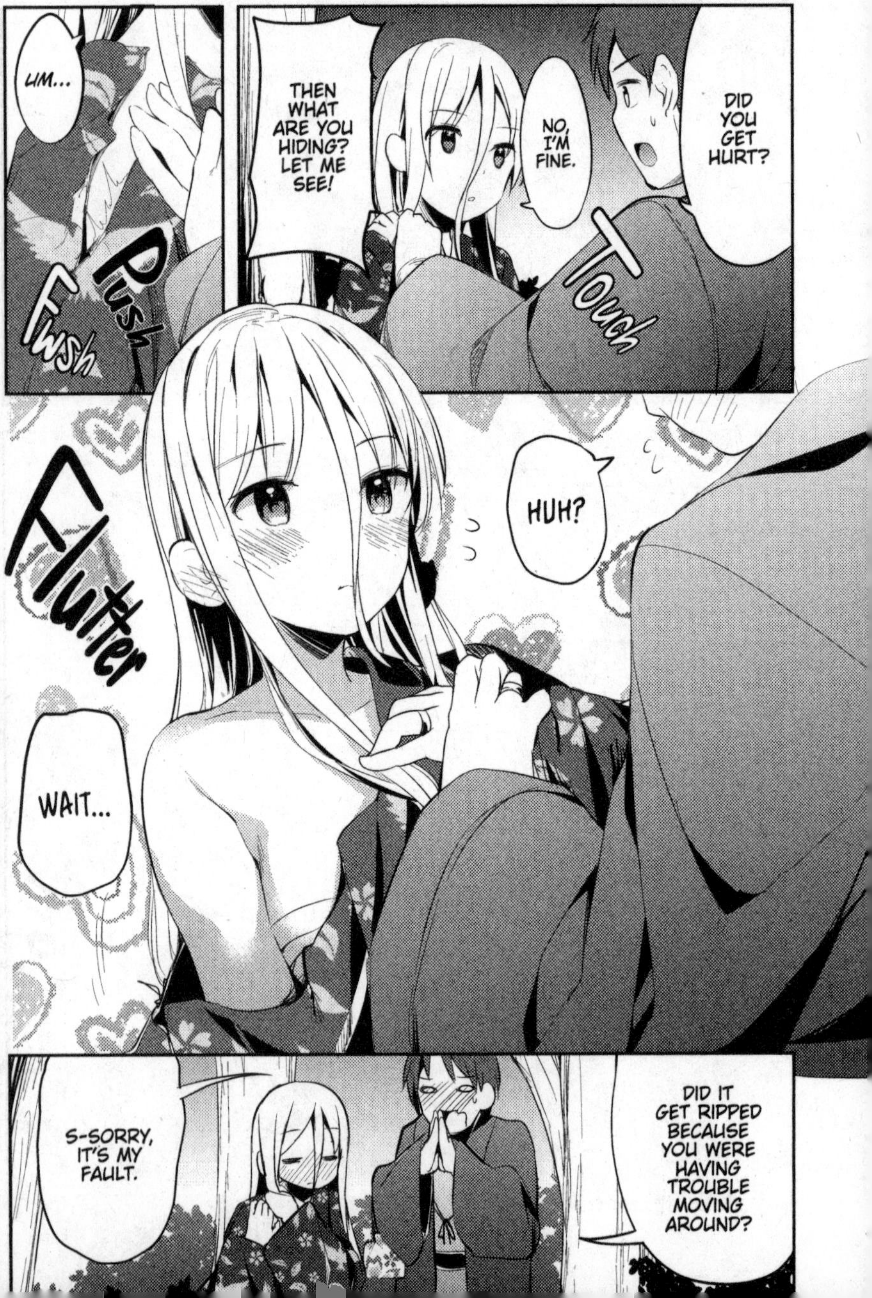
DID YOU GET HURT?
NO, I'M FINE.
THEN WHAT ARE YOU HIDING? LET ME SEE!
Touch
UM...
Push
Fwsh
HUH?
Flutter
WAIT...
DID IT GET RIPPED BECAUSE YOU WERE HAVING TROUBLE MOVING AROUND?
S-SORRY, IT'S MY FAULT.

SETSUNA-SAN'S INJURY.

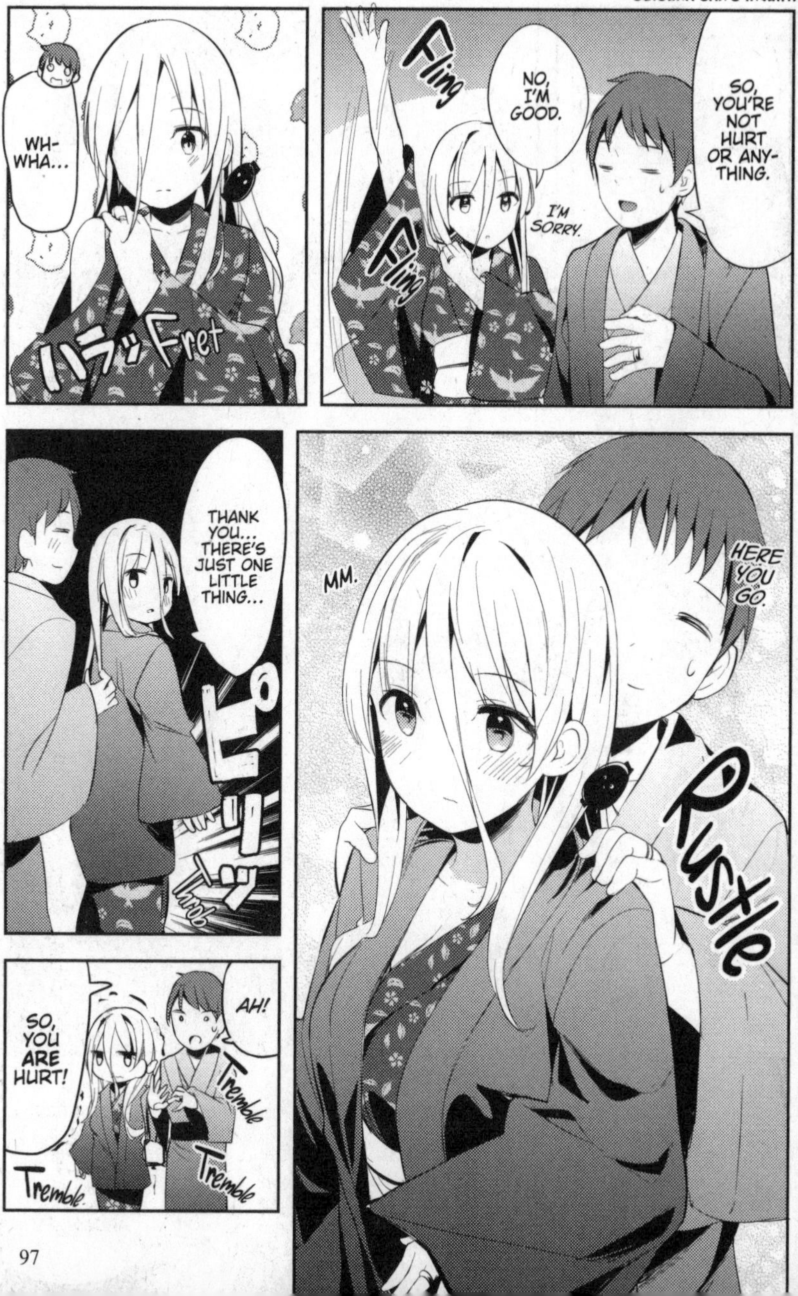
SO, YOU'RE NOT HURT OR ANY-THING.
NO, I'M GOOD.
I'M SORRY.
Fling
Fling
WH-WHA...
Fret
HERE YOU GO.
MM.
Rustle
THANK YOU... THERE'S JUST ONE LITTLE THING...
Throb
AH!
SO, YOU ARE HURT!
Tremble
Tremble
Tremble

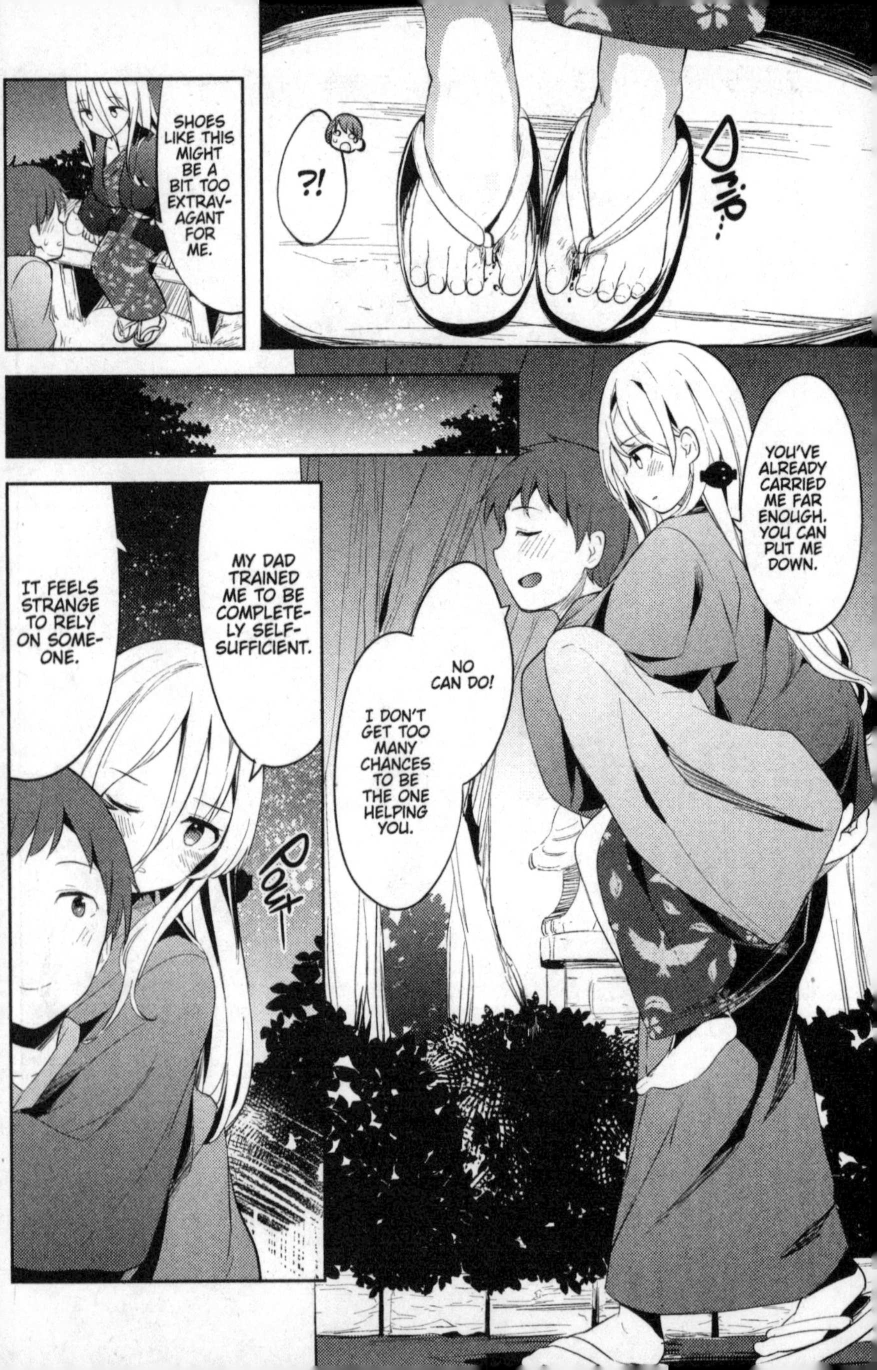
Drip...
?!
SHOES LIKE THIS MIGHT BE A BIT TOO EXTRAVAGANT FOR ME.
YOU'VE ALREADY CARRIED ME FAR ENOUGH. YOU CAN PUT ME DOWN.
NO CAN DO!
I DON'T GET TOO MANY CHANCES TO BE THE ONE HELPING YOU.
MY DAD TRAINED ME TO BE COMPLETELY SELF-SUFFICIENT.
IT FEELS STRANGE TO RELY ON SOMEONE.
Pout—

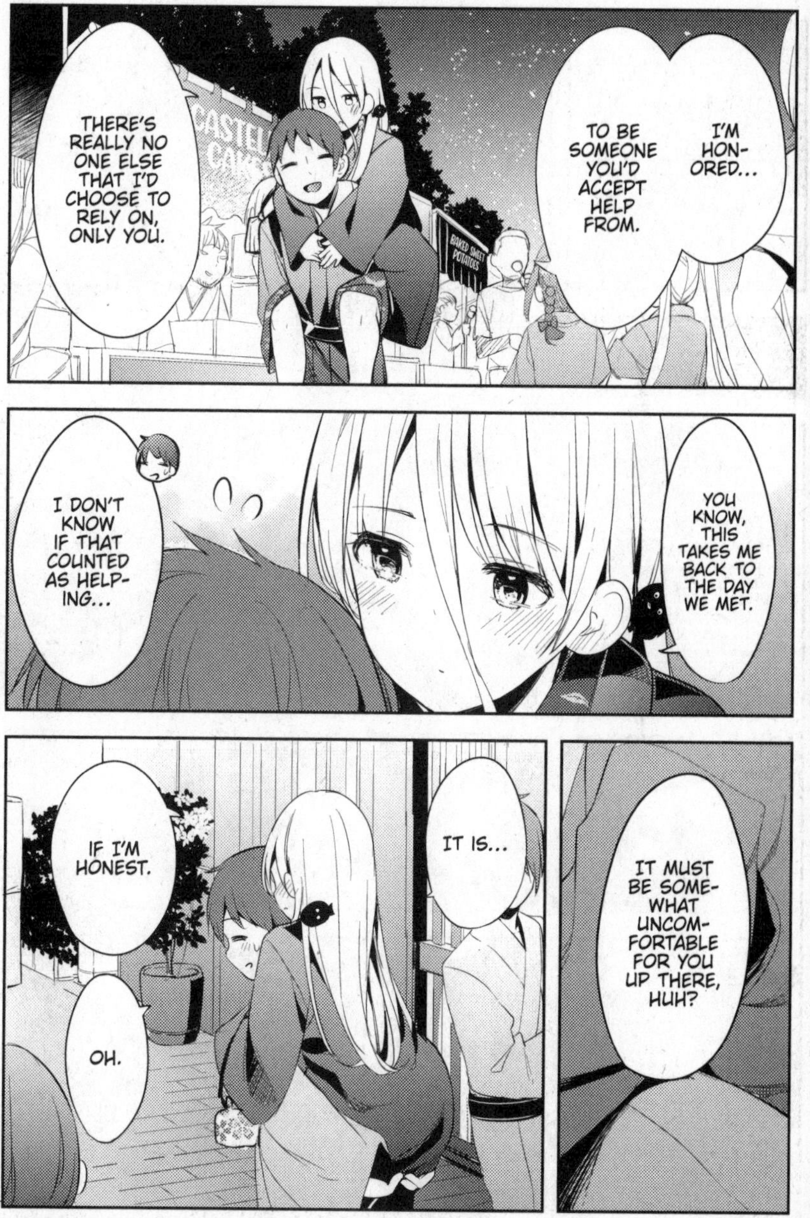
I'M HONORED...
TO BE SOMEONE YOU'D ACCEPT HELP FROM.
BAKED SWEET POTATOES
THERE'S REALLY NO ONE ELSE THAT I'D CHOOSE TO RELY ON, ONLY YOU.
YOU KNOW, THIS TAKES ME BACK TO THE DAY WE MET.
I DON'T KNOW IF THAT COUNTED AS HELPING...
IT MUST BE SOMEWHAT UNCOMFORTABLE FOR YOU UP THERE, HUH?
IT IS...
IF I'M HONEST.
OH.

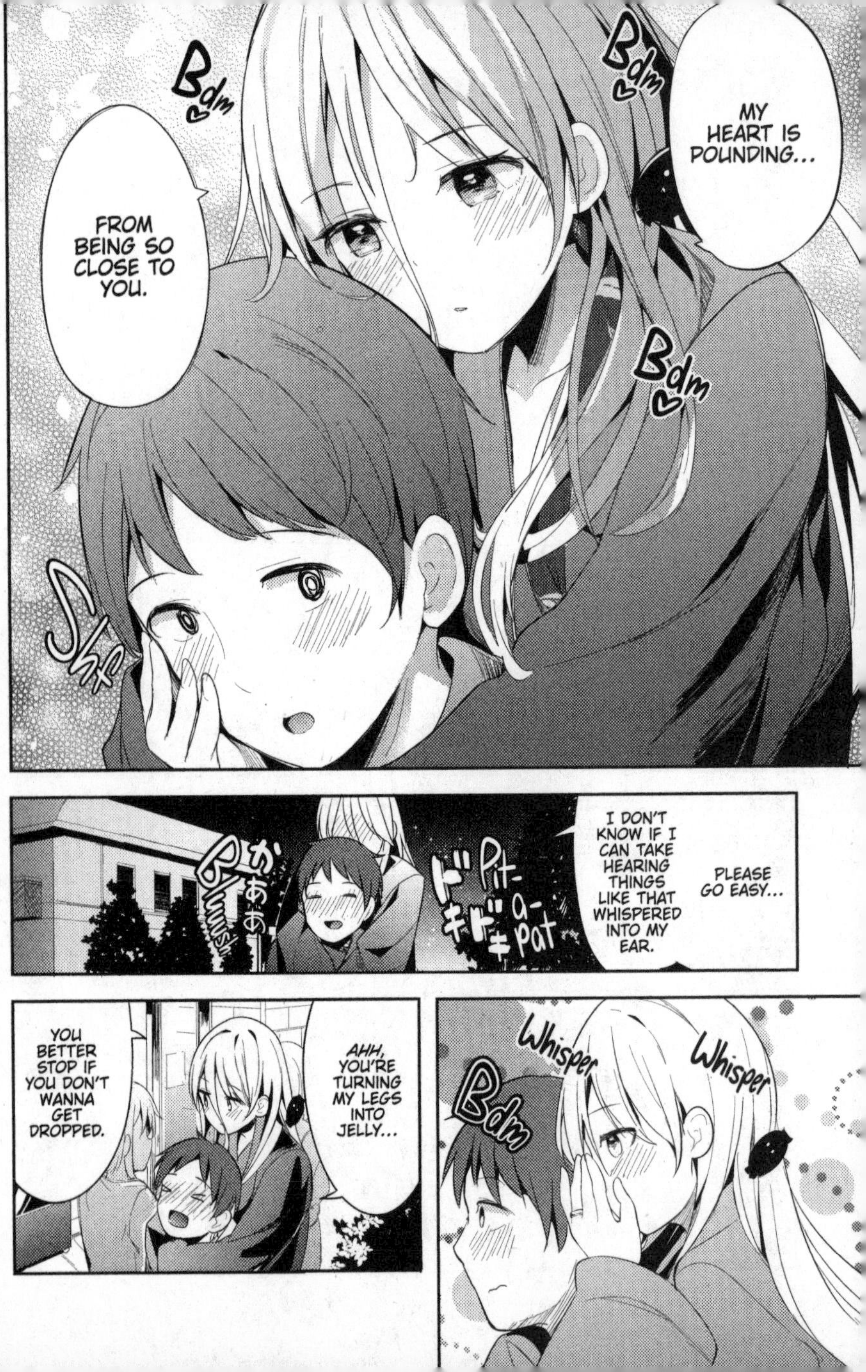
Bdm
MY HEART IS POUNDING...
Bdm
FROM BEING SO CLOSE TO YOU.
Bdm
Shf
PLEASE GO EASY...
I DON'T KNOW IF I CAN TAKE HEARING THINGS LIKE THAT WHISPERED INTO MY EAR.
ドキドキ
Pit-a-pat
かあああ
Blush
Whisper
Whisper
Bdm
AHH, YOU'RE TURNING MY LEGS INTO JELLY...
YOU BETTER STOP IF YOU DON'T WANNA GET DROPPED.

THE OMNIPRESENT OBSERVER.

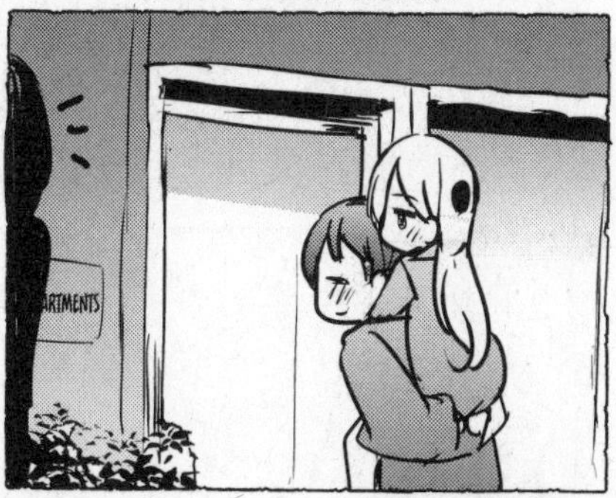

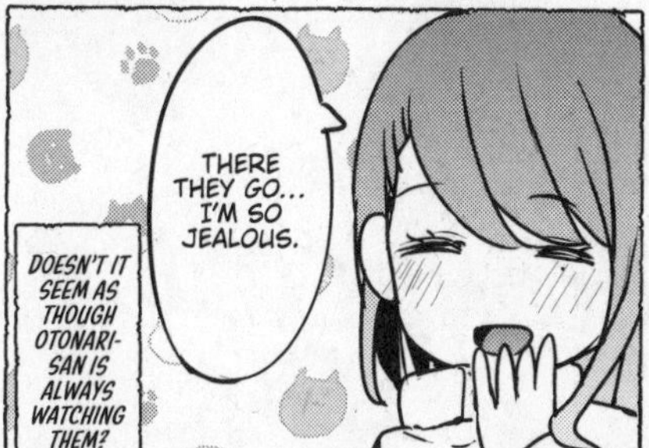
THERE THEY GO... I'M SO JEALOUS.
DOESN'T IT SEEM AS THOUGH OTONARI-SAN IS ALWAYS WATCHING THEM?

MY
Lovey-Dovey
Wife IS A
STONE COLD
KILLER

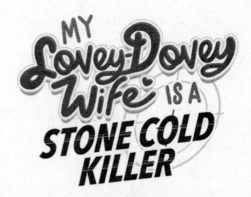

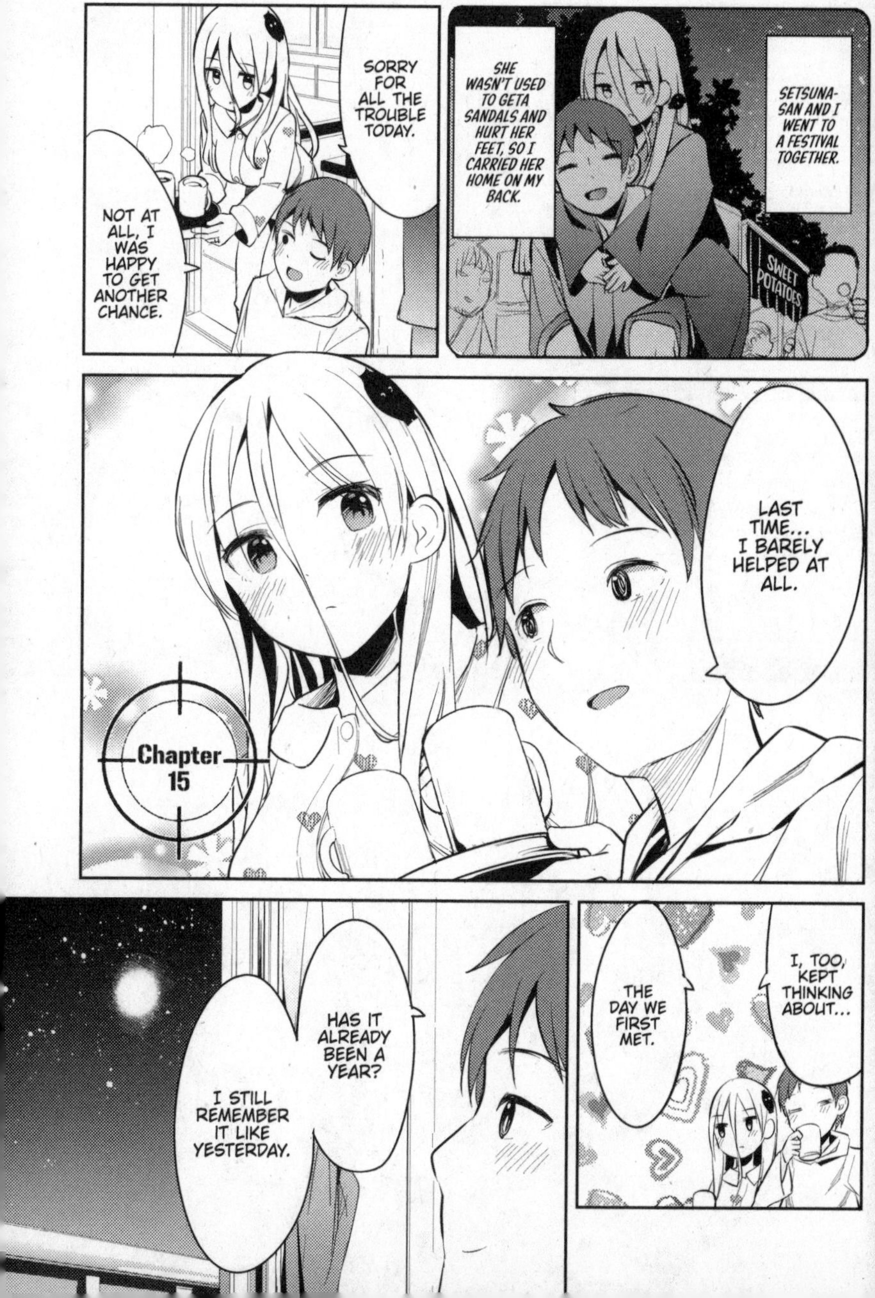
SETSUNA-SAN AND I WENT TO A FESTIVAL TOGETHER.
SHE WASN'T USED TO GETA SANDALS AND HURT HER FEET, SO I CARRIED HER HOME ON MY BACK.
SWEET POTATOES
SORRY FOR ALL THE TROUBLE TODAY.
NOT AT ALL, I WAS HAPPY TO GET ANOTHER CHANCE.
LAST TIME... I BARELY HELPED AT ALL.
Chapter 15
I, TOO, KEPT THINKING ABOUT...
THE DAY WE FIRST MET.
HAS IT ALREADY BEEN A YEAR?
I STILL REMEMBER IT LIKE YESTERDAY.

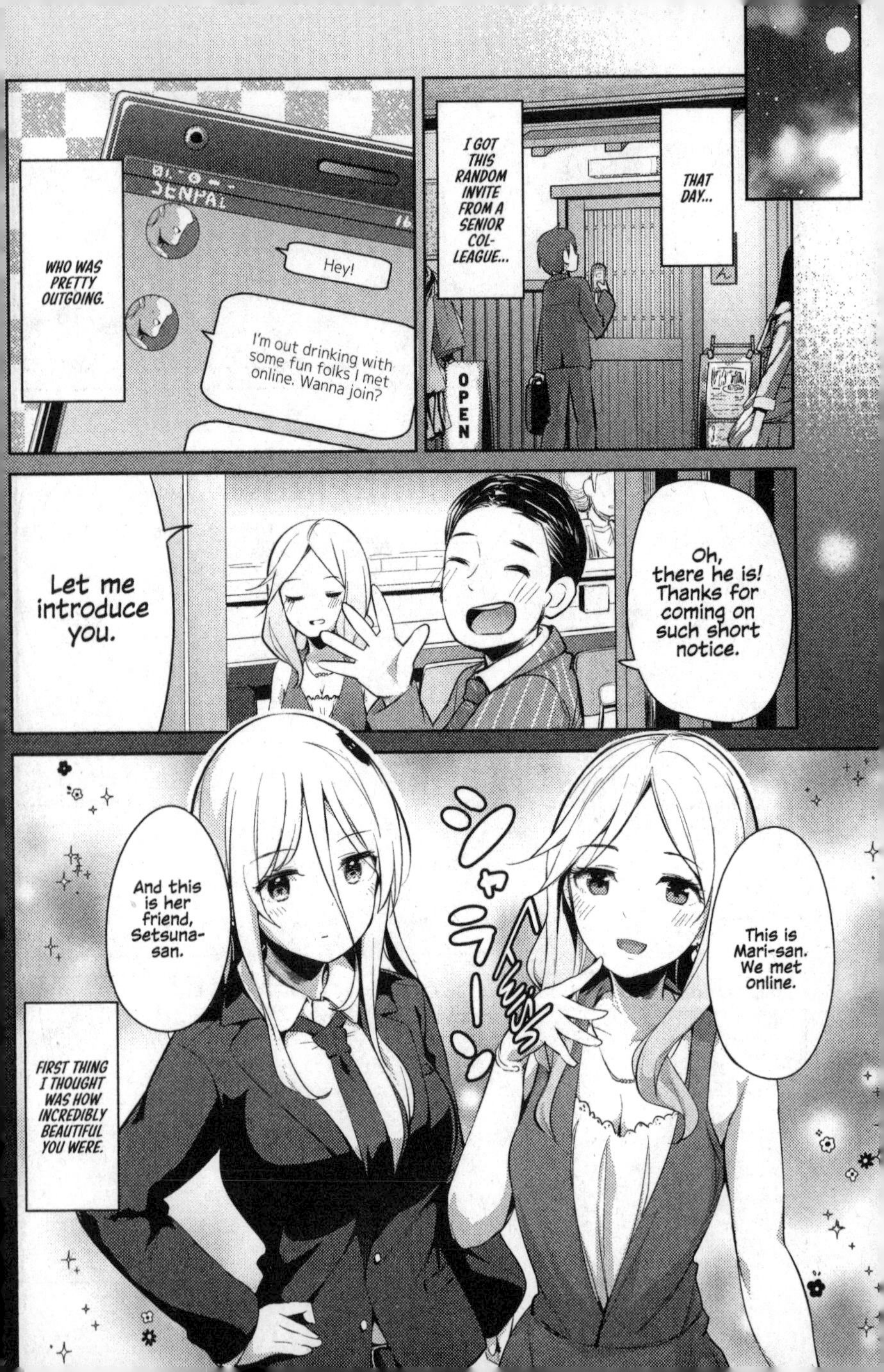
THAT DAY...
I GOT THIS RANDOM INVITE FROM A SENIOR COL-LEAGUE...
OPEN
SENPAI
Hey!
WHO WAS PRETTY OUTGOING.
I'm out drinking with some fun folks I met online. Wanna join?
Oh, there he is! Thanks for coming on such short notice.
Let me introduce you.
This is Mari-san. We met online.
Swish
And this is her friend, Setsuna-san.
FIRST THING I THOUGHT WAS HOW INCREDIBLY BEAUTIFUL YOU WERE.

SETSUNA-SAN.

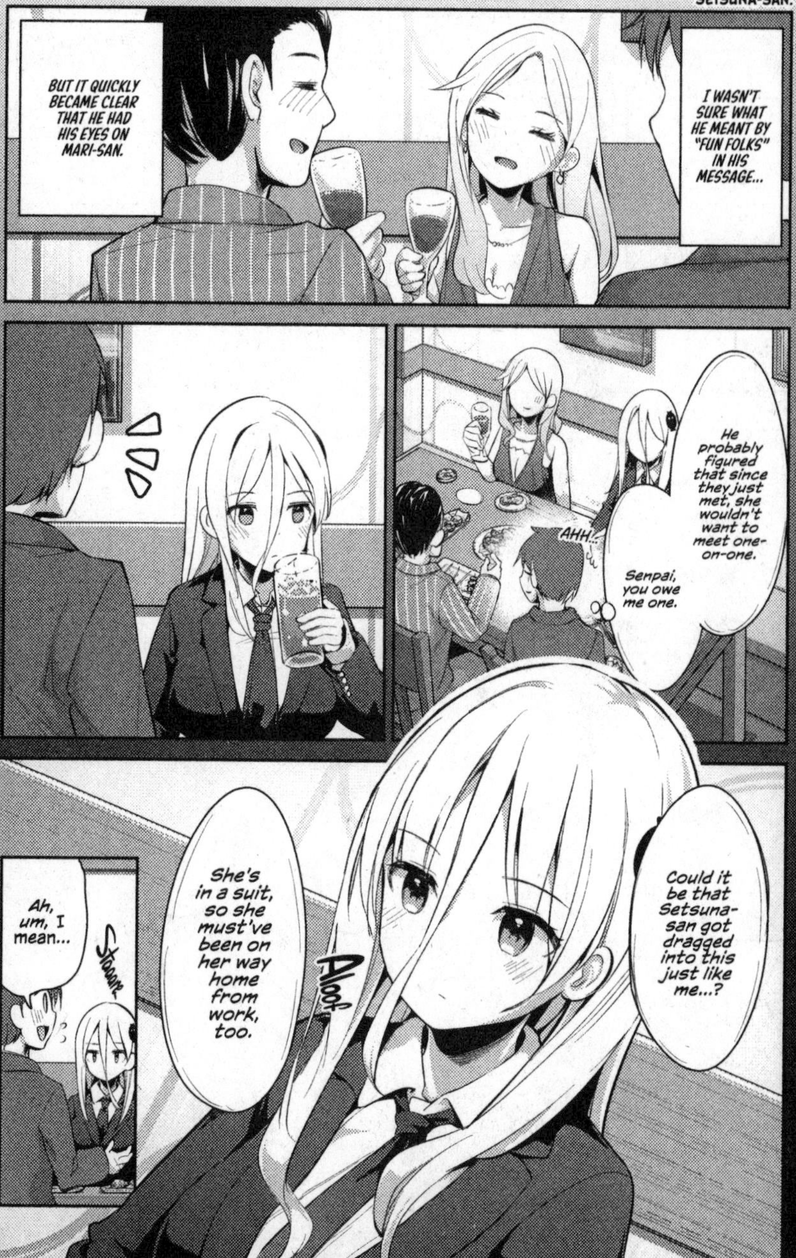

I WASN'T SURE WHAT HE MEANT BY "FUN FOLKS" IN HIS MESSAGE...
BUT IT QUICKLY BECAME CLEAR THAT HE HAD HIS EYES ON MARI-SAN.
He probably figured that since they just met, she wouldn't want to meet one-on-one.
AHH...
Senpai, you owe me one.
Could it be that Setsuna-san got dragged into this just like me...?
She's in a suit, so she must've been on her way home from work, too.
Aloof
Staaare
Ah, um, I mean...

STRAIGHT SHOOTER.

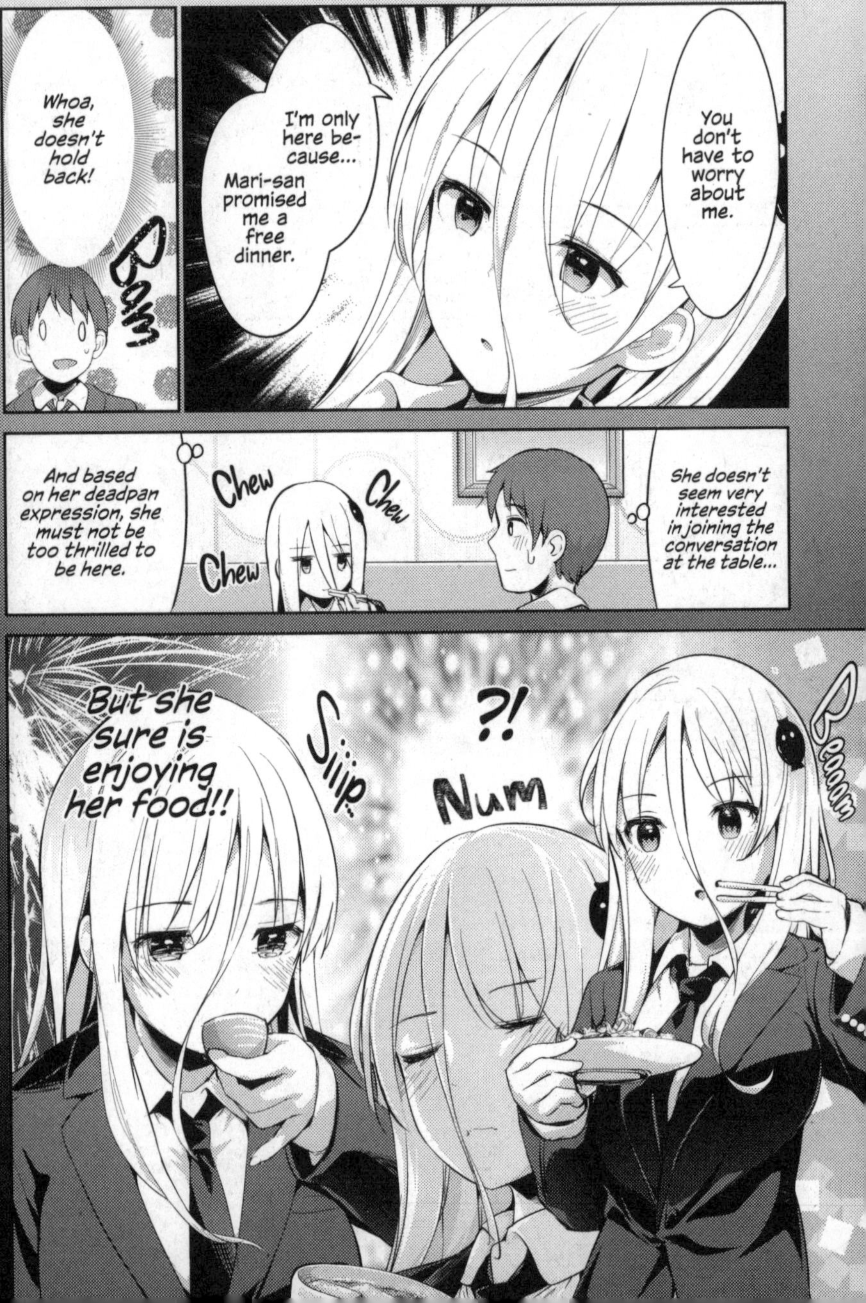
You don't have to worry about me.
I'm only here be-cause...
Mari-san promised me a free dinner.
Whoa, she doesn't hold back!
Bam
She doesn't seem very interested in joining the conversation at the table...
Chew
Chew
Chew
And based on her deadpan expression, she must not be too thrilled to be here.
Beaaam
Num
?!
Siiip...
But she sure is enjoying her food!!

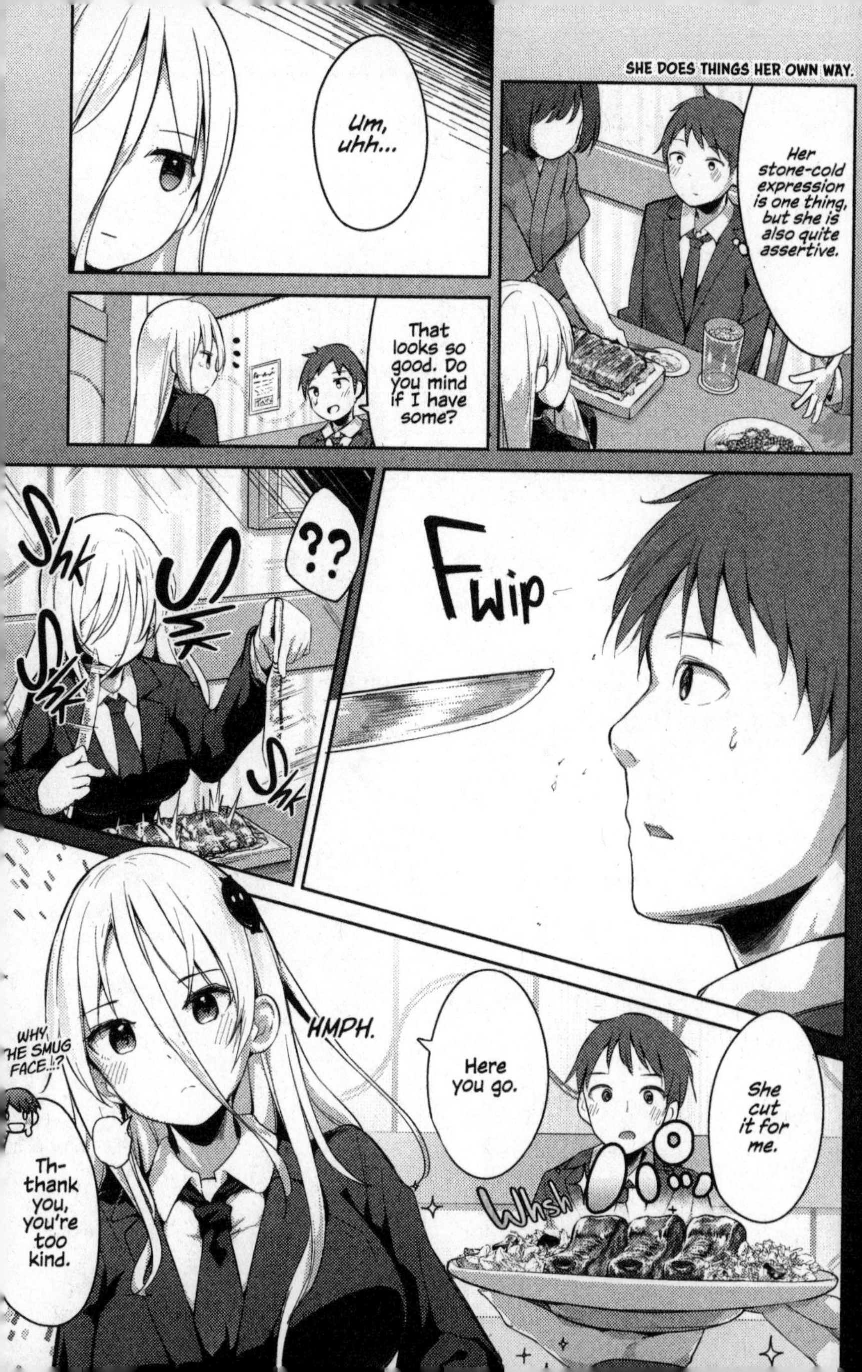
SHE DOES THINGS HER OWN WAY.
Her stone-cold expression is one thing, but she is also quite assertive.
Um, uhh...
...
That looks so good. Do you mind if I have some?
Fwip
??
Shk
Shk
Shk
Shk
She cut it for me.
Here you go.
Whsh
HMPH.
WHY THE SMUG FACE!!?
Th-thank you, you're too kind.

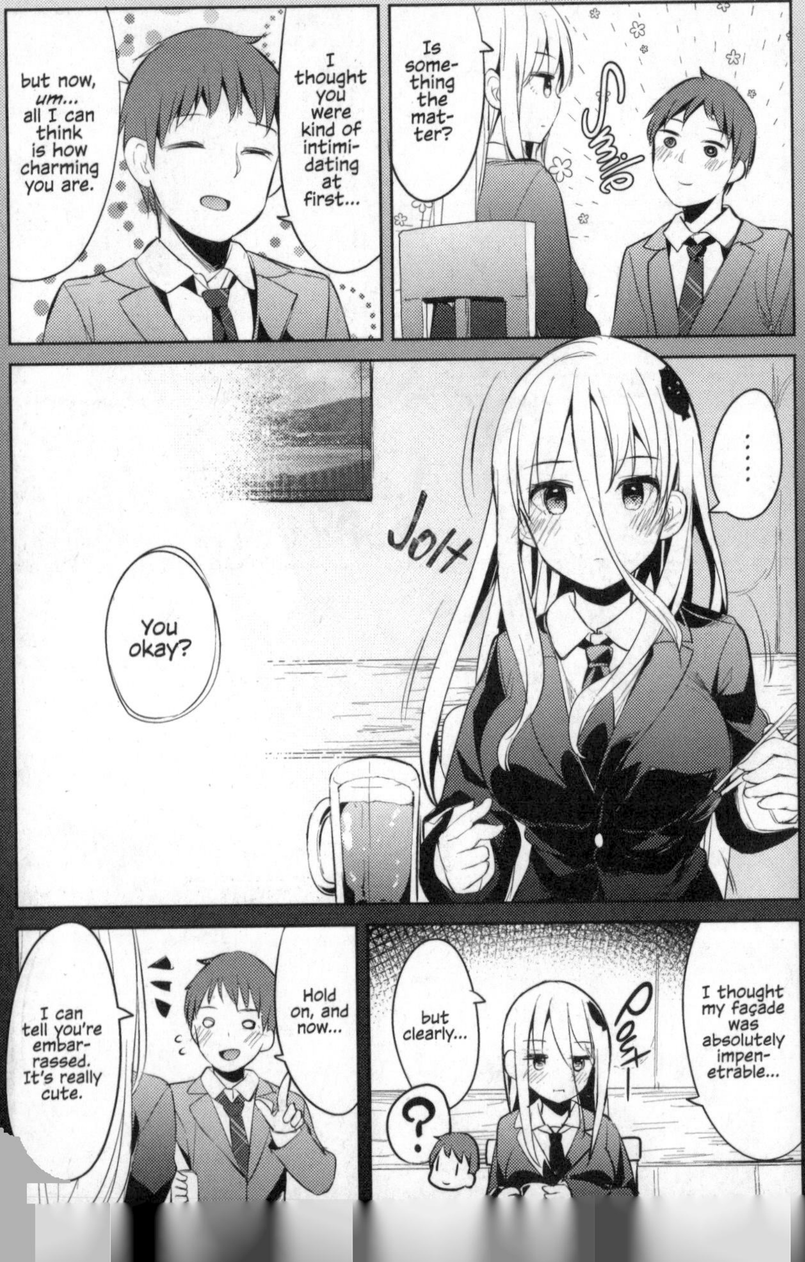
Is something the matter?
Smile
I thought you were kind of intimidating at first...
but now, *um*... all I can think is how charming you are.
......
Jolt
You okay?
I thought my façade was absolutely impenetrable...
Pout—
but clearly...
?
Hold on, and now...
I can tell you're embarrassed. It's really cute.

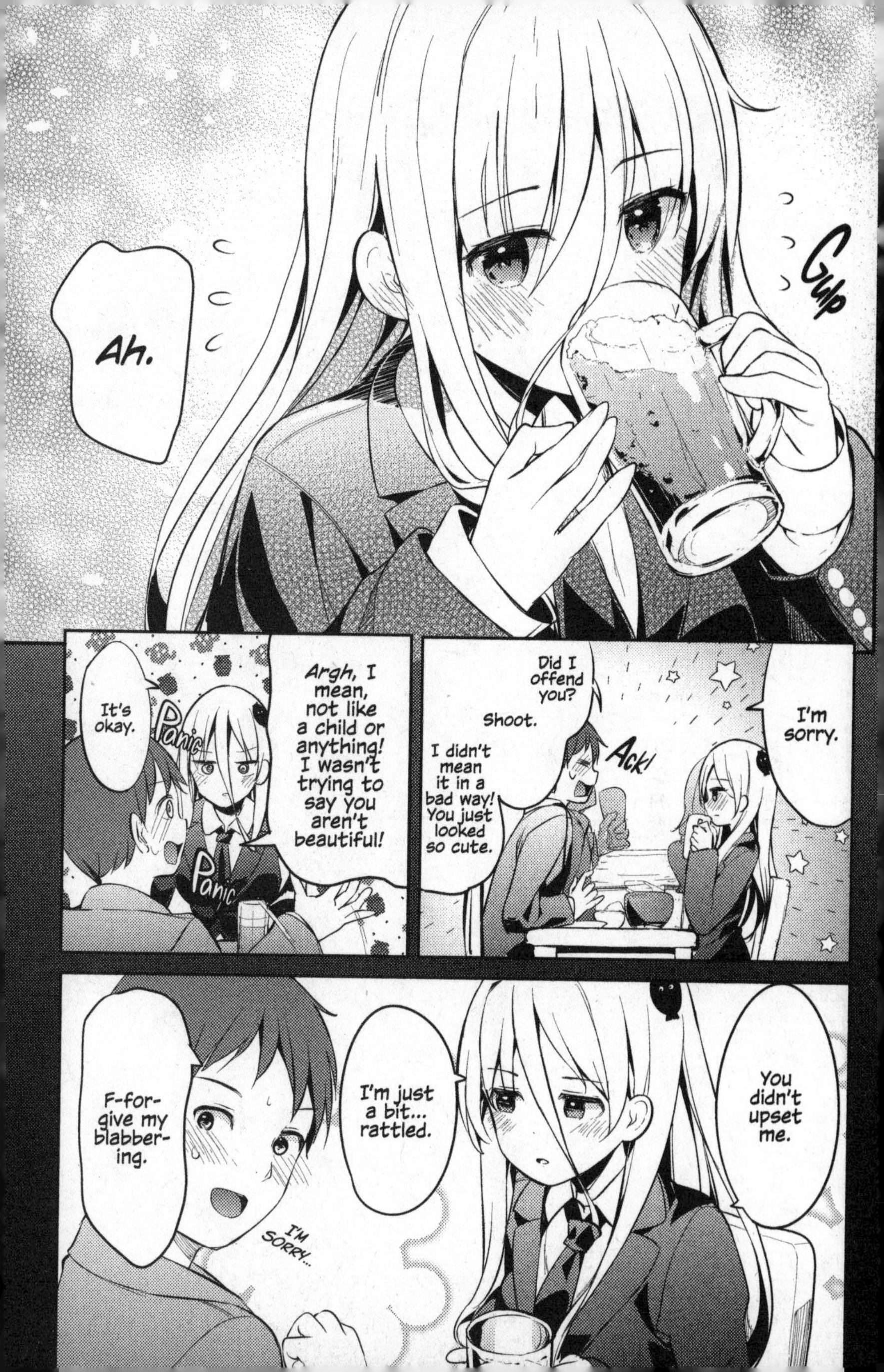
Gulp
Ah.
I'm sorry.
Ack!
Did I offend you?
Shoot.
I didn't mean it in a bad way! You just looked so cute.
Argh, I mean, not like a child or anything! I wasn't trying to say you aren't beautiful!
Panic
Panic
It's okay.
You didn't upset me.
I'm just a bit... rattled.
F-forgive my blabbering.
I'm sorry...

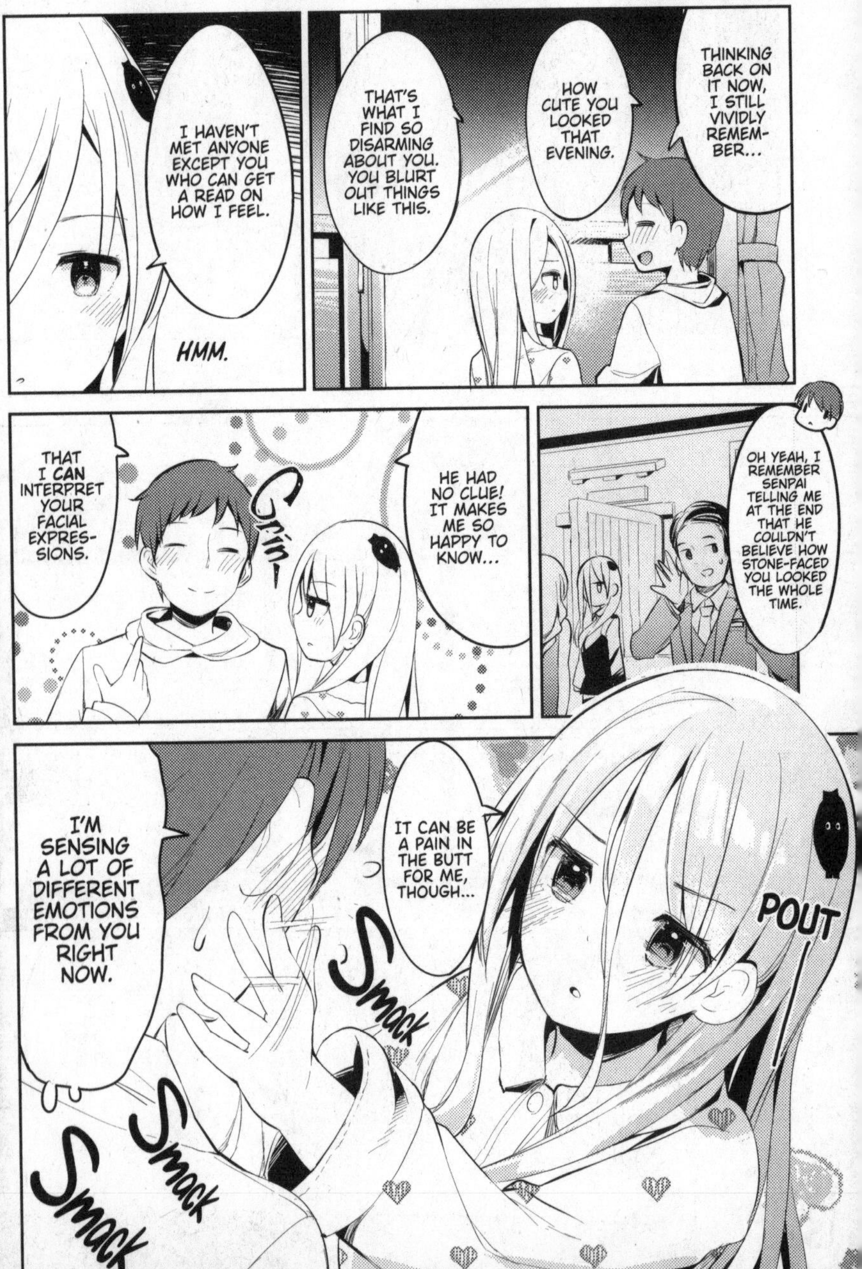
THINKING BACK ON IT NOW, I STILL VIVIDLY REMEMBER…
HOW CUTE YOU LOOKED THAT EVENING.
THAT'S WHAT I FIND SO DISARMING ABOUT YOU. YOU BLURT OUT THINGS LIKE THIS.
I HAVEN'T MET ANYONE EXCEPT YOU WHO CAN GET A READ ON HOW I FEEL.
HMM.
OH YEAH, I REMEMBER SENPAI TELLING ME AT THE END THAT HE COULDN'T BELIEVE HOW STONE-FACED YOU LOOKED THE WHOLE TIME.
HE HAD NO CLUE! IT MAKES ME SO HAPPY TO KNOW…
Grin
THAT I CAN INTERPRET YOUR FACIAL EXPRESSIONS.
IT CAN BE A PAIN IN THE BUTT FOR ME, THOUGH…
POUT
I'M SENSING A LOT OF DIFFERENT EMOTIONS FROM YOU RIGHT NOW.
Smack
Smack
Smack

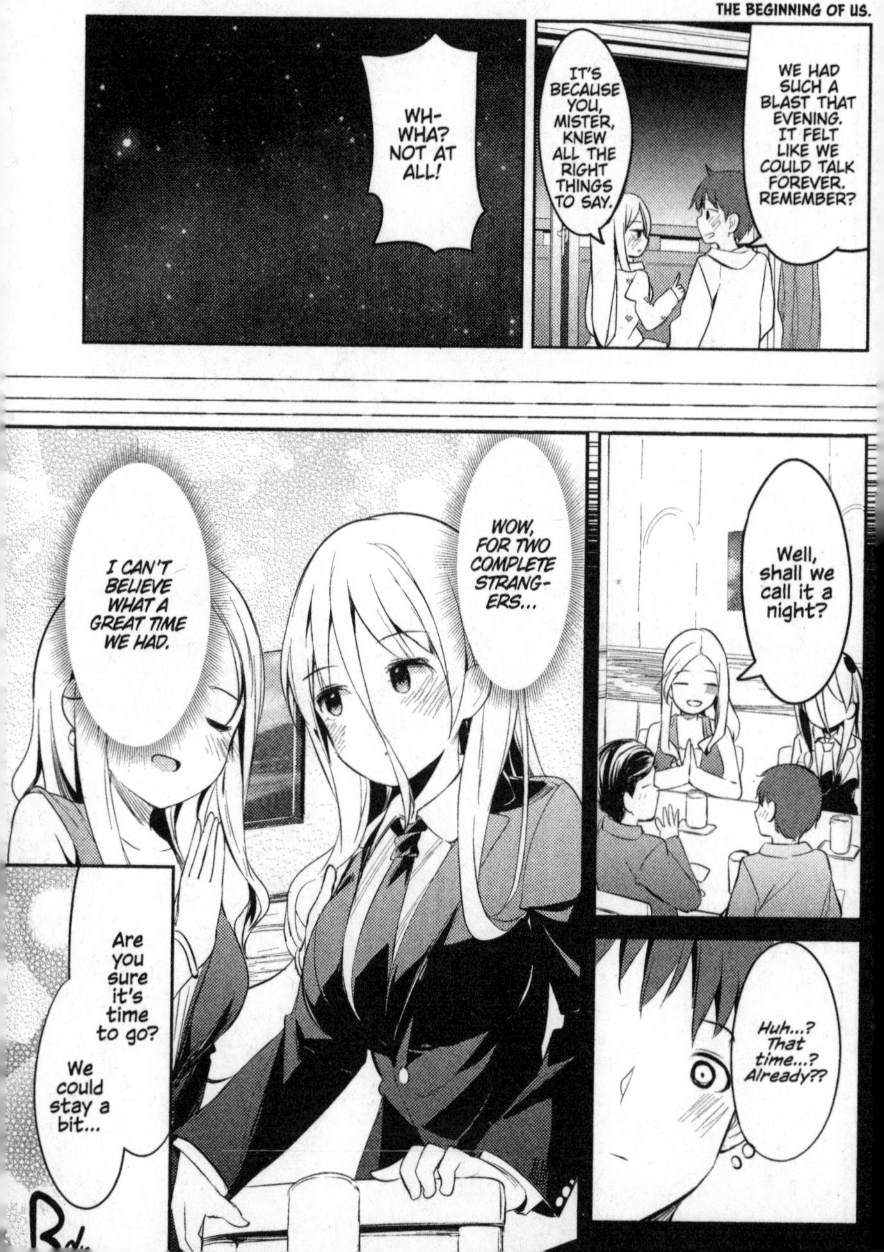
WE HAD SUCH A BLAST THAT EVENING. IT FELT LIKE WE COULD TALK FOREVER. REMEMBER?
IT'S BECAUSE YOU, MISTER, KNEW ALL THE RIGHT THINGS TO SAY.
WH-WHA? NOT AT ALL!
Well, shall we call it a night?
Huh...? That time...? Already??
WOW, FOR TWO COMPLETE STRANG-ERS...
I CAN'T BELIEVE WHAT A GREAT TIME WE HAD.
Are you sure it's time to go?
We could stay a bit...

WALKING TO THE SUBWAY.

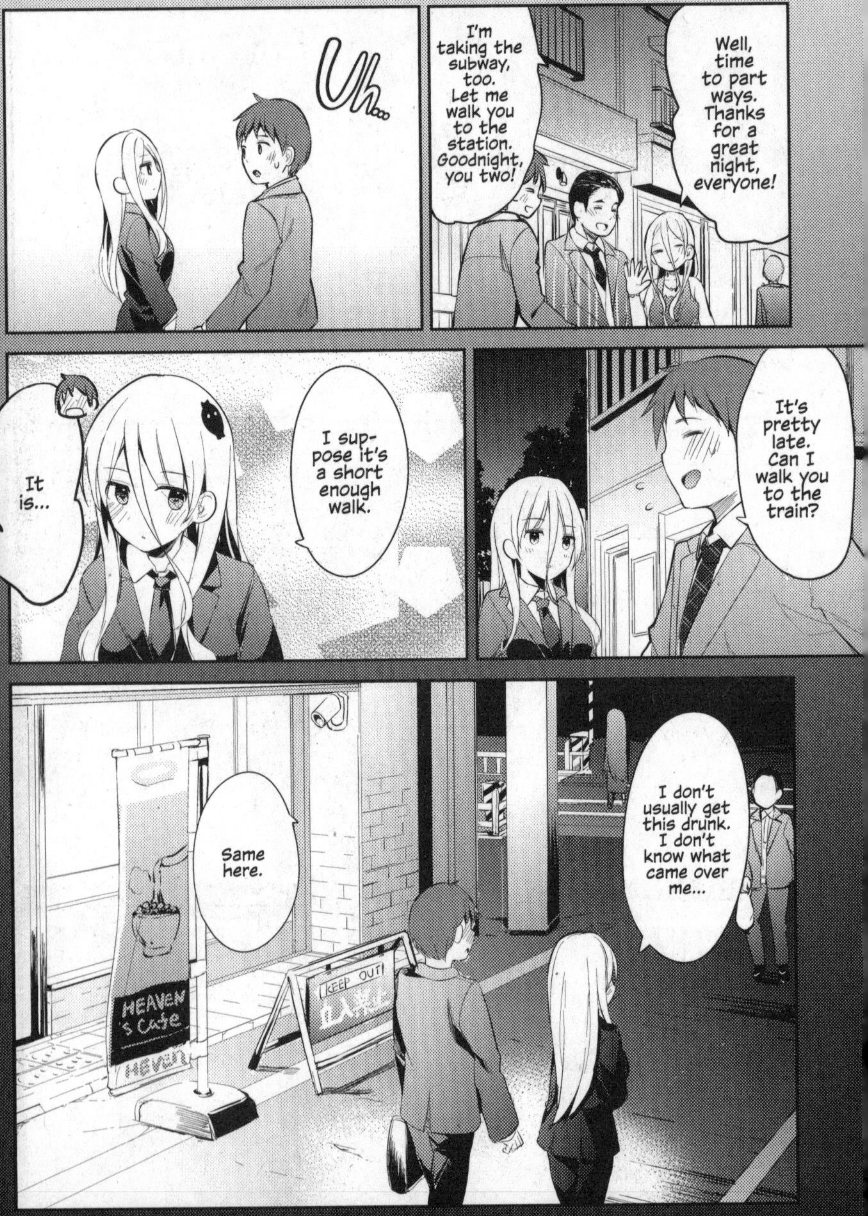
Well, time to part ways. Thanks for a great night, everyone!
I'm taking the subway, too. Let me walk you to the station. Goodnight, you two!
Uh...
It's pretty late. Can I walk you to the train?
I sup-pose it's a short enough walk.
It is...
I don't usually get this drunk. I don't know what came over me...
Same here.
KEEP OUT!
HEAVEN's Cafe
HEVEN

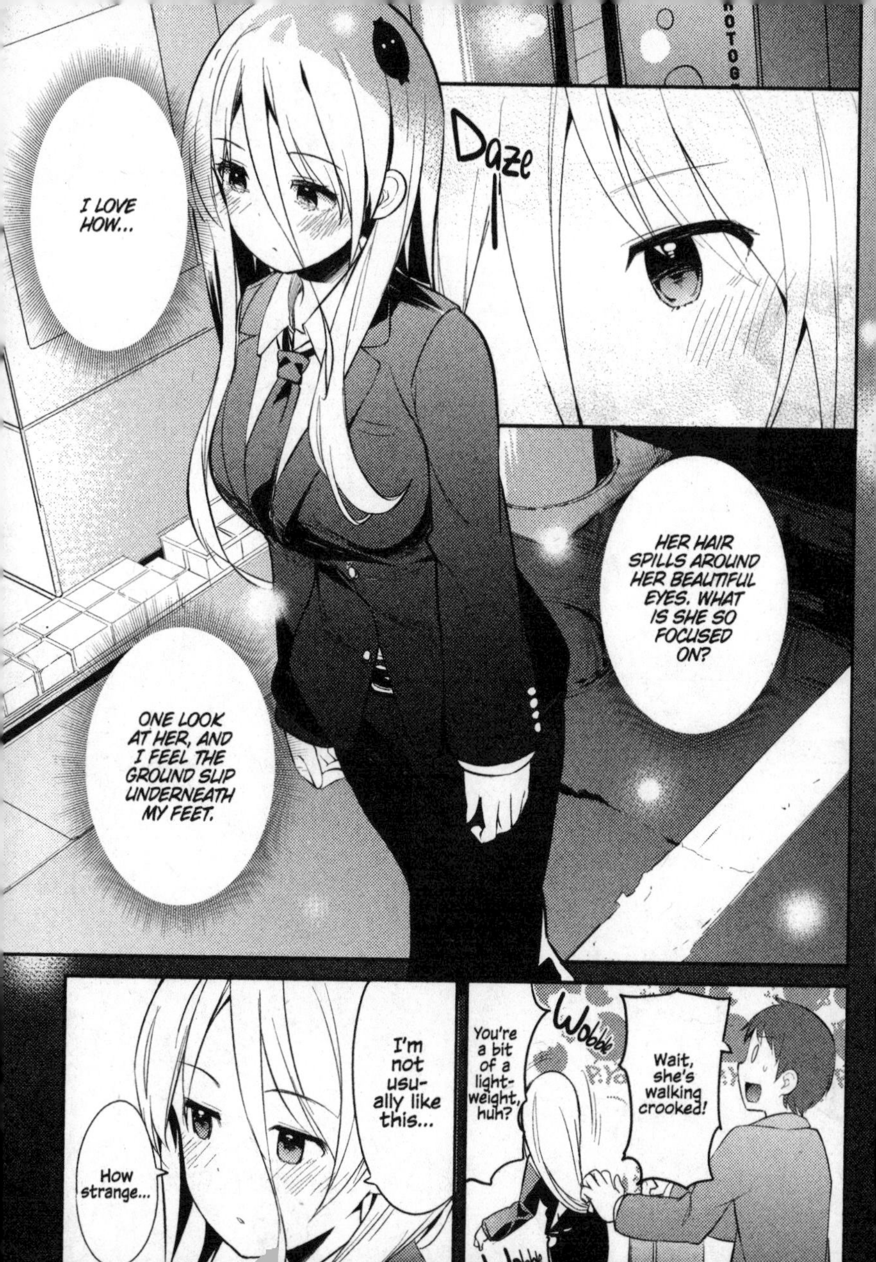

Daze
HER HAIR SPILLS AROUND HER BEAUTIFUL EYES. WHAT IS SHE SO FOCUSED ON?
I LOVE HOW...
ONE LOOK AT HER, AND I FEEL THE GROUND SLIP UNDERNEATH MY FEET.
Wobble
Wait, she's walking crooked!
You're a bit of a light-weight, huh?
Wobble
I'm not usu-ally like this...
How strange...

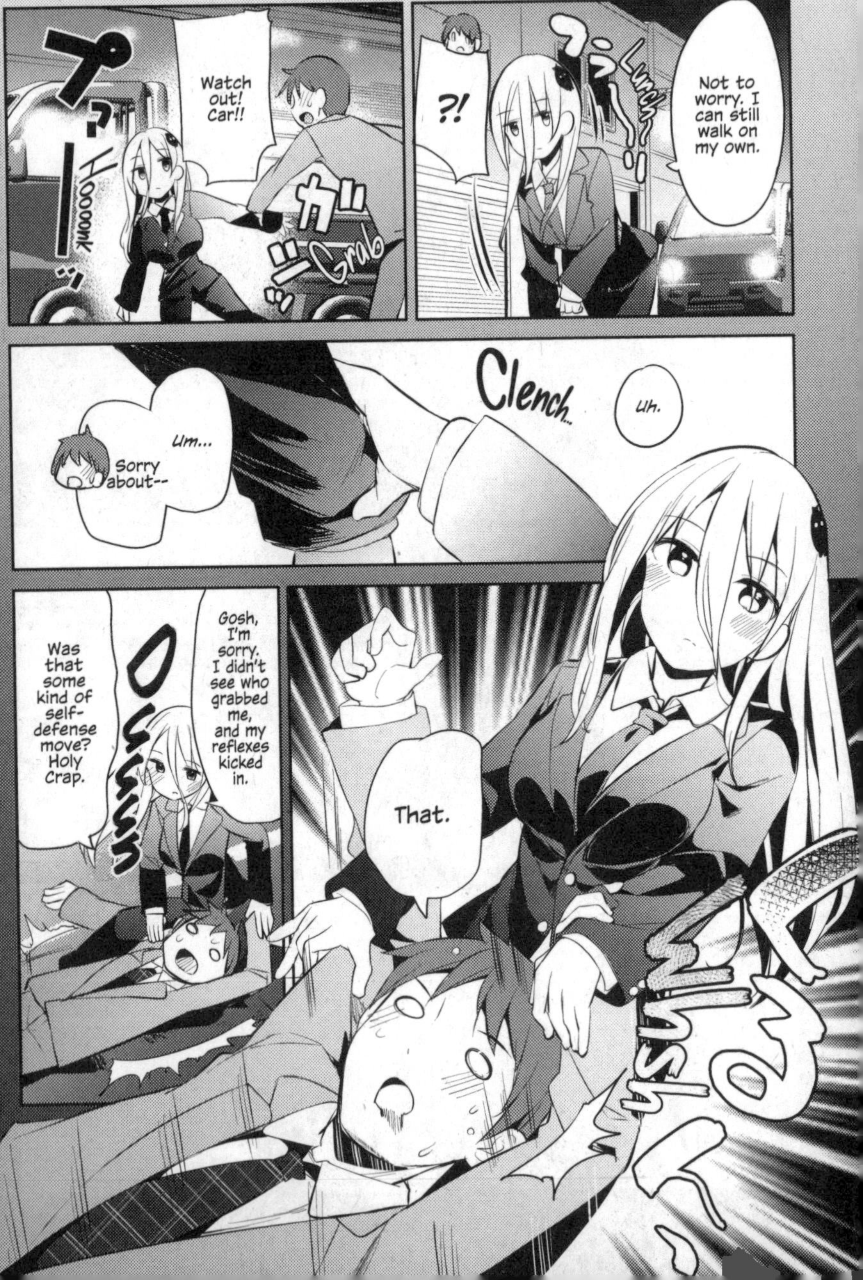
Not to worry. I can still walk on my own.
Lurch~
?!
Watch out! Car!!
Hoooonk
Grab
Clench...
uh.
um... Sorry about--
Gosh, I'm sorry. I didn't see who grabbed me, and my reflexes kicked in.
Was that some kind of self-defense move? Holy Crap.
Duuun
That.
Swish

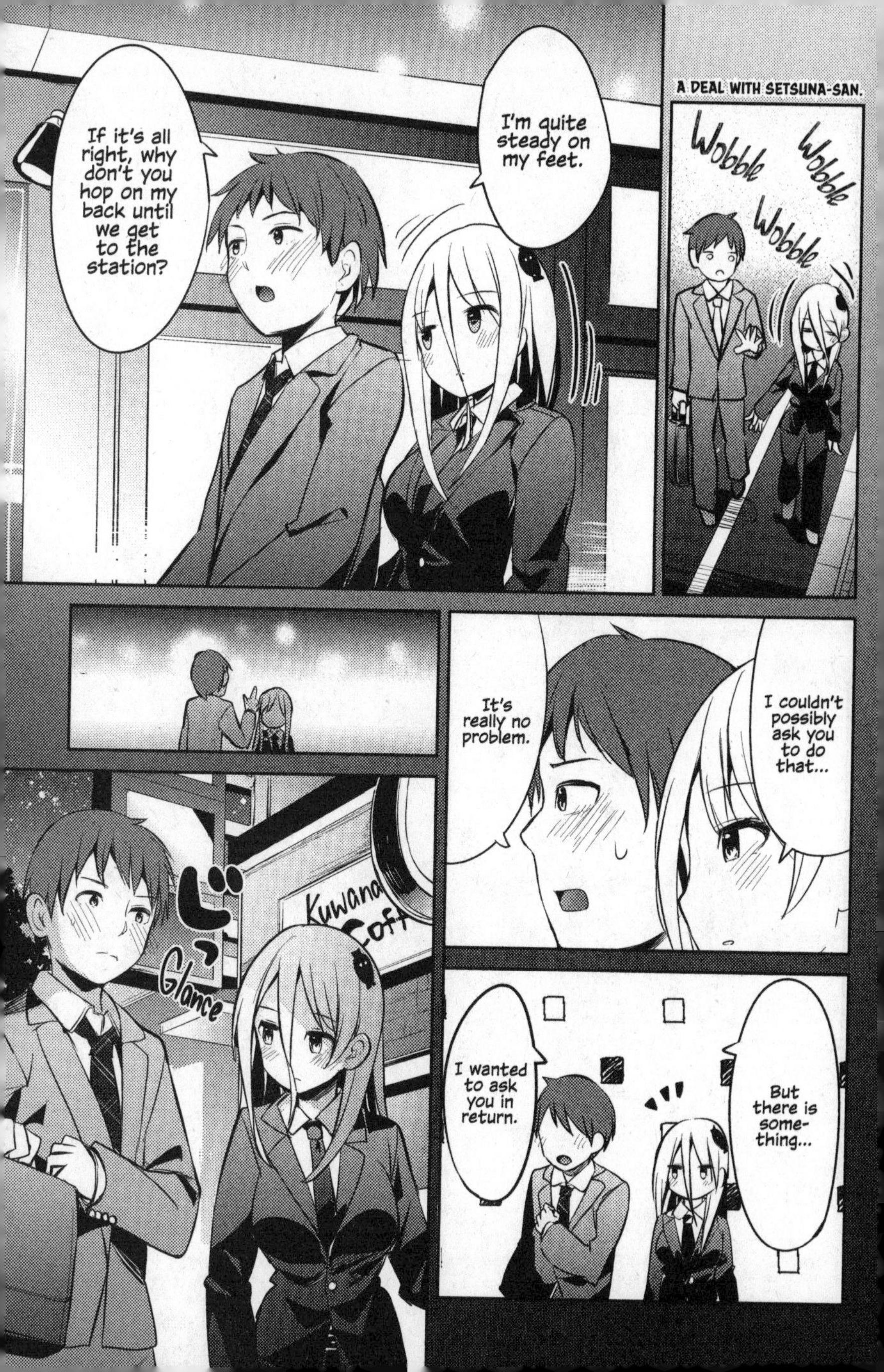
A DEAL WITH SETSUNA-SAN.
Wobble
Wobble
Wobble
I'm quite steady on my feet.
If it's all right, why don't you hop on my back until we get to the station?
I couldn't possibly ask you to do that...
It's really no problem.
But there is some-thing...
I wanted to ask you in return.
じ
Glance
Kuwana Coff

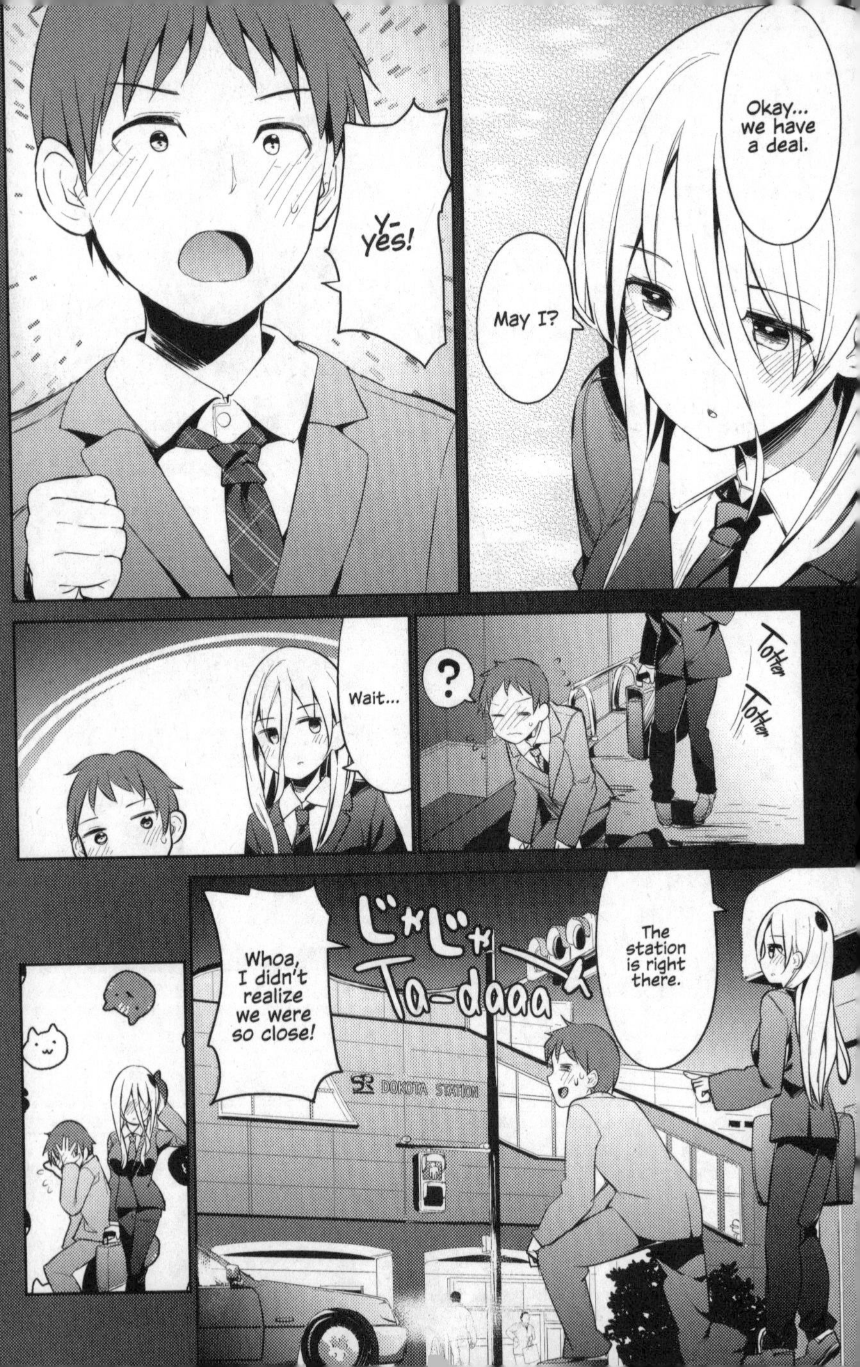
Okay... we have a deal.
May I?
Y-Yes!
Totten
Totten
?
Wait...
The station is right there.
じゃじゃーん
Ta-daaa
Whoa, I didn't realize we were so close!
DOKOTA STATION

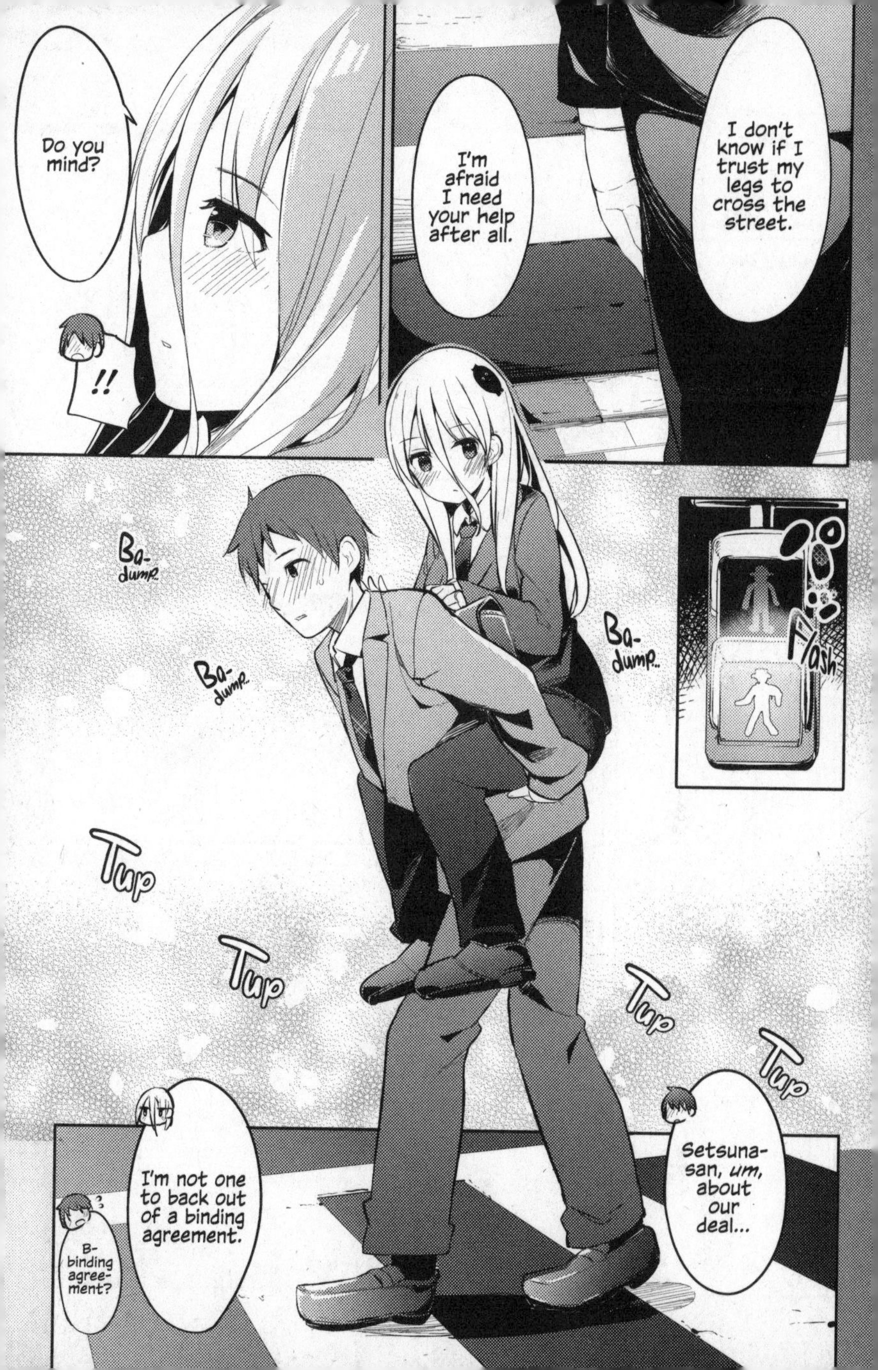
I don't know if I trust my legs to cross the street.
I'm afraid I need your help after all.
Do you mind?
!!
Flash
Ba-dump...
Ba-dump...
Ba-dump...
Tup
Tup
Tup
Tup
Setsuna-san, um, about our deal...
I'm not one to back out of a binding agreement.
B-binding agreement?

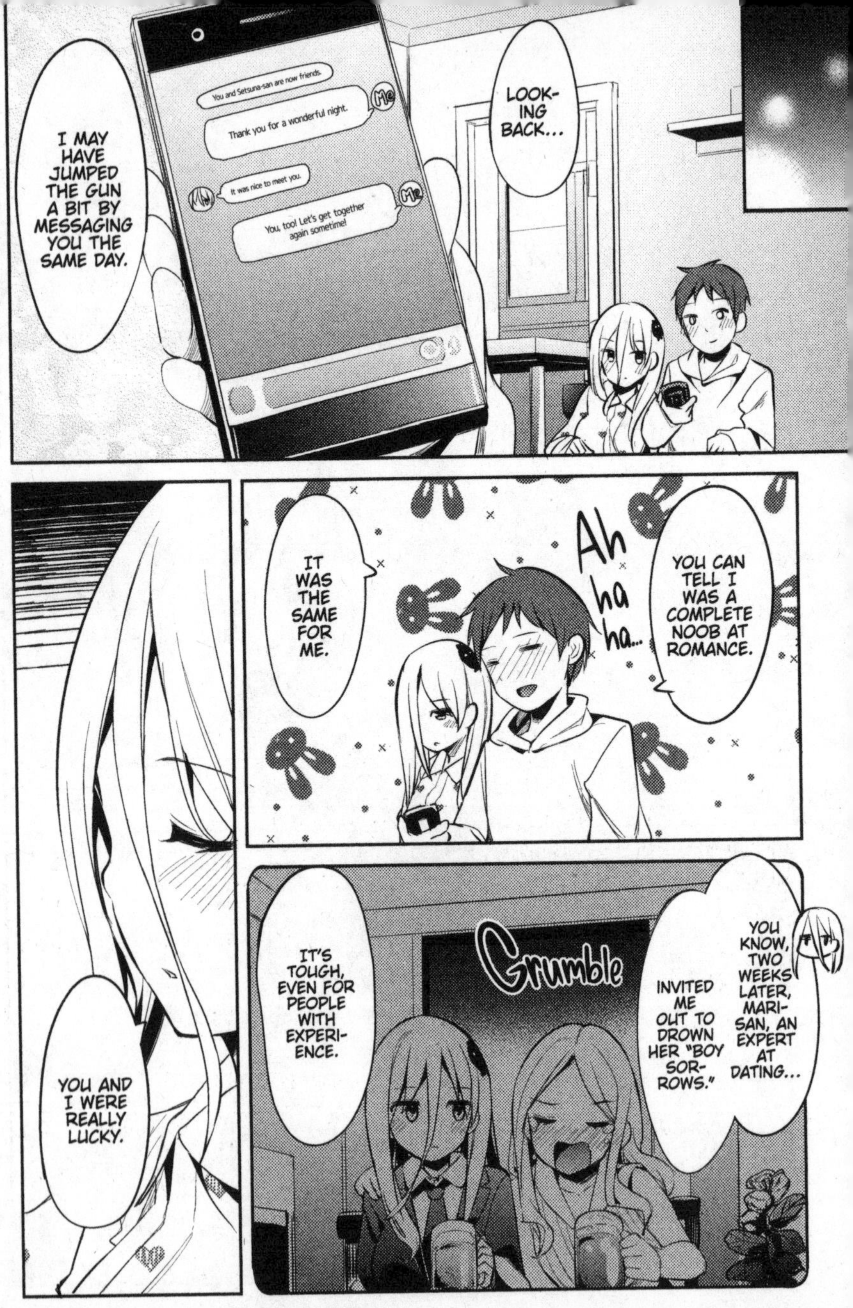
LOOKING-BACK...
You and Setsuna-san are now friends.
Thank you for a wonderful night.
It was nice to meet you.
You, too! Let's get together again sometime!
I MAY HAVE JUMPED THE GUN A BIT BY MESSAGING YOU THE SAME DAY.
YOU CAN TELL I WAS A COMPLETE NOOB AT ROMANCE.
Ah ha ha...
IT WAS THE SAME FOR ME.
YOU KNOW, TWO WEEKS LATER, MARI-SAN, AN EXPERT AT DATING...
INVITED ME OUT TO DROWN HER "BOY SOR-ROWS."
Grumble
IT'S TOUGH, EVEN FOR PEOPLE WITH EXPERI-ENCE.
YOU AND I WERE REALLY LUCKY.

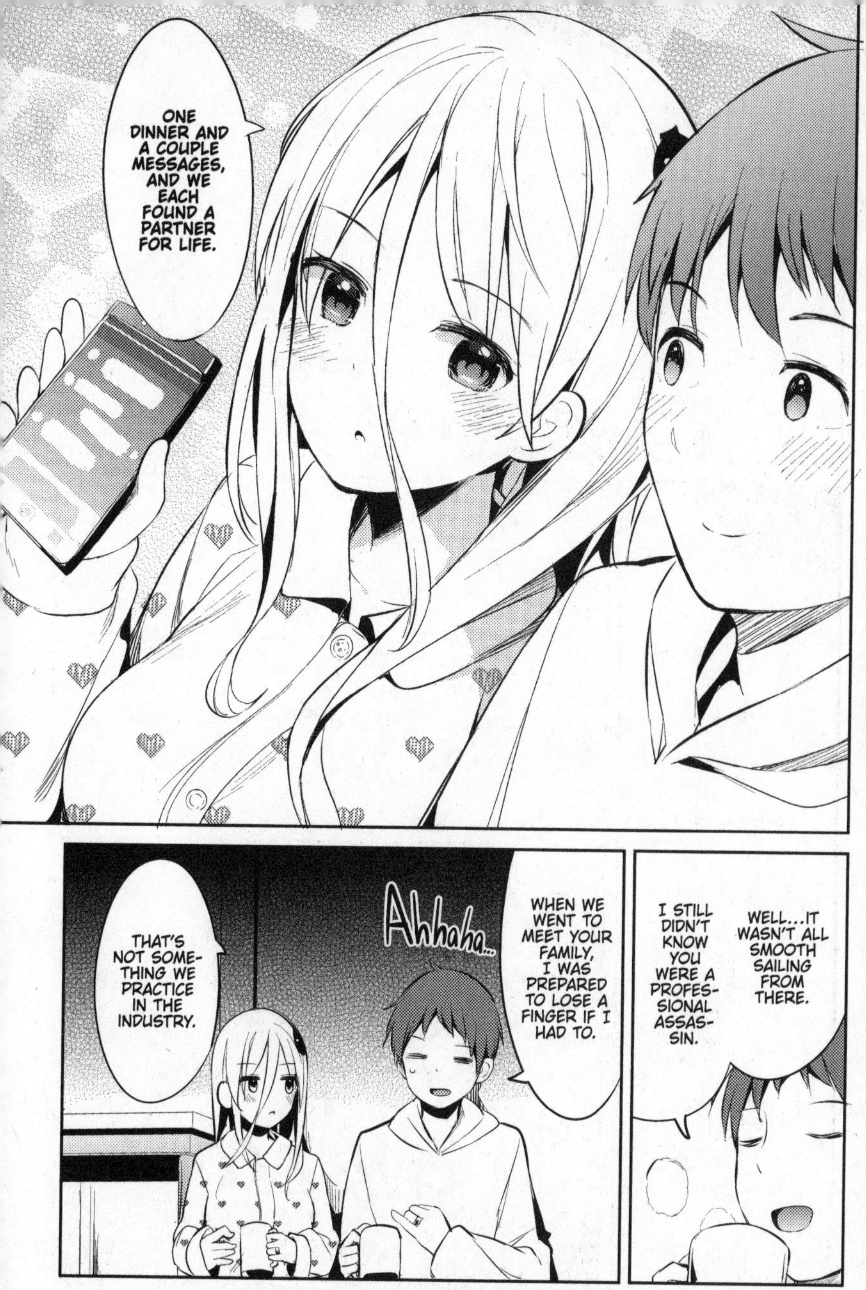
ONE DINNER AND A COUPLE MESSAGES, AND WE EACH FOUND A PARTNER FOR LIFE.
WELL...IT WASN'T ALL SMOOTH SAILING FROM THERE.
I STILL DIDN'T KNOW YOU WERE A PROFES-SIONAL ASSAS-SIN.
WHEN WE WENT TO MEET YOUR FAMILY, I WAS PREPARED TO LOSE A FINGER IF I HAD TO.
Ahhaha...
THAT'S NOT SOME-THING WE PRACTICE IN THE INDUSTRY.

MY
Lovey-Dovey
Wife IS A
STONE COLD
KILLER

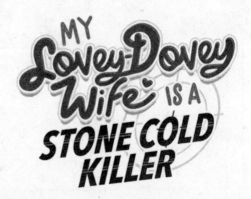

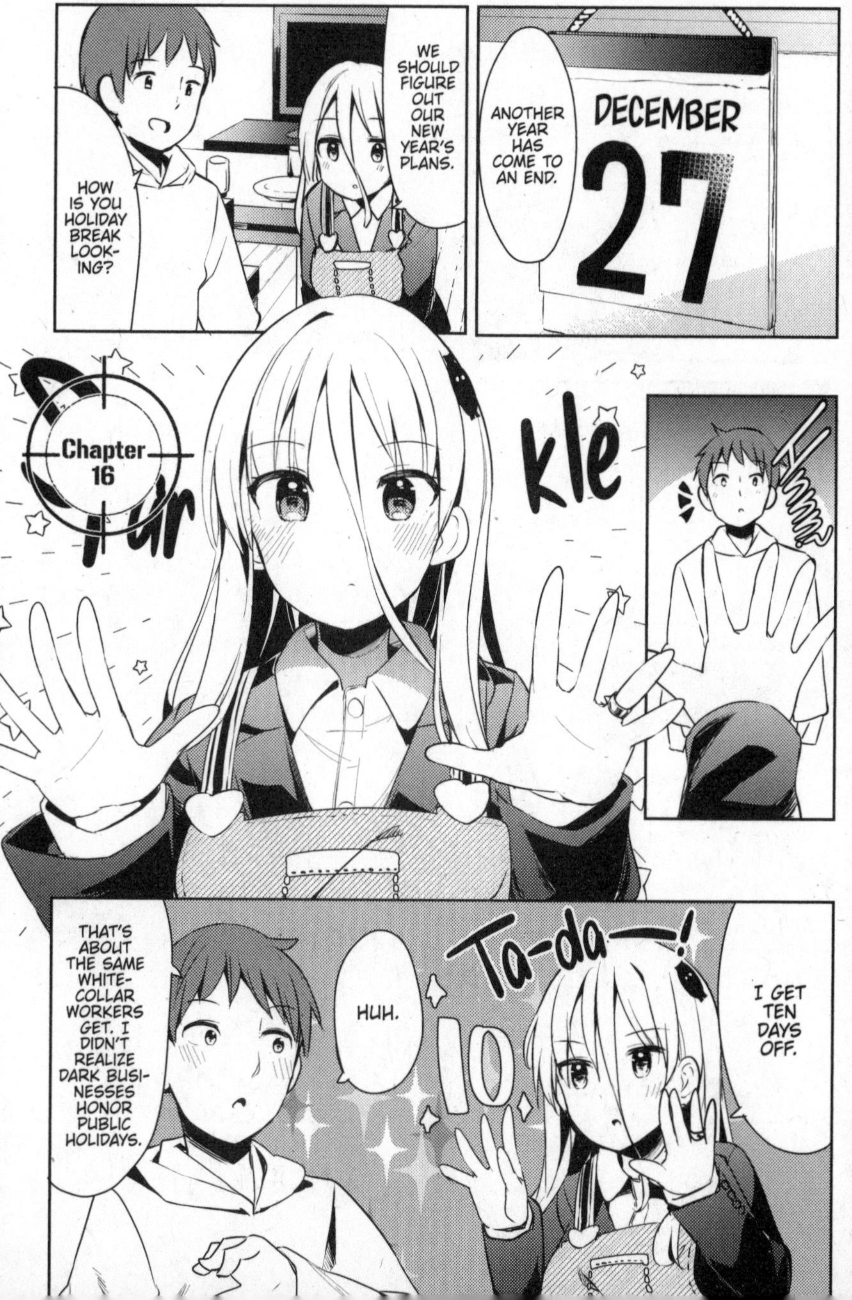
DECEMBER 27
ANOTHER YEAR HAS COME TO AN END.
WE SHOULD FIGURE OUT OUR NEW YEAR'S PLANS.
HOW IS YOU HOLIDAY BREAK LOOKING?
Hmm?
Chapter 16
kle
I GET TEN DAYS OFF.
Ta-da—!
10
HUH.
THAT'S ABOUT THE SAME WHITE-COLLAR WORKERS GET. I DIDN'T REALIZE DARK BUSINESSES HONOR PUBLIC HOLIDAYS.

LAST YEAR WITH SETSUNA-SAN.

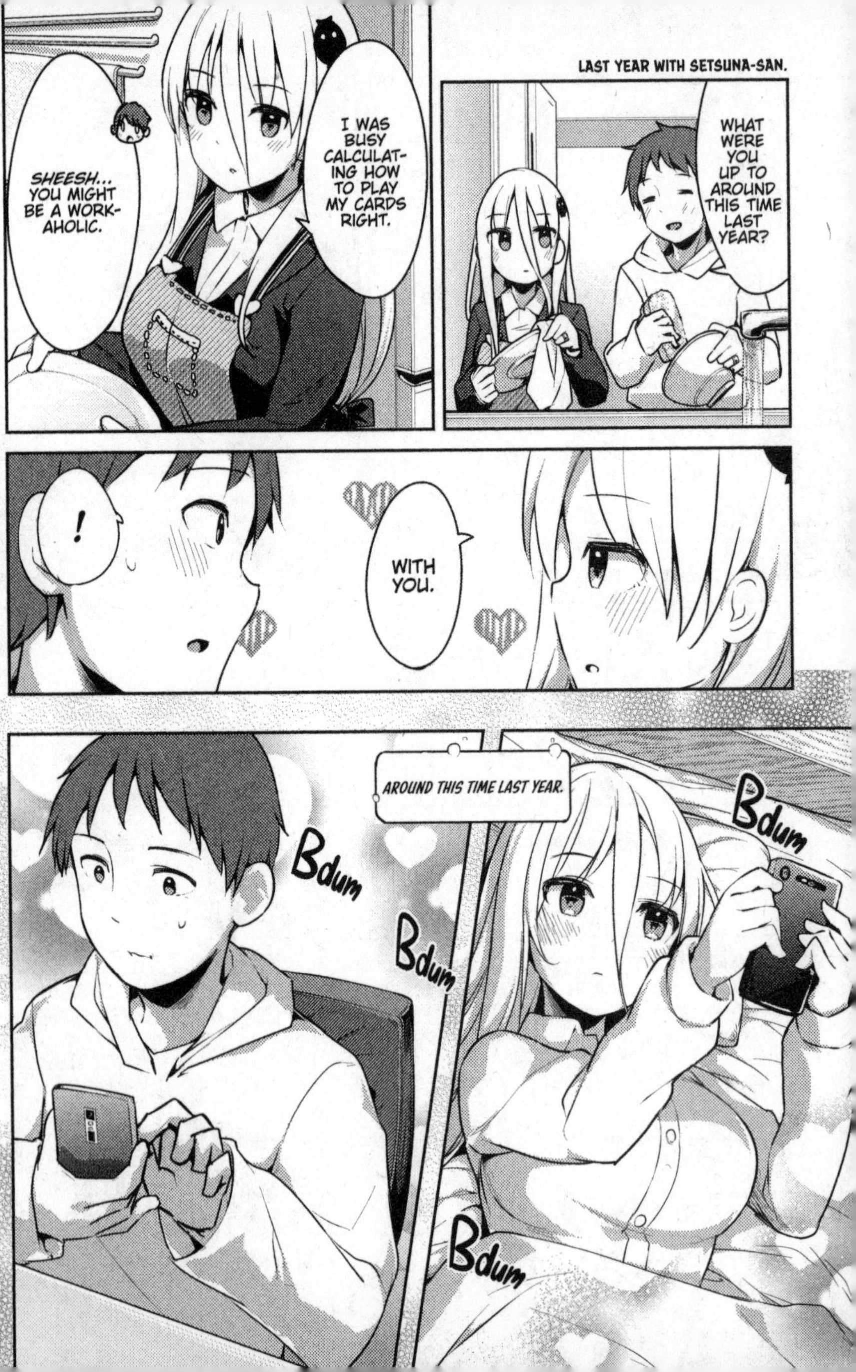
WHAT WERE YOU UP TO AROUND THIS TIME LAST YEAR?
I WAS BUSY CALCULATING HOW TO PLAY MY CARDS RIGHT.
SHEESH... YOU MIGHT BE A WORKAHOLIC.
WITH YOU.
!
AROUND THIS TIME LAST YEAR.
Bdum
Bdum
Bdum
Bdum

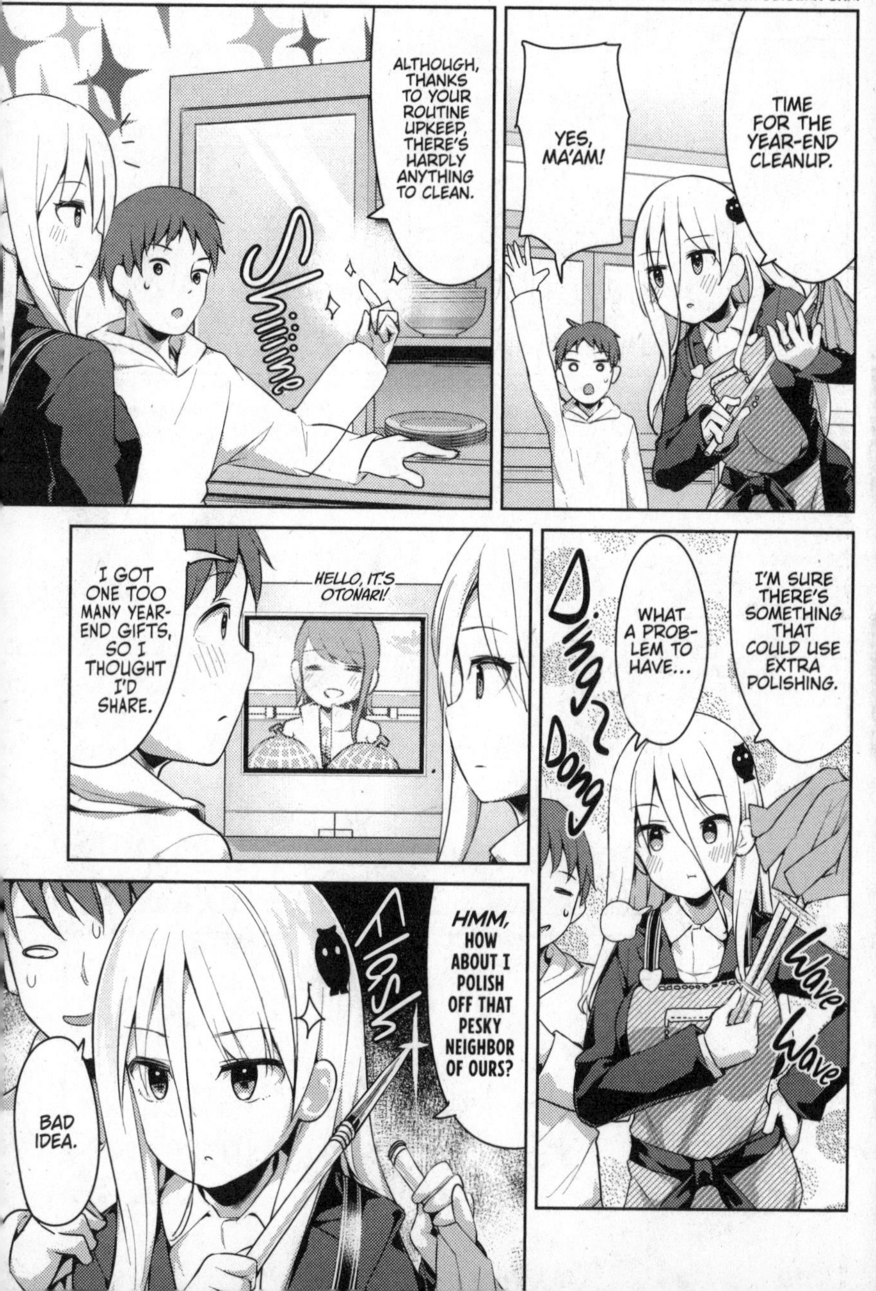
TIME FOR THE YEAR-END CLEANUP.
YES, MA'AM!
ALTHOUGH, THANKS TO YOUR ROUTINE UPKEEP, THERE'S HARDLY ANYTHING TO CLEAN.
Shiiiine
I'M SURE THERE'S SOMETHING THAT COULD USE EXTRA POLISHING.
WHAT A PROBLEM TO HAVE...
Ding~ Dong
Wave Wave
HELLO, IT'S OTONARI!
I GOT ONE TOO MANY YEAR-END GIFTS, SO I THOUGHT I'D SHARE.
HMM, HOW ABOUT I POLISH OFF THAT PESKY NEIGHBOR OF OURS?
Flash
BAD IDEA.

SETSUNA-SAN'S FAMILY'S HOUSE.

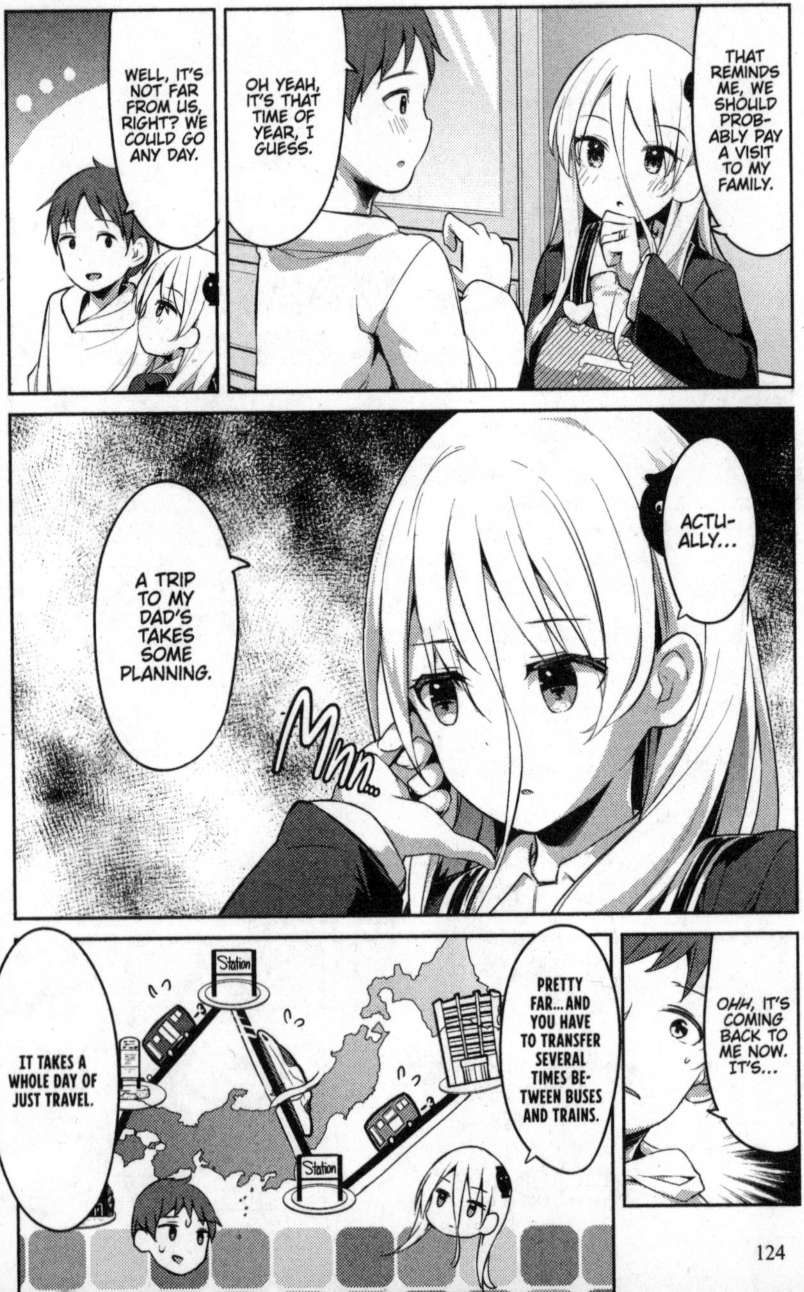
THAT REMINDS ME, WE SHOULD PROB-ABLY PAY A VISIT TO MY FAMILY.
OH YEAH, IT'S THAT TIME OF YEAR, I GUESS.
WELL, IT'S NOT FAR FROM US, RIGHT? WE COULD GO ANY DAY.
ACTU-ALLY...
A TRIP TO MY DAD'S TAKES SOME PLANNING.
Mnn...
OHH, IT'S COMING BACK TO ME NOW. IT'S...
PRETTY FAR... AND YOU HAVE TO TRANSFER SEVERAL TIMES BE-TWEEN BUSES AND TRAINS.
Station
Station
IT TAKES A WHOLE DAY OF JUST TRAVEL.

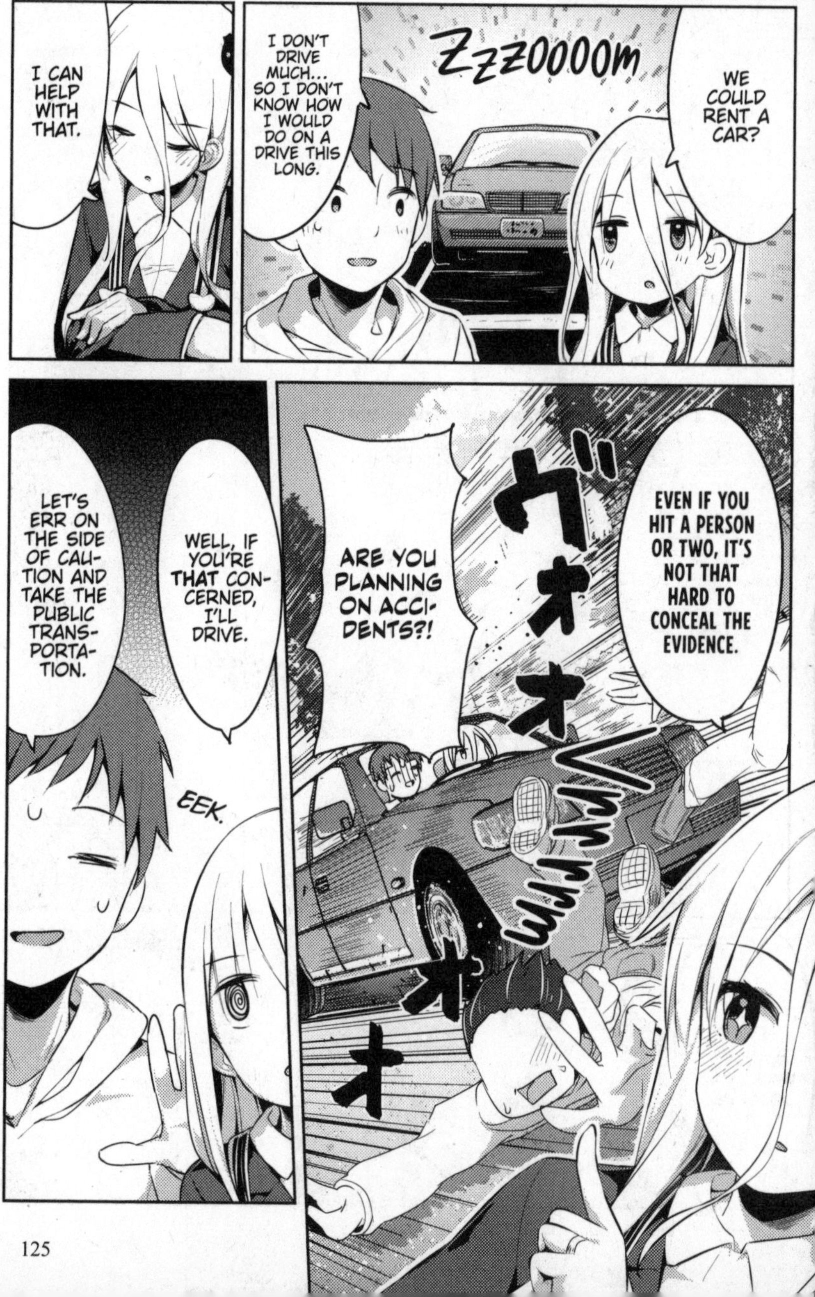
WE COULD RENT A CAR?
ZZZOOOOM
I DON'T DRIVE MUCH... SO I DON'T KNOW HOW I WOULD DO ON A DRIVE THIS LONG.
I CAN HELP WITH THAT.
EVEN IF YOU HIT A PERSON OR TWO, IT'S NOT THAT HARD TO CONCEAL THE EVIDENCE.
ヴオオオオ
ARE YOU PLANNING ON ACCIDENTS?!
WELL, IF YOU'RE THAT CONCERNED, I'LL DRIVE.
LET'S ERR ON THE SIDE OF CAUTION AND TAKE THE PUBLIC TRANSPORTATION.
EEK.

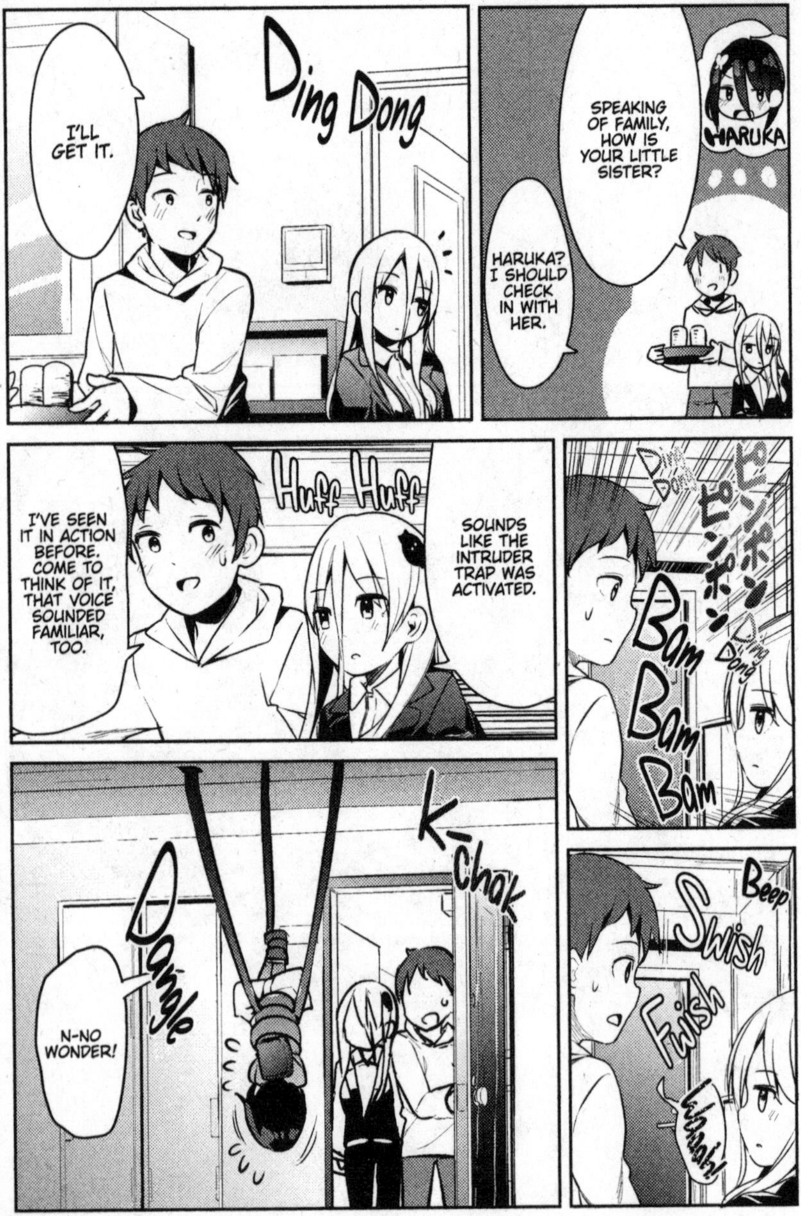
SPEAKING OF FAMILY, HOW IS YOUR LITTLE SISTER?
HARUKA
HARUKA? I SHOULD CHECK IN WITH HER.
Ding Dong
I'LL GET IT.
Ding Dong
ピンポンピンポン
Ding Dong
Bam Bam Bam
Huff Huff
SOUNDS LIKE THE INTRUDER TRAP WAS ACTIVATED.
I'VE SEEN IT IN ACTION BEFORE. COME TO THINK OF IT, THAT VOICE SOUNDED FAMILIAR, TOO.
Beep
Swish
Fwish
Whoah!
K-chak
Dangle
N-NO WONDER!

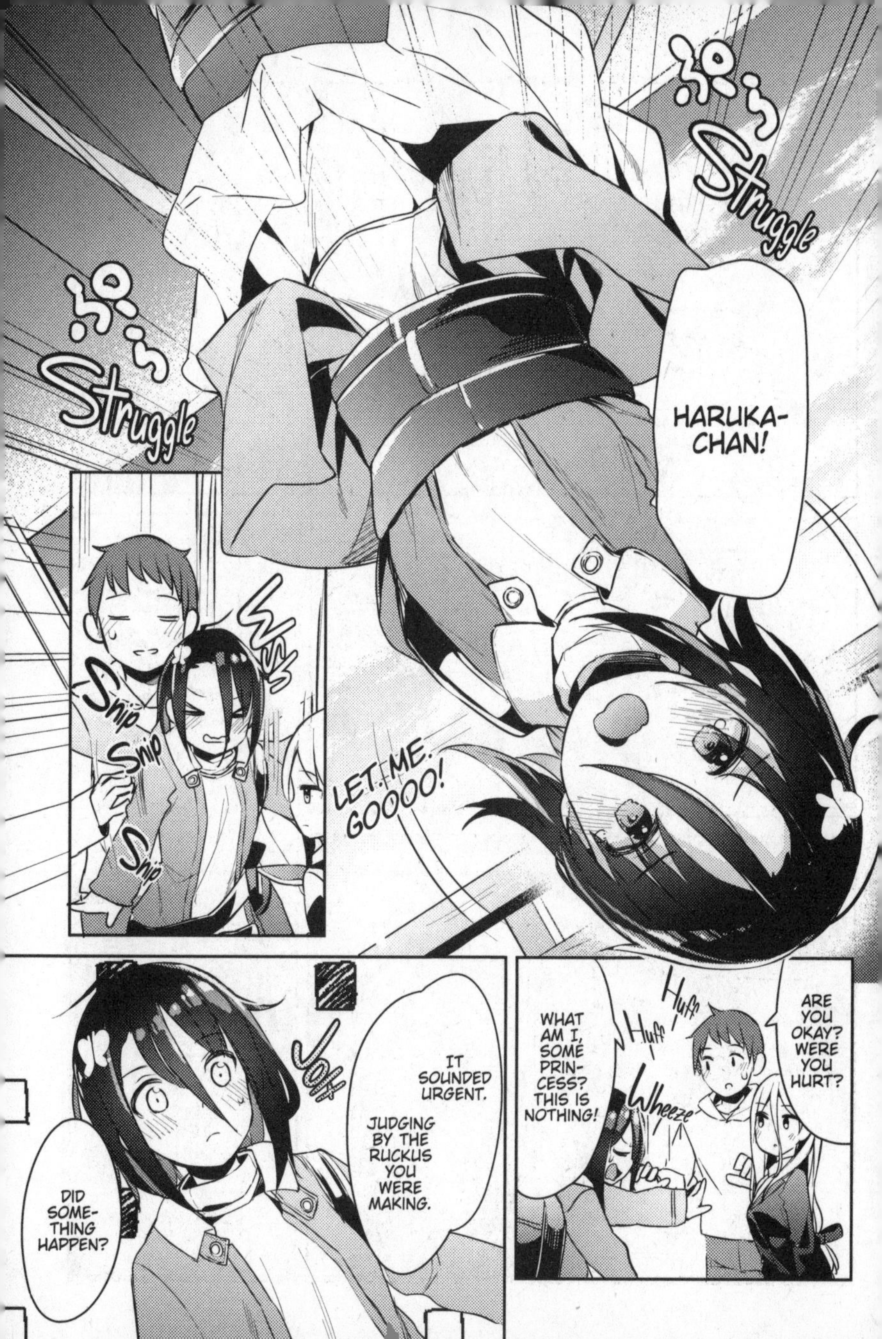
ぷぅ Struggle
HARUKA-CHAN!
ぷぅ Struggle
Wsh
LET. ME. GOOOO!
Snip Snip Snip
ARE YOU OKAY? WERE YOU HURT?
Huff Huff
Wheeze
WHAT AM I, SOME PRINCESS? THIS IS NOTHING!
IT SOUNDED URGENT.
JUDGING BY THE RUCKUS YOU WERE MAKING.
DID SOMETHING HAPPEN?

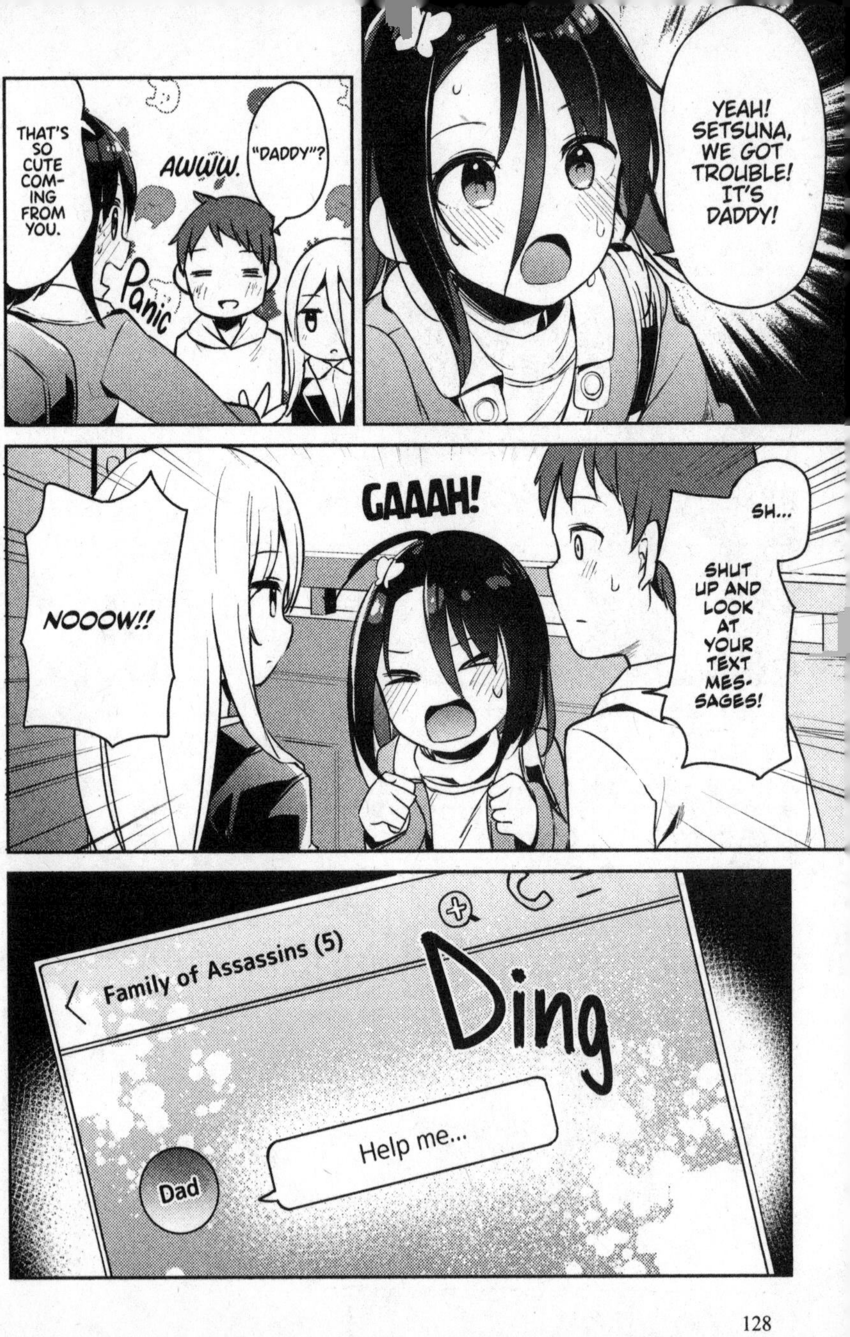
YEAH! SETSUNA, WE GOT TROUBLE! IT'S DADDY!
"DADDY"?
AWWW.
THAT'S SO CUTE COM-ING FROM YOU.
Panic
SH...
SHUT UP AND LOOK AT YOUR TEXT MES-SAGES!
GAAAH!
NOOOW!!
Family of Assassins (5)
Ding
Help me...
Dad

WHEN AN ASSASSIN STRIKES A DEAL.

HEY, I HAVE A BIG FAVOR TO ASK YOU.
……
TODAY AT SIX O'CLOCK, NEAR THE SUBWAY STATION A.
I NEED SOME-ONE AS BACK-UP...
YOU KNOW WHAT I MEAN?
……
PLEEEASE, SETSUNA. IF YOU DO THIS FOR ME...
THE DRINKS ARE ON ME!
HM... JUST THE DRINKS?
AFTER SOME HAGGLING, THEY SEALED THE DEAL WITH MARI PAYING FOR SETSUNA'S DRINKS AND DINNER.

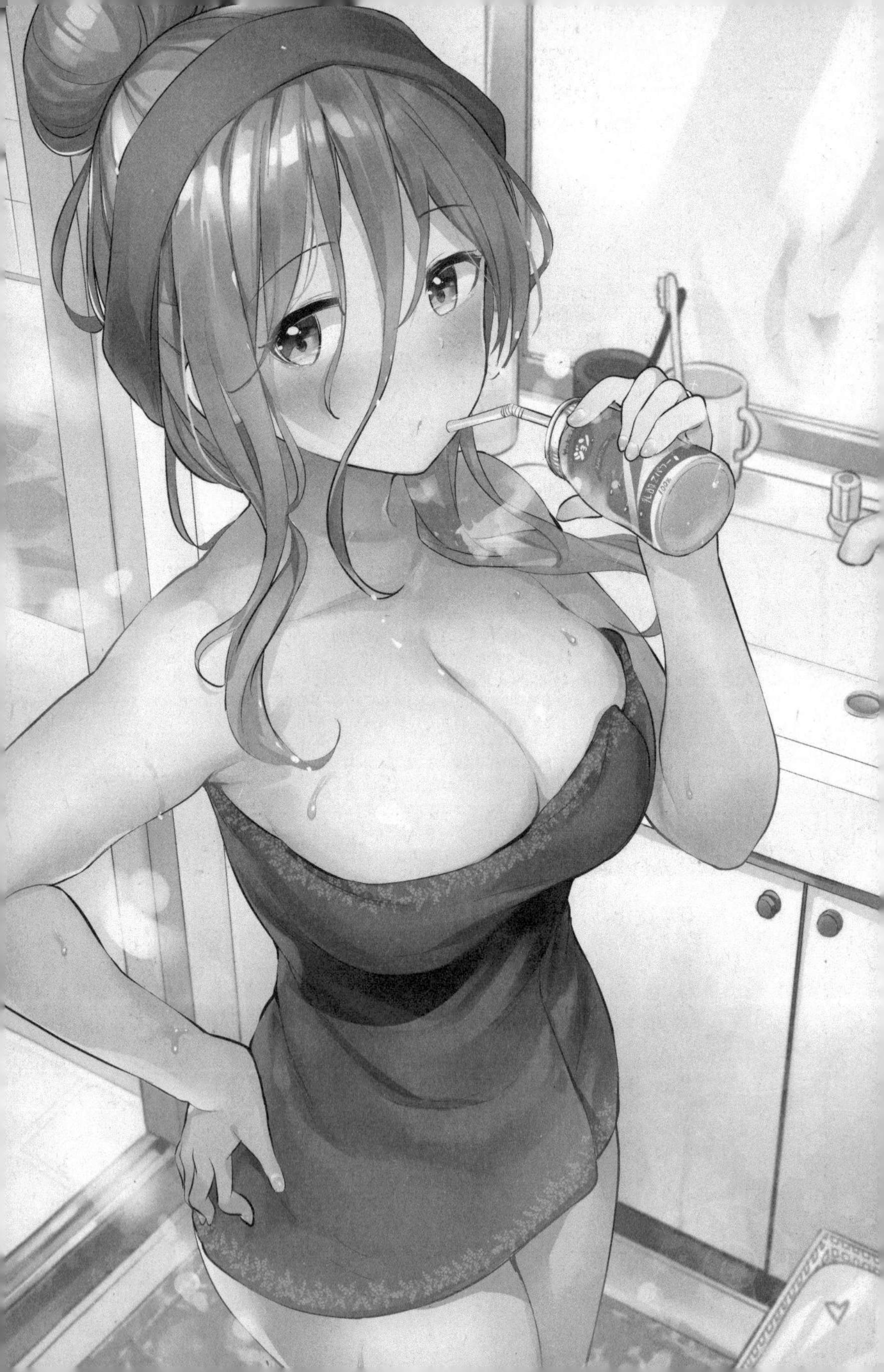

Afterword

Thank you for reading the second volume of *My Lovey-Dovey Wife is a Stone Cold Killer*.

I couldn't be happier with the response this volume received. To all my readers, thank you so much for your comments online and for sharing your thoughts about the book.

I wanted to tell the story of how Setsuna-san and the protagonist met from the very beginning, and I'm thrilled to see it in print. Now, some of you might be wondering...how on earth do two people go from meeting like this for the first time straight to married?! All in due time, dear reader. I would love to explore and present the answer to this question in the next volume.

Let's talk a bit about what is to become of the series moving forward. What's in the cards for our heroes in Volume 3? That's to be continued! As it is, the end of Volume 2 certainly invites a continuation. That said, should you expect this to become a long-running series...? I don't think so, *heh heh*.

This manga revolves around day-to-day challenges that Setsuna-san and the protagonist face. Whenever somethings serious comes up, Setsuna-san is usually able to react quickly and solve the problem. Yet, there's always room for improvement, such as better communication with their neighbor, Otonari-san, and building up courage to progress in their relationship. With all that in mind, I have a feeling that, in the next volume, the story will touch upon a set of values that are somewhat different from those of most people. Thank you all for your support and patience as I put these ideas into fruition.

You can trust that I am hard at work on the next volume. Stay tuned for updates on its release!

HAVE A LOOK!

Special Thanks

[Production]
dosiro-do-san
https://twitter.com/DosiroD

[Editor in Chief]
Yamamoto-san

[Designer]
Kusume-san

Tsutsuikyuu-san
Omegane-sensei

And all of you who picked up this book!

About The Author

My Twitter → https://twitter.com/higheast

I might or might not make frequent posts...!

← Art Site

My page on pixiv fanbox. Do I share original sketches of Setsuna-san and others? Maybe!

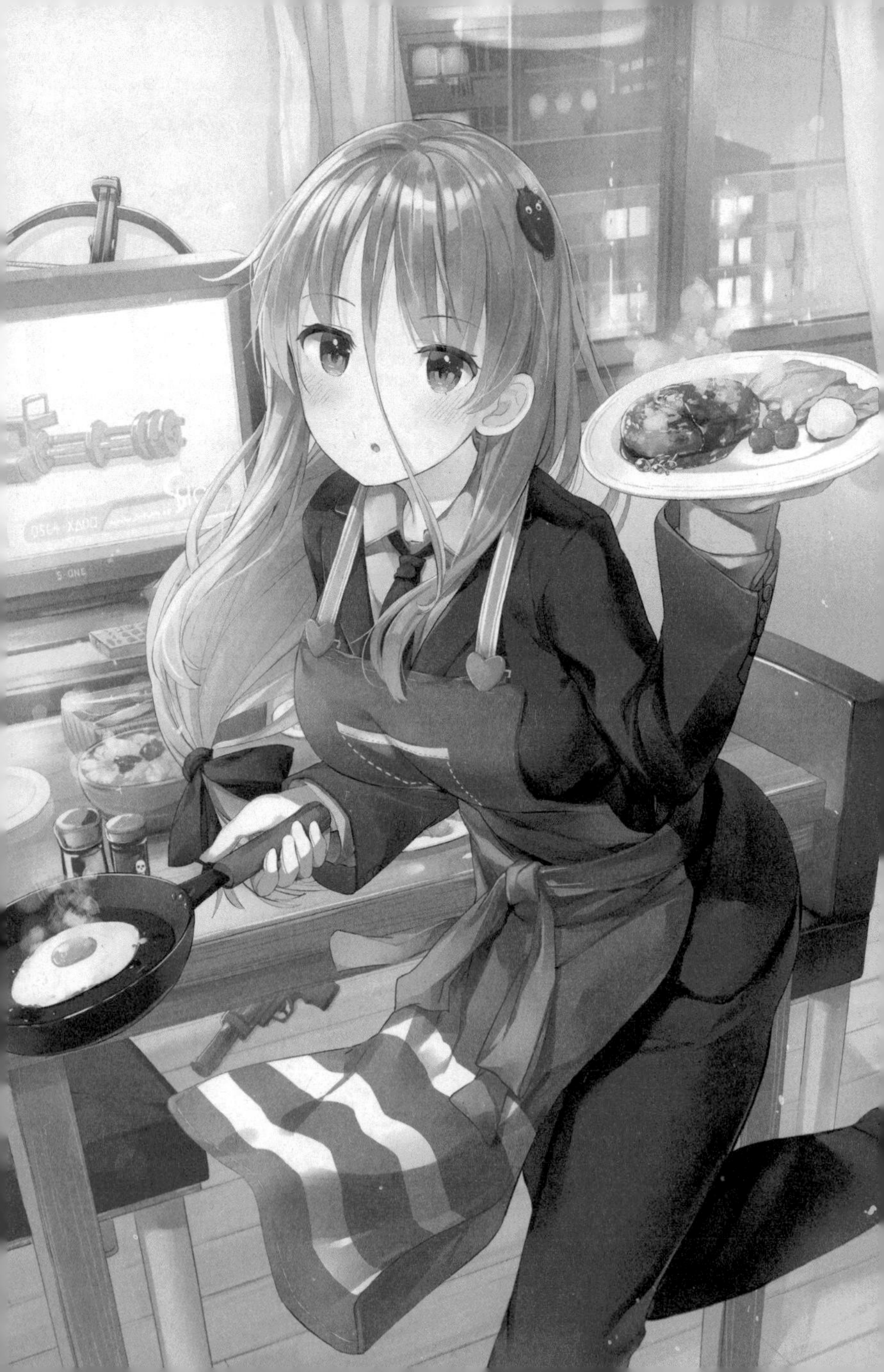

MY Lovey-Dovey Wife IS A STONE COLD KILLER

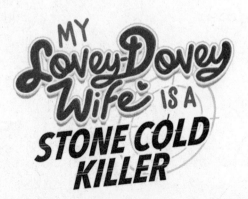

MY Lovey-Dovey Wife IS A STONE COLD KILLER

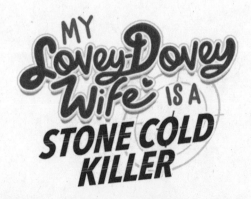

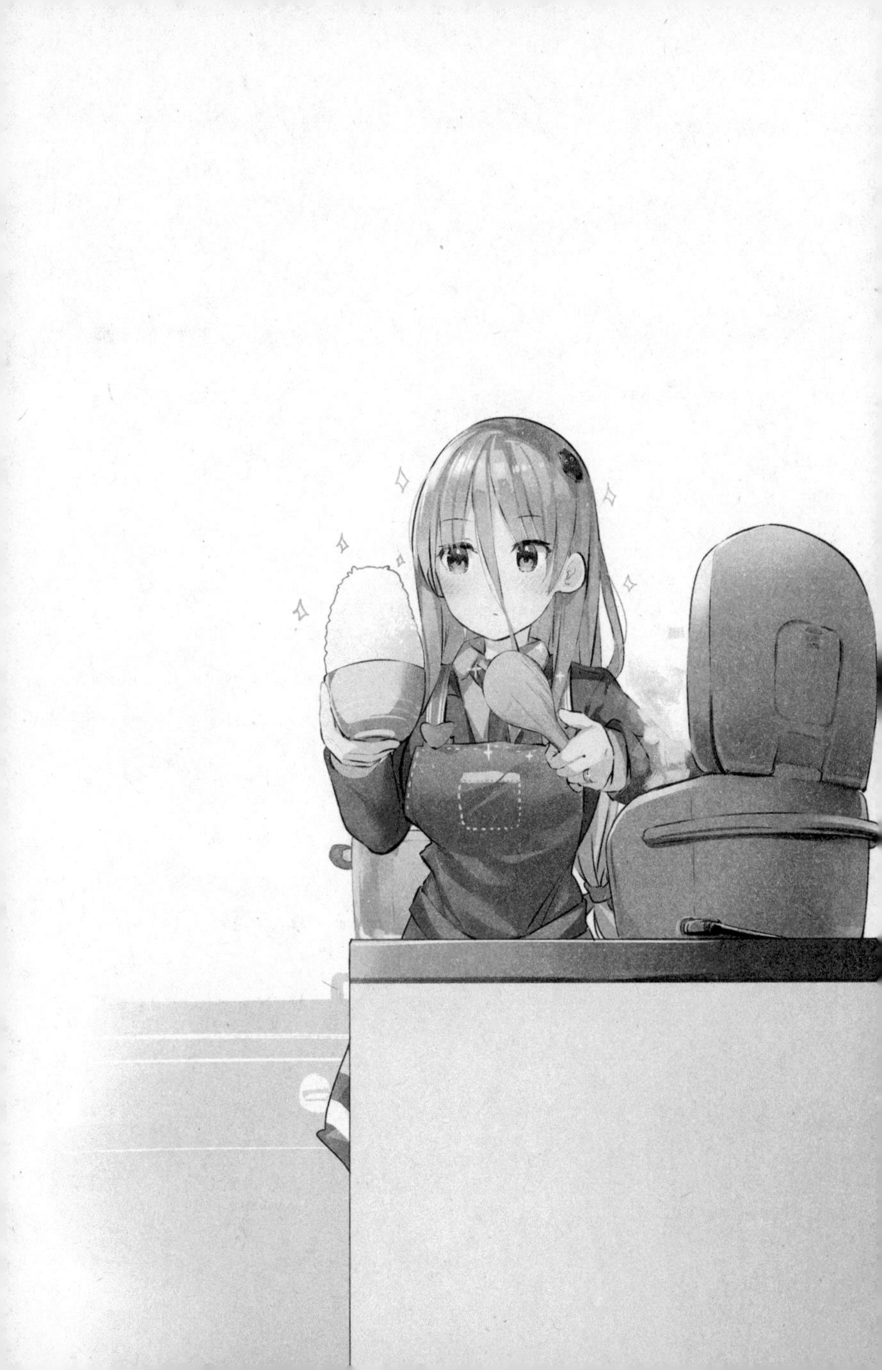

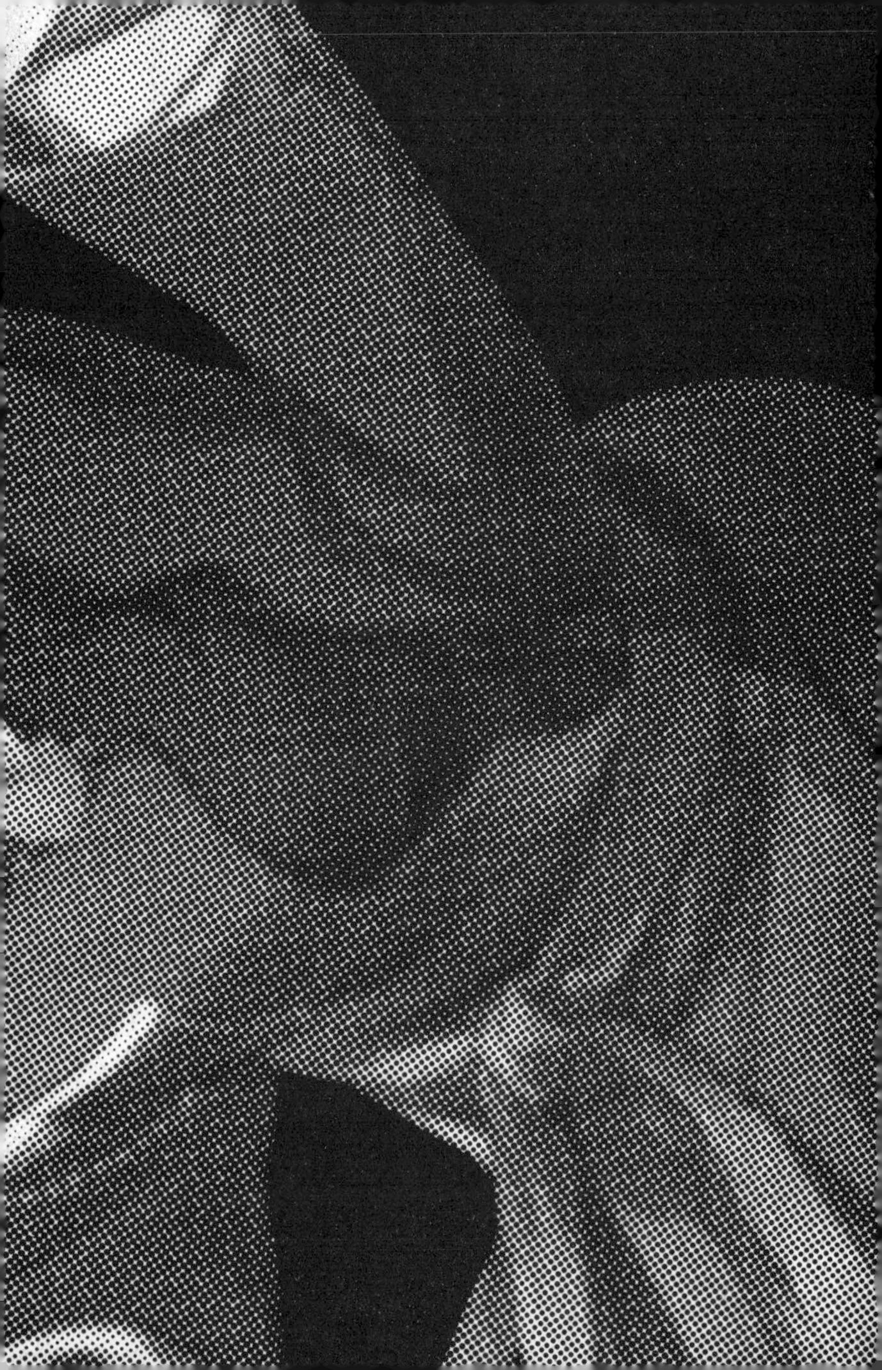

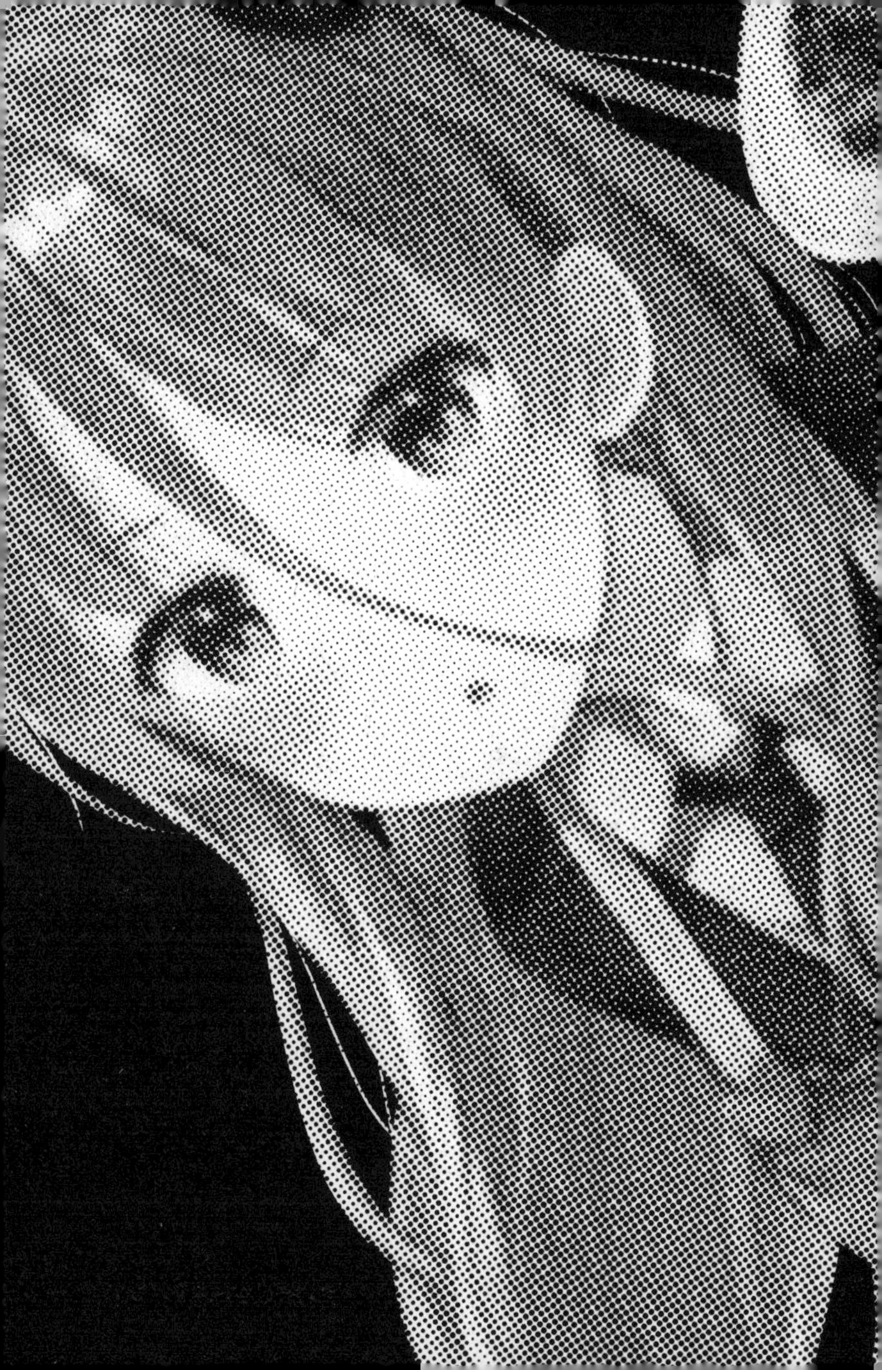

MY
Lovey-Dovey
Wife IS A
STONE COLD
KILLER

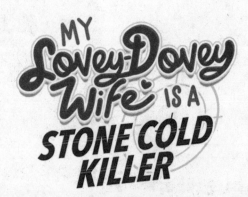

SEVEN SEAS ENTERTAINMENT PRESENTS

MY Lovey Dovey WIFE IS A STONE COLD KILLER

story and art by DONTEN KOSAKA   VOLUME 2

TRANSLATION
Elena Kirillova

ADAPTATION
Tabby Wright

LETTERING
Mercedes McGarry

COVER DESIGN
Hanase Qi

LOGO DESIGN
Shi Briggs

PROOFREADER
James Rhoden

COPY EDITOR
Dawn Davis

EDITOR
Kristiina Korpus

PREPRESS TECHNICIAN
Melanie Ujimori

PRINT MANAGER
Rhiannon Rasmussen-Silverstein

PRODUCTION ASSOCIATE
Christa Miesner

PRODUCTION MANAGER
Lissa Pattillo

EDITOR-IN-CHIEF
Julie Davis

ASSOCIATE PUBLISHER
Adam Arnold

PUBLISHER
Jason DeAngelis

HAIKEI... KOROSHIYASAN TO KEKKONSHIMASHITA Vol.2
©Donten Kosaka 2021
First published in Japan in 2021 by KADOKAWA CORPORATION, Tokyo.
English translation rights arranged with KADOKAWA CORPORATION, Tokyo.

Seven Seas press and purchase enquiries can be sent to Marketing Manager Lianne Sentar at press@gomanga.com. Information regarding the distribution and purchase of digital editions is available from Digital Manager CK Russell at digital@gomanga.com.

Seven Seas and the Seven Seas logo are trademarks of Seven Seas Entertainment. All rights reserved.

ISBN: 978-1-63858-142-0
Printed in Canada
First Printing: March 2022
10 9 8 7 6 5 4 3 2 1

////// READING DIRECTIONS //////

This book reads from *right to left*, Japanese style. If this is your first time reading manga, you start reading from the top right panel on each page and take it from there. If you get lost, just follow the numbered diagram here. It may seem backwards at first, but you'll get the hang of it! Have fun!!

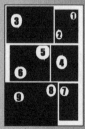